T0291158

Failed
GLOBALISATION
Inequality, Money, and
the Renaissance of the State

Failed
GLOBALISATION
Inequality, Money, and the Renaissance of the State

Heiner Flassbeck
University of Hamburg, Germany

Paul Steinhardt

W🌐 World Scientific

NEW JERSEY · LONDON · SINGAPORE · BEIJING · SHANGHAI · HONG KONG · TAIPEI · CHENNAI · TOKYO

Published by

World Scientific Publishing Co. Pte. Ltd.
5 Toh Tuck Link, Singapore 596224
USA office: 27 Warren Street, Suite 401-402, Hackensack, NJ 07601
UK office: 57 Shelton Street, Covent Garden, London WC2H 9HE

Library of Congress Cataloging-in-Publication Data
Names: Flassbeck, Heiner, author. | Steinhardt, Paul F., author.
Title: Failed globalisation : inequality, money, and the renaissance of the state /
    Heiner Flassbeck, University of Hamburg, Germany, Paul Steinhardt.
Description: Hackensack : World Scientific, 2020. |
    Includes bibliographical references and index.
Identifiers: LCCN 2019054522 | ISBN 9789811215759 (hardcover) | ISBN 9789811215766 (ebook) |
    ISBN 9789811215773 (ebook other)
Subjects: LCSH: Economic development--Social aspects. | Equality. |
    International economic integration.
Classification: LCC HD75 .F573 2020 | DDC 338.9--dc23
LC record available at https://lccn.loc.gov/2019054522

British Library Cataloguing-in-Publication Data
A catalogue record for this book is available from the British Library.

For any available supplementary material, please visit
https://www.worldscientific.com/worldscibooks/10.1142/11702#t=suppl

Desk Editor: Ong Shi Min Nicole

Typeset by Stallion Press
Email: enquiries@stallionpress.com

Printed in Singapore

About the Authors

Heiner Flassbeck is a German economist. He was State Secretary (Deputy Minister) in the German Federal Ministry of Finance during 1998–1999 and Chief Economist of the United Nations Conference on Trade and Development (UNCTAD) from 2003 to 2012.

Paul Steinhardt has held management positions at German banks and their subsidiaries in Germany and abroad. Together, Flassbeck and Steinhardt publish *Makroskop* magazine.

Contents

Preamble

Globalisation was a wonderful idea. After the Berlin Wall came down and the political division between East and West Germany was overcome, and centrally planned economies gave way to the free market, nothing seemed to stand in the way of peaceful cooperation between people all around the world. After all, why should people everywhere not communicate and work together freely, to their mutual advantage?

The big idea was simple: It would be enough to remove national institutional obstacles to doing business. A spontaneous global economic order would then emerge in which every individual would contribute according to his or her abilities, to the benefit of all. A global division of labour among free people would represent the crowning triumph of liberalism, with personal freedom and economic efficiency maximised in glorious tandem. The achievement of an ancient dream seemed within reach: A world populated by free and prosperous global citizens of the Earth.

Alexis de Tocqueville, author of the classic text *Democracy in America*, had already predicted in 1840 that democracy would create an open and globally networked society:

> *Dans les siècles démocratiques, l'extrême mobilité des hommes et leurs impatients désirs font qu'ils changent sans cesse de place, et que les habitants des différents pays se mêlent, se voient, s'écoutent et s'empruntent. Ce ne sont donc pas seulement les membres d'une même nation qui deviennent semblables; les nations elles-mêmes s'assimilent, et toutes ensemble ne forment plus à l'œil du*

spectateur qu'une vaste démocratie dont chaque citoyen est un peuple. Cela met pour la première fois au grand jour la figure du genre humain.

In democratic times, the extreme mobility of people, and the impatience of their desires, lead them to constantly change locations. People from different countries mix; they see, hear, and imitate each other. It is not only the members of the same ethnicity who become more similar; different ethnic groups assimilate, and together they form what in the eye of the beholder is a vast democracy in which every individual citizen is a unique ethnicity. For the first time, a clear light is shone on the face of the human race.

But Tocqueville's high hopes for the consequences of the "democratic age" have been bitterly disappointed by the real course of history. The miserable failure of the economic and political liberalism that has shaped the world more than any other idea in the last 40 years would have been clear even without the election of the likes of Donald Trump to the Presidency.

The dissatisfaction of so many people that was expressed in the election of an openly reactionary president has not only demonstrated the political inability of liberalism to maintain the necessary balance between freedom and equality. More than that, it has shown liberalism's inability to comprehend the interactive dynamics of social and economic factors in complex modern societies, or to serve as a framework for developing viable policy prescriptions.

While the philosophical and political problems of liberalism have been intensively discussed, what has not yet been clearly understood is why it has failed so blatantly in what it claims as its own core domain — the structuring of economic cooperation. To this day, the vast majority of economists continue to adhere to the dogma that "the market" should take the lead in nearly all important social decisions; the state's role should be limited to setting the legal framework for the market, and filling a few gaps.

This has always been an inadequate conception of the tasks of the state — and by now, it has been clearly refuted by reality. Indeed, it is no exaggeration to say that the decline of liberalism was inevitable from the outset, since its proponents never developed a satisfactory intellectual framework either for guiding the indispensable global cooperation of nation-states or for the resulting national-level policy consequences.

What is still not understood today is that the economic theory behind liberalism is not merely in need of a bit of improvement in some areas. No, this "theory," which really should not be granted the dignity of being titled as such, is incapable even in principle of understanding the dynamics of a market-economy system — and it is therefore wholly unsuitable for deriving valid policy guidelines.

Anyone who relies on the theoretical framework of economic liberalism to carry out a historical or political analysis is necessarily going to go wrong. The problem is that theories of economic liberalism, especially so-called neo-classical economics, mischaracterise social systems that are in reality dynamic and historically unique as being, instead, recurring sequences of equilibrium states whose basic characteristics are completely static and ahistorical.

Instead of understanding the economy as a dynamic process that consists of sequences of interrelated events that can only be understood in the context of real historical time, liberal economics has developed an artificial theory in which supply and demand curves intersect without reference to time or history. Liberal economics is essentially a failed attempt to explain almost all economic phenomena as solutions to the problem of distributing scarce goods through a perfect market.

The intellectual failure of economic liberalism became widely apparent in the wake of the global crisis of financial markets which began in 2007 and shook the world economy in the two years that followed. Capital markets showed themselves to be highly inefficient, and this demonstrated that the dogma of the superiority of market-economy control of all economic relations could not be correct. But the fundamental wrongness of the liberal interpretation of the world was also revealed in never-ending unemployment, in obscene and dysfunctional wealth and income inequality, in the helpless failure to integrate developing countries into the world economy, and in the ever-increasing pressure of citizens in many countries of the world to escape their poverty through emigration.

Nevertheless, economic liberalism made a roaring comeback after a brief interlude of state intervention and insight into the fundamental failure of markets. The forces of brute economic power made it clear to political decision-makers immediately after the crisis that, although the state may be permitted to play the saviour role in an emergency, this certainly did not mean anyone would be permitted to infer that the distribution of powers and responsibilities between market and state needed to be rethought.

The systemic crisis that was revealed at the time has now largely disappeared from public discourse as a topic. But the crisis has by no means been overcome. Ten years on, deflationary trends, zero interest rates, persistently high unemployment, a crisis of free trade, and an inability to revive the investment dynamics of earlier times prove that there can be no pretence of a return to normality.

This book shows in detail why the neoliberal hope of being able to reduce the state to the role of a framework-setter and gap-filler has failed. The capital markets, for example, need help from the state every day in order to be able to function at all; the so-called labour markets need direct, ongoing stabilisation by the state; and the monetary system — contrary to what liberalism would have us believe — is a domain of the state.

The paramount importance of state management of market processes leads nation-states into a dilemma: There currently exists no mechanism that could ensure that the prices, wages, and interest rates found at the national level complement each other in such a way that serious conflicts between states can be prevented.

International policy coordination is therefore essential if a world order is to be sought which enables intellectual and cultural exchange between people from different countries, trade in goods and services to the benefit of all those involved, and freedom of movement of individuals across national borders.

In short, the democratic nation-state needs a global order, and the global order needs nation-states capable of taking action. Only in a democratic nation-state can prices be found that are both efficient and democratically legitimate, and only with the help of a global framework can a fair balance of interests between states be achieved.

Coping with this challenge will be much more demanding and difficult than the liberal myth of spontaneous self-regulation of social systems has misled policymakers to believe for the past 40 years. To begin, a central prerequisite for harmonious and peaceful coordination of cooperation between nation-states is a common understanding of basic causal interrelationships in economics.

Such an understanding has only existed once in the past three hundred years: Among the delegates from nearly fifty countries who met in the small town of Bretton Woods in the US state of New Hampshire at the end of the Second World War. At Bretton Woods, nations successfully agreed (albeit without German participation) on the broad outlines of a global monetary system that enabled a global economic miracle for more than 20 years in the post-war era.

Today, the tasks to be accomplished at the global level are much more comprehensive and complex. In particular, the environmental and economic dimensions of global cooperation must be reconciled. It is no exaggeration to say that today the international community of states is facing the greatest challenges in the history of humankind.

I

Globalisation and Digitisation — The Challenges of Our Time

If one were to ask people from all over the world what they consider to be the biggest challenges of our time, the answers would likely be quite similar. Most would identify globalisation and digitisation as phenomena that have the potential to change their lives for better or for worse.

That is rather surprising. Digitisation is a new phenomenon, but the rationalisation of work has been shaping human history for centuries; so, one would think we would have learned to deal with it by now. It is also surprising that neither international organisations nor international politics has succeeded in presenting even the skeleton of "global governance" for so-called globalisation. No serious discussion has even begun on the issues raised.

Why is it that the world is incapable of understanding the consequences of an age-old phenomenon such as displacement of human labour by technological progress, or of agreeing on the broad lines of an international economic order? Can this be explained by pointing to the conflicting interests of societal actors? Also, who or what is preventing employees and their organised representatives from at least proposing possible solutions? And why should the interests of different governments, united as they are by the belief in the beneficial effects of free trade, free markets, and free enterprise, be so different that agreement on an international economic order appears impossible?

There must be deeper reasons why politicians have not understood — or do not want to understand — how a functioning economic order could be shaped at national and international levels.

In any event, it is obvious that such an economic order can only be designed on the basis of an empirically validated economic theory. A comprehensive economic theory of this kind does not yet exist. But whatever such a theory may look like, we will explain in this book that it is indispensable that the theory must redefine the relationship between "labour" and "capital," and that it must recognise the key role of "money" as the central control instrument of the economy.

Why has Liberal Globalisation Failed?

In recent years, there has been a flood of statements to the effect that globalisation and digitisation are overwhelming the mass of people, unsettling citizens and voters, who are therefore increasingly prey to "populism," to the siren songs of those who spuriously promise to alleviate or even prevent the inevitable adjustment pains caused by globalisation and digitisation.

The election of Donald Trump in the USA and the gains in vote-share of "extremist" parties throughout Europe, such as most recently the "Alternative for Germany" (AfD), are almost unanimously attributed to this globalisation/digitisation complex by the leading media and the "centrist" parties.

Conventional wisdom claims that the gamut of economic ailments — whether these be increasing material inequality or dissatisfaction with one's own economic situation — is ultimately the result of people's unwillingness to face the adjustment requirements of the globalised neoliberal world order: an order which may hurt some individuals in the short run, but on the whole increases general prosperity. If, according to the subliminal message of those who warn against populism, the people refuse to swallow the bitter pill of "flexibility" and "willingness to adapt," populism, with its unbearable lightness of being, will send people to hell in the end.

The gamut of critiques of globalisation that can be read in popular media seems comprehensive. But in reality, it is vague and unstructured, because regardless of the different perspectives and criticisms brought to bear, the proposition that free trade is always good is almost never questioned. The well-known German economist Peter Bofinger, for example, says that globalisation may harm individuals, but it benefits nations (Kaufmann, 2016). A leading German business newspaper, *Handelsblatt*, claims that corporate managers in Germany and elsewhere are alarmed because more and more people find it difficult to cope with a rapidly changing world (Reuters, 2016). Corporate managers fear new trade wars because populist politicians are not prepared to push through the tough measures necessary for global structural change against the resistance of the people. Thomas Fricke, an economic columnist, sees "derailed globalisation" as the decisive problem of our time (Fricke, 2016), and even finds a close connection between globalisation and suicide rates in certain regions of the USA (*Ibid.*), but — in that essay, at least — does not arrive at the idea of asking where and why globalisation has gone off the rails.

Another leading German economic columnist, Mark Schieritz, writing in *Die Zeit*, fears that Germany will find few international partners for its efforts to "heal the wounds of globalisation" as chair of the G20 (Schieritz, 2016), but somehow forgets that Germany itself creates new wounds every day with its massive trade surpluses. His colleagues in the same gazette fear a popular uprising against free trade, even though there are (they firmly believe) more winners than losers from free trade in Germany (Nienhaus & Tönnesmann, 2016). But they forget to ask whether Germany might perhaps be a special case — one of the few nations that are among free trade's winners.

Pascal Lamy, a former Director General of the World Trade Organisation, joins in and says that "populists" say that imports are bad and exports are good, although every third-class economist knows that this is nonsense. But how is it Lamy knows with such confidence that imports are good is not known (Lamy is not an economist).

With the help of the Bertelsmann Foundation and the Cologne Institute for Economic Research (Institut der deutschen Wirtschaft), the large-circulation German magazine *ARD Plusminus* (Krull, 2016) "explains" to the public that free trade is definitely good. The prominent Munich-based philosopher Julian Nida-Rümelin believes that historical phases of deglobalisation are very dangerous, which can be seen in the fact that such a phase ended in the middle of the last century in "National Socialism and the Second World War" (Nida-Rümelin, 2016). *Frankfurter Allgemeine Zeitung* (FAZ), the leading newspaper in Frankfurt, Germany's financial centre, describes in detail how free trade is based on reciprocity, and so cannot present a unilateral burden on certain countries — although, unfortunately, hardships for individuals cannot be avoided (Armbruster, 2017). Here again, the special case of Germany is not examined.

Richard David Precht, philosopher, world-explainer, author, and entertainer, has discovered that digitisation takes people's work away (e.g. Phoenix, 2017). He never tires of warning us that we will run out of work, more or less the day after tomorrow. The digital industrial revolution is on the near horizon, threatening chaos and upheaval. Trade unions are becoming obsolete, the centrist German social democratic party SPD is losing its traditional core clientele of workers, and none of the country's political parties have answers to the enormous new social challenges that are arising. The CDU has understood nothing, the Left wants to go back to the 1970s, and the right-wing AfD back to the 1950s, in Precht's assessment.

In the *FAZ*, Philip Plickert impressively demonstrated just how far wide off the mark the current discussion on so-called digitisation lies (Plickert, 2015). The "experts" quoted in his article clearly do not understand that they have succumbed to an old prejudice, an unexamined economic cliché. Harvard University employment researcher Richard Freeman says: "As soon as robots and computers can carry out a task more cheaply than human workers, they take people's jobs away — unless the workers are prepared to accept less pay."

This is false. It is true that technical progress destroys certain jobs — but not "jobs" in aggregate. When machines can do something better, more reliably, and faster than people, machines replace people in those functions. This has not changed since the beginning of human history. Had people successfully resisted mechanisation and rationalisation from the beginning (it began well before industrialisation) in efforts to prevent the loss of a certain job (their job) by accepting reduced wages in order to outcompete machines, there would have been no increase in material prosperity.

Even Plickert, author of the *FAZ* piece, recognises this when he correctly states:

> In the long run it has not come true that the new industrial world no longer offers jobs — on the contrary. As a result of increasing productivity, prosperity has also increased among the general population over time. The use of modern machines made production cheaper, prices fell, and demand increased as a result. Instead of the old trades in agriculture and crafts, which had become superfluous, new industrial trades emerged.

However, he cannot draw a logical inference from this observation, because he cannot admit that rising wages are what is needed to cushion rationalisation. He writes vaguely about "rising prosperity and rising productivity," but fails to explain why prices have to fall in order for prosperity to rise. What escapes him is that rising prosperity can be better achieved with rising wages and constant prices.

The Poisoned Offer of Neoliberalism

The new economic liberalism began in the 1970s with the promise to solve all economic problems with the help of a single central adjusting screw. The keyword was "flexibilisation." This meant making all areas of life more flexible, but first and foremost it was about the so-called labour market. Inflexible wages had emerged as the decisive focus of the new macroeconomic thinking from the great controversy between Keynesianism (born in the 1930s) and the old conceptual world of "classical" economics. Classical economics had developed at the beginning of the 19th century (based on the older economic theories of Adam Smith and David Ricardo), but was later decisively modified and transformed into a general theory of markets by Léon Walras in the late 19th century.

In the Keynesian conceptual world, inflexible wages were regarded as a problem that could be lived with, or even as a social achievement that for political reasons should not be questioned. Keynesianism, for the first time in the history of economics, concentrated on developing an analysis of macroeconomic dynamics. (Even Karl Marx had remained stuck in microeconomic modes of thinking.)

Yet even in the course of the Keynesian revolution, inflexible wages were only rarely explicitly described as a decisive prerequisite for successful economic development. That is why in the 1970s there was only half-hearted opposition to the attempt by neoliberals — the new representatives of the old liberal paradigm — to promote the notion that flexibility of all prices, including wages, was the most important factor in successful economic development.

When high inflation and high unemployment occurred simultaneously in the wake of the oil price explosions in the 1970s — a phenomenon that came to be known as "stagflation" — the neoliberals' time had come. They were able to claim that stagflation convincingly demonstrated that systems in which the most important price of a market economy is inflexible, namely the price of labour, entail insoluble conflicts that cannot be fought with the recipes of Keynesianism.

The message of the "new economic liberalism" was that only flexible prices and independent central banks could create the conditions that would make it possible to get the twin problems of inflation and underemployment under control. Neoliberalism allied itself with monetarism, thereby creating a theoretical bulwark that was difficult to overcome. Monetarism is the age-old teaching that it is possible to quantitatively define a money supply and then control it technocratically in such a way that inflation would be relegated forever to being a minor, peripheral phenomenon.

But what this "neoliberalism" offered in terms of constructive solutions to overcome the problems of economic development was extremely meagre, and not even particularly new. In addition to making all prices more flexible, neoliberalism knew and knows only free trade as the further necessary and sufficient condition for prosperity and economic development. Consequently, globalisation was seen as the ultimate means of ensuring that free entrepreneurs in free markets all over the world would be allowed to do what economic liberals believe they can do better than any state: Consistently make good use of the opportunities presented by technological progress by means of entrepreneurial investment, thereby ensuring an optimal supply of all kinds of economic goods to all people.

Let us therefore take a closer look at the solutions proposed by neoliberalism, beginning with the question of whether "free trade" as invoked by economic liberals really exists at all. Do we really need flexible wages and prices to meet the challenges of globalisation effectively? And to what extent are the issues discussed under the heading of "digitisation" really making unmanageable demands on people today?

Free Trade as a Solution?

Hardly any issue has brought more protesters onto the streets in recent years than the Transatlantic Trade and Investment Partnership (TTIP), the planned free trade agreement between the USA and Europe. Many people seem to share an intuition that such agreements sacrifice important values to an ideology.

On the other side of the debate, a large majority of economists defends "free trade" tooth and claw. In their view, free trade is an absolute necessity for the economy to function efficiently. According to their doctrine, if each country specialises in the production of those goods that it can most cheaply produce, the world as a whole gains.

Nothing is as sacred to liberal economists and politicians as free trade. After all, free trade is the only thing they have to offer to explain the "prosperity of nations." This "theory" is based on a doctrine the English economist David Ricardo postulated 200 years ago. At that time, it was feared that free trade could be harmful, because some countries were able to produce all tradable products more efficiently than all other countries. In order to compensate for the superior countries' absolute advantages in the realm of production, it was thought that inferior countries would have to use protectionism to ensure their own producers would have a chance of survival.

Arguing against this view, David Ricardo proposed his famous "principle of comparative advantage," according to which it is not the absolute but rather the comparative advantages that matter in international trade. So if, for example, a producer in one country produces shoes particularly well, but a producer in another country is especially efficient in the production of cloth, then the two can trade with each other even if the manufacturer of shoes could also produce cloth more cheaply. Specialisation, i.e. the shoe manufacturer's concentration on the production of shoes and the cloth manufacturer's on cloth, will produce a better overall result for both, if they engage in trade with each other.

This example — which was Ricardo's original example — shows how unrealistic his idea is. He apparently assumes that the shoemaker is fully occupied with the production of shoes and that it would not occur to him to produce both shoes and cloth at the same time. But in the real world, no economy is ever working at full capacity. Every producer or national economy, given absolute advantages and free capacities, will use all available advantages and will not limit itself to one product.

In addition, Ricardo assumes that — at full employment — the remuneration of the workforce precisely reflects the respective scarcity of labour and capital, at all times and in all participating countries. That is another heroic assumption. In reality, nominal values are decisive for international trade because, together with currency relations (exchange rates), they determine prices.

Consider: What happens if, as is very often the case, inflation rates vary widely between countries? Let us assume, for example, that annual increases in wages paid in one country exceed productivity growth far more than in another. Then the products of the first country will become more expensive year-on-year, and the demand for these products will decline, even though the availability of labour and capital have not changed, or are the same in both countries.

In this situation, in order to rebalance demand, there should at least be a functioning mechanism to ensure that the two countries' widely divergent prices and wages remain equal when they are calculated in an international trade currency. One might expect that this mechanism is the currency market.

However, this assumption is wrong. In our era, currencies have become the playthings of speculators. The relative values of currencies are often driven in the completely wrong direction for years, as speculators take advantage of inflation and interest rate differences in different currency areas to make short-term profits. In this way, currencies of countries with high inflation appreciate, and those of countries with low inflation depreciate, which is exactly the opposite of what would be necessary to rebalance trade. Ricardo's defence of free trade is therefore invalid on this point too.

But that is not all. Consider the phenomenon of offshoring, when producers from countries with high productivity shift production to countries with low productivity and low wages. The neoclassical theory of international trade assumes that the composition of direct investments (i.e. the relocation of fixed assets) is always driven by the relative prices of labour and capital. It is thus assumed that an American manufacturer of mobile telephones, for example, which is relocating its production to China, will invent a completely new production technology system for deployment in China, one which is much more labour-intensive than the one used at home in the USA, in order to take advantage of the lower price of labour in China. This assumption is beyond questionable — it is ridiculous.

Neoclassical equilibrium theory further assumes that companies make no profits. In the assumptions-driven logic of neoclassical economics, companies must not and cannot make any profits due to monopolistic advantages. So if mobile phones are produced in China, then, according to this notion, the successful Western production system will be discarded, and a new, more labour-intensive system will be invented for implementation in China. This is then used to produce the same product of the same quality, and offer it on the world market at exactly the same price.

According to neoclassical theory, the producer thus forgoes the profits he would have made if he had combined higher-productivity Western production system technology with lower Chinese wages. Had he done that, he could have significantly reduced his unit labour costs, i.e. wages paid per hour divided by the value of goods produced per hour. However, the entrepreneur does not seize this opportunity, as he is, by assumption, not allowed to make an "extra profit."

Direct investments are of such enormous scale today that Chinese exports can in no way be compared with the composition of trade goods of a Western industrial country. Chinese trade consists largely of exports of products of Western companies whose factories are located in China; these account for an estimated 60%–70% of the total value of China's exports.

This fact reveals that the neoclassical economists' justification for free trade is nonsense. It follows that the globally regnant free trade ideology is based on a theory that is not only unrealistic but manifestly wrong. International trade may be free, but we know nothing about whether it is also efficient. Yet it is the claim that freedom necessarily implies efficiency that is presented as the reason and justification for implementing TTIP and other free trade agreements.

We do not know whether trade liberalisation is efficient. The idea that any intervention in free trade is necessarily harmful and inefficient is simply wrong. For example, a country should not be condemned for defending itself against accepting massive imports from another country whose companies take in extremely high monopoly profits by combining high productivity with low wages. In such cases, protectionist measures can improve the welfare of the world as a whole, by preventing healthy domestic companies from being harmed by overseas rivals' monopoly profits.

Making matters even worse, some countries tend to export much more than they import, in a manner reminiscent of mercantilism. This phenomenon of "global imbalances" stands in stark contrast to the free trade doctrine. As the so-called world champion exporting nation, with the largest excess of exports over imports by value, Germany is the world's biggest sinner in this respect.

Surpluses or deficits in trade are much more important than potential Ricardian "productivity effects" when it comes to assessing the economic success or failure of international trade for participating countries. The reality is that once significant and sustained external trade imbalances exist, the trading partners of a country that defends its surpluses have no incentive to enter into a free trade agreement with that country.

Neither huge swings in currency exchange rates, nor direct investment (offshoring), nor wage dumping, are subjects of serious analysis in free trade ideology. What this means is that defenders of "free trade" make their judgments on the basis of a doctrine that has nothing to do with the real world. What the globalised economy needs much more urgently than a doctrinal debate on trade policy is an international currency system that prevents individual countries from gaining unjustified absolute advantages over long time periods by means of wage-dumping or similar measures.

Rigid Wages and the Threat of Globalisation

Economic liberals set the agenda early on in the debate over the consequences of globalisation, by linking an epochal political shift to a massive threat. According to their thesis, in the wake of the fall of the Berlin Wall, the West would not be able to carry on as before, given that many countries in Eastern Europe and Asia (with China as a new economic superpower) had opened their borders for the exchange of goods. In view of the emergence of new participants in the international division of labour, the relative scarcity of capital and labour had changed fundamentally on a global basis.

Because labour is abundant in developing and transition economies, while capital is scarce, prices for capital and labour at the global level must adapt and conform to these new ratios, neoliberals claimed. Labour must become cheaper and capital more expensive. Inflexible wages in industrialised countries would inevitably lead to unemployment. Struggles over distribution of income between labour and capital in the rich developed countries would drive capital out of the country, because for capitalists there would always be the alternative of investing their capital overseas, in an emerging economy.

Probably no other thesis has dominated the international discussion about the consequences of globalisation as strongly as this simple, even primitive argument, which was derived directly from the neoclassical "theory" of a "labour market." Although this theory cannot be sustained on close inspection, the arguments put forward against it were also extremely feeble. The decisive reason: "Progressive" economists refused to completely reject neoclassical labour market theory.

If they had not taken up the scarcity theory, but had instead emphasised the role of wages as a stabiliser of domestic demand, progressive economists could have shown that it is by no means the case that Chinese workers determine wages in Germany. In reality, the globalisation of markets is all about structural change and economic dynamism. Neoliberalism recognises neither phenomenon, and therefore has no policy prescription for either.

The Great Fear

Unemployment is without doubt the greatest economic and political threat to modern societies. Unemployment is quite rightly seen, by many observers as well as those directly affected, as a decisive signal that we cannot continue as before, and changes are necessary. But the conclusions drawn from this are mostly wrong. Economists and non-economists, corporate spokespeople and trade unionists, well-meaning philosophers and critical intellectuals all see our world as being awash in a powerful current of globalisation and digitisation that will inevitably wash away the beloved amenities of the welfare state.

In their view, only diehards living in the past and blind isolationists refuse to accept the historical necessity to radically question our standard of living, and the need, in future, for citizens to secure themselves against individual life risks such as unemployment, old age, and illness by private means, instead of relying on the state.

Is the welfare state finished because more poor countries want to actively participate in world trade? Are millions of Chinese overrunning the borders of rich countries and forcing them to share their prosperity? How can it be that all rich countries have dramatically increased sales of their goods to China?

One does not have to answer such questions if one wants to strike a pose as a doomsday prophet of globalisation or digitisation. Apparently, it is enough for sages and policymakers to parrot a few buzzwords, and the fateful cycle of belt-tightening is activated in response to the cliché that developed-world societies are living beyond their means. That cycle always ends with a further diminishment of the welfare state.

What does Globalisation Demand?

If we move beyond doomsaying and public displays of fearful trembling in the face of globalisation and engage in sober analysis instead, it turns out that it is possible to establish very simple rules for the peaceful economic coexistence of nations. All economic rules, regardless of who lays them down, in the end reduce to a single principle: A requirement that each country and each individual adapt to their own circumstances — i.e. that none live beyond their own means.

No state can demand more than this from another, and no global regulatory regime can demand more than this from individual countries or their citizens. To demand more would mean that one person is required to consciously live below his means, which logically means that another person is forced to live at a level above his means — because taken together, as a single global population, the people as a whole can live neither below nor above their means (Flassbeck & Spiecker, 2016).

Translated into economic terminology, this means that each country must adapt its demands precisely to its own productivity. At the individual economic level, this rule is immediately obvious: in the long run, an economic entity cannot spend more than it takes in, which means that everyone has to do the work necessary to earn the goods and services they claim. If someone spends more than the value of what he produces, he is living beyond his means, and that requires him to get into debt, which means he has to find a creditor. The creditor is someone who believes that one day the debtor can repay his debts — in other words, that the latter's future productivity will be sufficient to repay the value of the goods and services he has previously claimed.

The same applies in the other direction: In the long run, you cannot spend less than you earn. If you want to live below your means, you have to find a debtor, i.e. someone who is willing to live beyond their current means. If you want to become a creditor (or net saver), you have to find others who want to get into debt. If no one is prepared to get into debt in the amount in which you would like to save, then there is no customer for what you, as a prospective saver, want to produce beyond your own current needs or wants. The demand for your produce that you would prefer to see in order to generate your net income is missing; you lack buyers, and your savings plan fails.

The rule, then, is that countries must in the long run live in conformity with their own productivity and within their own means. What does this rule imply for international trade?

What it implies is that in the long run, everyone can benefit from the international division of labour only if no country increases its competitiveness at the expense of other countries through protectionism or similar measures. Countries can trade with one another on an equal footing only if no country lives either beyond or below its means in the long run.

If this happens nevertheless, i.e. if large creditor and debtor positions are built up in the long term through massive violations of the general rule that countries should live in close conformity with their means, then exchange rates will sooner or later be adjusted between countries — assuming that each has its own currency. If a country loses creditworthiness due to a constantly growing external debt position, its currency will be devalued.

Conversely, a country with an immense creditor position must sooner or later see its currency revalued upward — which means the creditor country sees a devaluation of its assets abroad, in terms of those assets' purchasing power as measured in the creditor country's own currency. The exchange rate valve, although problematic in many respects, is a form of proof that better means of balancing the differential economic performances of nations have failed (or have not been attempted).

However, countries are not in themselves economic entities; rather, they consist of a large number of economic entities such as corporations and households. Consider a situation in which different countries are locked within the same currency area, as is the case with the 17 countries of the Eurozone. Without the emergency exchange rate valve, how is it possible to ensure the implementation, at the national level, of the rule that in the long run, every economic player must live in conformity with their means — which is to say, with their productivity?

Let us assume that, in the general case, labour productivity increases over time due to improvements in technology. Taken as a whole, a national economy automatically adapts to its productivity in the long term if the average real income per capita (measured in terms of the average wage per hour, for example) grows at the same rate as the average productivity (i.e. the increase in real income per hour). Logically — and this has been confirmed by a wealth of empirical experience — this is best achieved by nominal average wages growing in the economy by the sum of the expected average increase in productivity and the target inflation rate.

This simple wage rule implies that not only the employees, the "labour factor," but also the capital side, must participate appropriately in the fruits of economic development. Moreover, linking wages and productivity in this way enables a stable inflation rate. That is because the gap between nominal wage increases and increases in real labour productivity (the development of so-called "unit labour costs") is the decisive determinant of overall cost development, which in turn largely determines unit price development (as will be shown later).

The participation of the broad mass of the population in the benefits of increasing productivity through corresponding increases in their wages is thus the key mechanism for ensuring that a country's economic development occurs in harmony with the basic rule for a sustainable international division of labour, i.e. the rule that countries must live neither beyond nor below their means.

In contrast, a strategy of living below one's means, i.e. a years-long attempt to deny the broad mass of the workforce its proportionate share in the benefits of productivity increases, necessarily ends up in a national and international blind alley. Germany has been in this situation for years, because it decided to attempt to meet the challenges of globalisation by tightening its own belt and living below its own means — thus necessarily relying on the willingness of its trading partners in the rest of the world to accept an ever-increasing burden of international trade debt.

Trade Between High- and Low-Wage Countries

In Germany, a typical full-time worker earned gross annual wages of about 25,000 euros in 2000, whereas a Chinese worker earned the equivalent of about 1,150 euros. How can two countries trade with each other when their wage levels are so far apart? Would all products not have to be manufactured in China, and would Germany not have to import all goods from the Far East?

The answer is no, because the decisive factor for the competitiveness of a product on the world market, at a given level of quality, is its price — and this is not determined by the absolute level of wages at which it is produced but rather by wages in relation to productivity, i.e. by labour costs per unit of production. How much money is spent on wages in the production of a single "piece" of a given product therefore depends on the amount and quality of capital stock (production machinery and processes) used to produce it.

For example, if a particular item is produced exclusively by manual labour, and one piece is produced by a craftsman in one day, the unit labour cost of that product amounts to the daily wage of the craftsman. However, if the same product is produced with a machine operated by a worker, and she can produce 10 pieces a day with the aid of this machine, then the unit labour costs of the product amount to one-tenth of her daily wage. Even if this machine-equipped worker earns an hourly wage five times as high as that of the craftsman, she can still offer a single piece at a lower price than her craftsman competitor (assuming for now that the machine has already been paid for and can be treated as a sunk cost).

It follows that the current high wage costs in Germany no more fell magically from heaven than did the relatively low Chinese wage rates. Both developed in small steps from the past. Wage rates mirror productivity, which in turn is based on the capital stock generated by a country. Anyone who declares the current level of unit labour costs in Germany to be generally too high is either ignoring the historical development of the nation's productivity and capital stock, or is implicitly claiming that the (West) German capital stock has suddenly become obsolete due to the gradual opening of markets since the end of the East–West conflict, having been devalued by increasing globalisation. This proposition is obviously absurd, given the leading position of many German export goods on world markets (including markets in low-wage countries).

Of course, the price of a good depends not only on unit labour costs but also on the cost of capital, i.e. the cost of the capital stock used in production. To stay with our example: The worker must have her machine before she can produce anything with it. If the wage and capital costs of capital-intensive production added together prove too high, and these costs outweigh the productivity advantage over labour-intensive production, the capital-intensive goods will not be competitive. Were this the case, the capital-intensive mode of production would then either not have developed at all, or it would be displaced by a more labour-intensive mode of production.

But has anyone ever observed mechanical looms giving way to hand-looms? On the contrary, humanity has always sought (and continues to seek) to build up the largest possible capital stock, because technological progress makes comparatively labour-intensive productive activities superfluous, usually at an acceptable price. As technology improves, workers turn to more productive jobs with which higher incomes, and thus greater prosperity can be achieved.

This means that in the medium to long term, the development of economies towards a constantly increasing use of capital (capital in the sense of machinery and automated processes) is a kind of natural law. Is it plausible that weavers could be paid so little, indefinitely into the future, that an investment in the construction of a machine loom would never pay off? No, that is not remotely plausible — and what this implies is that neither the historical development of our capital stock nor that of our wages, both of which have increased over time, was a mistake.

If the existing highly developed capital stock (the stock of production machinery and attendant processes) in Germany is so much higher than in China that unit labour costs per piece produced are the same despite the very different wage levels between the two countries, then no displacement of high-wage producers on the world market need result — i.e. the high-wage country does not automatically import everything from the low-wage country. In those sectors in which unit labour costs are higher in Germany than in China, however, cheaper suppliers replace the more expensive ones on the world market — and international trade takes place. Germany has so far performed outstandingly well in the context of these international structural changes.

High-wage countries specialise in goods that can only be produced with specialised technology (machinery and production process) that cannot easily reproduced elsewhere — at least not in the short run. Only firms that have a large and highly specialised capital stock, and the corresponding expertise necessary to operate it, can offer highly specialised goods on the world market. As a rule, these firms are not situated in low-wage countries, since those countries are characterised precisely by the fact that they are not (yet) so strongly industrialised and specialised.

Most economic textbooks, in examining international trade, limit their analysis to the toy example of two commercial goods on the world market. This leads to a story of tough international cut-throat competition, in which rich nations with high wage rates inevitably lose. As soon as one considers the realistic scenario of a vast and ever-changing global market with enormous numbers of specialised goods and services, however, this zero-sum story loses all plausibility.

The usual theoretical model assumes manufacturers are able to choose at will between different production techniques (i.e. more or less labour- or capital-intensive systems) in order to optimally adapt to the factor–price ratio for labour and capital (the wage-to-interest ratio). But this model is unrealistic and misleading.

It isn't merely adjustment frictions or a temporary geographic immobility of factors of production that are responsible for the fact that countries and companies cannot make continual arbitrary adjustments to the location of production, or to the details of production processes, in response to factor–price ratios. Much more fundamental forces are at work. It isn't possible to produce a mobile phone or a Mercedes with just any old arbitrary division of work between labour and machines. If the Daimler-Benz corporation wanted to build a car more labour-intensively than it does today, it would first have to invent a completely new production system. That would not only be expensive, it would be pointless.

The more capital-intensive production method is always superior in the long term, because it creates more potential for prosperity. It's the prerequisite for rising wages all over the world. A hypothetical parallel development of labour-intensive production processes for implementation in low-wage countries, created in an attempt to out-compete more highly mechanised production systems on price by taking advantage of cheap labour rates, will always lose in the long run. Anyone who doesn't believe that should go looking for an entrepreneur in China or India who uses 1970s-era technology to produce modern computers, for example.

Even if it were technically possible to maintain a more labour-intensive production method, it would not happen in reality. The reason is that it's much more profitable to combine today's capital-intensive production techniques with the low wages of emerging economies like China, India, or Vietnam. Temporary monopoly profits result from this arrangement — and these make any other solution uneconomical in comparison.

The standard economic models assume that monopoly profits play no role in the calculations of companies. This is nonsense. By making this assumption, the prevailing doctrine renders itself incapable of realistic analyses of international trade or of factor migration. The tragedy is that intellectuals from other disciplines — without knowing what they are doing, of course — adopt the assumptions of the standard neoclassical economic models, and try to analyse globalisation on that basis.

Trade in the Context of Easy Capital Migration

Advocates of wage-cost reductions in rich countries routinely argue that wage dampening is necessary because otherwise capital will emigrate to low-wage countries. Domestic unemployment is cited as proof that too little is being invested in high-wage economies like Germany — supposedly because the profitability of capital investments is too low, due to comparatively high domestic wages. If more profitable investment opportunities exist in lower-wage jurisdictions outside Germany, these will be used, and investment capital will flow out of the country — hence the argument.

Since the end of the East–West conflict and the associated increase in the participation of poorer economies in world trade, this mechanism of investment-capital outflow has achieved a new dynamism, to which Germany must adapt, the argument continues. The relative scarcity of production factors has changed fundamentally: A much larger global labour pool is available to be harnessed and put in the service of production for sale of goods in global markets. At the same time, the countries offering this huge surplus labour pool do not have a correspondingly large capital stock. The factor price ratio of labour to capital is much lower in the labour-rich countries than in the old industrial nations. On a global basis, the capital factor has become much scarcer in relation to labour. This increased scarcity makes it necessary to persuade capital to stay in the industrialised countries through lower wages, since very low wages in the emerging economies exert an enormous attraction on investment capital from wealthy industrialised countries (see Sinn, 2003, p. 91 ff.).

This view is partially correct in that it can indeed be worthwhile for entrepreneurs from rich countries to engage in "offshoring," i.e. to combine their capital-intensive production technologies with the cheap wages prevailing in emerging economies. This has always been a way of achieving temporary monopoly profits, and it has arguably become easier to achieve since 1989.

There is also a strong incentive for domestic entrepreneurs in low-wage countries to copy Western technologies, i.e. to import them and then generate above-average profits in combination with low domestic wages. If wage developments in the low-wage country follow the average growth in year-on-year productivity in the economy as a whole, considerable monopoly profits can be achieved over years, and perhaps even decades. That is because the overall productivity level in an emerging economy will remain well below what has already been achieved in rich countries for many years, due to the low starting value of a poor country's capital stock at the outset of its economic transition.

It is nonetheless wrong to blame the migration of capital to low-wage countries for high unemployment in wealthy industrialised nations. Anyone who examines the economic development of the German Federal Republic after the Second World War, for example, or that of Poland since the fall of the Berlin Wall, will see that capital movements do not take place suddenly and on a large scale; in fact, they take place rather gradually. Were that not the case, the build-up of West Germany's capital stock after the war would have been much quicker. Thirty years after its transition to a market system, Poland, with its cheap wages, should likewise have been highly industrialised long ago, if it were really the case that net capital flows going from high- to low-wage countries occur on as massive a scale as globalisation pessimists claim.

The manageable extent of capital shifts over recent decades can be explained in part by the fact that such shifts cannot be managed without risk. For one thing, the necessary human capital must be available in the low-wage country, i.e. the relevant know-how at all levels of the production process. Moreover, economic and political framework conditions in the emerging economy must be stable enough to encourage companies to make long-term investments there. Frequent changes in government resulting in major swings in economic policy can act as a deterrent to domestic and foreign investors. The same is true of a lack of internal security.

However, there is a more fundamental argument against the supposed risk of massive investment capital outflows to low-wage countries, and the threat of corresponding capital shortages in high-wage countries. If one sees economic development as a process in the course of which profits are gradually generated, savings accumulated, and investment capital is consequently acquired, then economic development is primarily about competitions between entrepreneurs, employees, or countries over a pool of investment capital which can allegedly be increased only very slowly. (In this view, investment capital can only be accumulated slowly because it can only be increased through accumulation of savings.)

But this is not what actually happens. Instead, if opportunities for extraordinary profit can be exploited in low-wage countries, then savings will accumulate more quickly, and investment capital that is urgently needed in the development process of emerging economies will recursively increase through the process itself. This will occur in a way that does not burden the capital account of the low-wage country, by allowing it to import more goods — including production machinery — from high-wage countries than would otherwise be possible.

The import of capital and know-how into emerging economies is therefore advantageous in the long term from the perspectives of both developing and rich countries. From the perspective of a low-wage country, a key consideration is that initially, the country will only be competitive on world markets in a very limited range of goods, due to its low stock of production capital. Every foreign investor who builds production capacity contributes to building up the emerging economy's capital stock, and with it, the basis for increased income and prosperity.

This will, of course, entail structural changes on all sides, but as a rule, these changes will be much greater in emerging economies than in high-wage countries. This is because the reproduction (copying) of existing production processes for making products meant for global markets can be implemented much more quickly than the invention and implementation of new technologies.

Developing countries do not need to reinvent the wheel. They can make enormous technological leaps in a short time as they build up their capital stock — leaps that are not possible for highly developed economies, which have no one to copy from. China's industries have not needed to apply

Western technologies from the 1960s over the past few decades of the country's development; foreign investors and their Chinese partners have directly implemented current technologies.

In the discourse of high-wage industrialised countries like Germany, it is often overlooked that structural changes associated with the globalisation of markets cause immense changes in the lives of the populations of low-wage emerging economies. These changes are usually not supported by a social safety net comparable to that of a wealthy country. Nevertheless, the combination of low wages and efficient technologies from industrialised countries represents a great opportunity for emerging countries to catch up economically and reduce their prosperity gap with rich countries. The locational advantage emerging economies offer in the form of low wages makes it possible to import technological knowledge, gradually expand their range of globally marketable products, and thus benefit from global trade.

A demand for wage cuts in high-wage countries therefore implicitly seeks to reduce developing countries' opportunity to catch up economically, or even to prevent it altogether. Ironically, those who demand wage-cuts in wealthy countries are usually the same people who are strictly against protectionism, and who promise poorer countries all the opportunities and benefits in the world if they only fully open their markets. At the same time, if the competitiveness of industrialised countries on world markets increases due to wage-cuts-induced reductions in the prices of goods produced in developed countries, then market opportunities are taken away from developing economies. The industrialised countries might even take away market share from poorer countries in the narrow product palette which the latter already sell internationally.

Moreover, if one were to move in the direction of an equalisation of German wages with Chinese or Indian wages, the exchange rate valve would clearly be activated, because then Germany would violate the central rule of international trade and capital movements. A further drastic appreciation of the euro would be unavoidable if wage cost reductions were made in Germany. Exchange rates can and must systematically compensate for unit labour cost differences, but never for absolute wage levels. Unlike many economics professors, foreign exchange traders know what is important in an international comparison.

Given that Germany is a high-wage country, its wage-restraint strategy entails serious consequences for countries that are somewhat lower on the ladder of industrialisation than the global market leaders, yet higher than developing countries. The consequences are especially severe for countries that use the same currency as Germany, i.e. the euro — as is the case with Italy, Spain, Portugal, or Greece, for example. If German companies try to become more competitive on world markets by cutting wages, this will affect their competitors in countries whose wages are only slightly lower than those prevalent in Germany. Companies in these countries had pursued a strategy of paying lower wages to compensate for their less-advanced capital stock (production machinery and processes). If German companies now reduce the wages of German workers, their competitors in other Eurozone countries must follow suit and reduce their own workers' wages if they do not want to lose all their market share. But this will inevitably lead to an appreciation of the euro in the medium term, undermining the efforts of the Germans to achieve greater competitiveness by moving closer to the Chinese wage level.

That is a stroke of luck for the developing countries, but it is a disaster for the poorer members of the Eurozone monetary union, since their global market competitiveness declines with a rising euro. This is apparently only gradually dawning on the managers of the European Central Bank, which is responsible for the monetary union. They have also been slow to understand that depressing wages across the Eurozone is generating a risk of deflation (cf. Europäische Zentralbank,[1] 2005).

These arguments may not really seem convincing to those workers in a high-wage country who have lost their jobs due to the relocation of a factory to a low-wage country. That does happen, and it is undoubtedly a difficult situation for those affected. In such cases, society must have a functioning social safety net and must create opportunities for those affected to find employment in other sectors of the economy.

Despite these negative impacts on the fates of some individuals, the consequences of the rise of emerging economies for Germany as a whole, from an overall economic perspective, have been further gains, not losses: Germany

---

[1] Although the relevant data were carefully compiled by the European Central Bank in this report (e.g. Table 2, p. 64), the obvious conclusion was not drawn. The unique opportunity to avoid the euro crisis at an early stage was missed.

exports considerably more goods than it imports. The increase in sales of goods abroad supports the German economy, and on balance, it creates jobs. As a rule, these job increases have occurred in other sectors than those that have relocated factories and workplaces to lower-wage jurisdictions abroad. But all in all, in regards to job numbers, Germany is better off, not worse off, as a result of international trade.

The necessary process of adaptation to international structural change certainly must be cushioned through social policy. However, it is simply wrong to pretend that an economy like Germany's suffers job losses, on balance, as a result of globalisation. Anyone who identifies globalisation as the problem when analysing the causes of Europe's serious labour market problems either has not thought the situation through carefully enough, or is pursuing a hidden political agenda by stirring up fear.

Trade in Times of Labour Migration

What happens if individual workers, or even entire groups of workers from low-wage countries decide not to wait until capital is made available to them in their home countries, and instead make their way to capital, i.e. emigrate to high-wage countries? We will refrain from discussing whether this could plausibly become a large-scale phenomenon, what legal framework might be applied to limit it, or whether, for demographic reasons, it might even be desirable. But let us examine the economic mechanisms in place between the countries concerned, and ask what economic rules should apply in order to make labour migration a beneficial process for countries of origin (i.e. low-wage countries) and countries of immigration (i.e. high-wage countries).

Workers from low-wage countries migrate to high-wage countries because they expect more available jobs, or higher wages, or both. In a normal labour market in a high-wage country, a so-called "destination country principle" applies *de facto*, i.e. immigrants in a high-wage country earn the same wage as local workers with the same qualifications. What are the economic consequences of this in a high-wage country? If there is no significant unemployment, and immigrant workers easily find jobs, immigration is no problem for the high-wage country; it even increases overall economic growth potential.

However, if there is significant unemployment in the high-wage country, it is unlikely that immigrants will find work at the prevailing wage. After all, why should an immigrant with otherwise equal qualifications be preferred to a native worker, given that the latter usually has no language difficulties or other adaptation problems? If immigrants are unable to find work, they will claim benefits from the social security systems. However, no society will tolerate this on a large scale for very long. The minimum standard of living that a rich society tries to guarantee its members through social security systems, with a view to ensuring social peace and cohesion, cannot be made available to the rest of the world, or even a noticeable part of it. In any case, if a rich society is prepared to spend money on a significant scale to help the poor from other countries, it can demonstrate its solidarity much more effectively through a massive increase in development aid than by importing people and paying them unemployment or welfare benefits.

But what happens when immigrants are prepared to work in a high-wage country at a much lower wage than the domestic workforce, and the host country is prepared to tolerate this? This willingness increases the likelihood of immigrants obtaining work in the host country. The fact that people often improve their standard of living compared to what they had experienced in their countries of origin, even if they have to accept lower wages compared to native workers in their new host country, is clearly a central motivator for migration.[2] And which entrepreneur in a high-wage country would not want to seize this opportunity to combine his highly efficient capital stock with low-wage workers who would not demand wages that correspond to the nation's overall labour productivity? The entrepreneur can thus achieve the benefits normally associated with investing capital in a low-wage jurisdiction without even having to offshore production facilities, with all the risks and costs that entails.

If the "country of destination principle" is abolished, and instead a "country of origin principle" is established for wage rates, immigrants will displace native workers. The latter either become unemployed and have to be financed by social security systems — a situation that is hardly acceptable to

---

[2] In reality, this deal does not always work out as advantageously as immigrants hope or expect; often, the cost of living is underestimated, housing is scarce and correspondingly expensive, or social integration fails.

society, and cannot be sustainable financed in the long term — or they adjust their wage expectations downwards. If the wage level in the high-wage country slips in this way, all the negative consequences already described above will occur: Declining domestic demand, falling corporate profits, wasted opportunities for growth and prosperity, more cut-throat competition on world markets, and/or appreciation of the domestic currency.

Immigrants' countries of origin will also be harmed by the wage cuts they have triggered in their new host countries. While labour markets in their countries of origin may find some marginal relief from excess unemployment,[3] migration does not create an additional capital stock in the low-wage country, as happens in the case of capital migration. The stay-behind populations in migrants' countries of origin do not benefit from the migrants' exit (except insofar as the migrants send part of their wage packets to relatives back home). The average productivity level does not increase, nor does the average wage level. No economic catching-up process is stimulated.

Instead, producers from the low-wage country are faced with even stiffer competition on the world market, because wage reductions create scope for global market share gains for entrepreneurs from the higher-wage country, achieved by means of price reductions. Although an appreciation of the currency of the high-wage country may ultimately reduce or eliminate this profit: the damage done in the meantime is often enormous — and not only in the low-wage country: Wage dumping causes a downward spiral in all those countries that are part of a monetary union with the high-wage country, or that have fixed their exchange rates to the high-wage country's currency for other reasons.

Only the consistent application of the country-of-destination principle, even in the face of high unemployment in high-wage countries, can prevent this vicious circle from damaging all participants in the trading system. This means that an unchecked flow of immigrants cannot be tolerated in Germany. This is in the interests of all concerned, notably including the low-wage countries surrounding Germany. The "law of one price," i.e. the principle of equal pay for equal work, must apply strictly to every individual nation, every

---

[3] Moreover, if it is particularly the most able and flexible workers who are willing to migrate, emigration should be seen as a brain drain.

culturally defined society, or every geographical region with a homogeneous level of development (i.e. an area with a fairly uniform capital stock level).

Where this principle is broken, economic crisis results, and neoliberal economic dogma prescribes crisis remedies that inevitably trigger a downward spiral: Wage cuts weaken domestic demand, causing the general level of domestic profits to fall, and with them, entrepreneurs' willingness to invest. Although wage cuts temporarily boost exports, the upside of this, in terms of producers' net income, is usually more than offset by the downside caused by the reduction in domestic demand.

At the same time, the state's ability to finance social security, welfare, and unemployment benefits is degraded and overstretched. Welfare and unemployment benefits systems were not, after all, designed to deal with a permanent failure of economic policy; they were only meant to temporarily cushion intertemporal and international structural changes. With the state's finances in trouble, the neoliberals' faulty analysis of the economic crisis immediately makes its next mistake: Neoliberalism says that the state as a whole must be radically shrunk if the challenge of globalised markets is to be mastered. The safety net is weakened, and people at the bottom of the economic pyramid are put under further pressure.

Given all this, it should be no surprise that the population is increasingly afraid of globalisation, and xenophobia is on the rise. Those who question the very foundations of Western society and its social-market institutions should be aware not only of the economic but also of the political consequences of their advice.

Digitisation as a Threat? Robots as Job Killers?

A topic that is both new and old is making the rounds at accelerating speed. Automation — the displacement of human workers by robots — is being hyped as a great danger. A confused debate "on machinery," as the English economist David Ricardo called it 200 years ago, is celebrating a renaissance.

The point at issue is so simple that one wonders how it can be that much of humanity still does not understand it. In their book *The End of Mass Unemployment*, Friederike Spiecker and Heiner Flassbeck described the connection between machinery and employment as follows:

Isn't it obvious? Unemployment is an inevitable fate: What was done yesterday by several workers on an assembly line is now done by a single robot. Where yesterday workers had to at least pack and label finished goods, today a computer-controlled packaging machine wraps and addresses them. More and more people are losing their jobs and — in some cases despite repeated retrainings — are unable to find new opportunities to earn a living. They become members of the class called "the long-term unemployed." Are we not systematically making ourselves unemployed through the increasing use of machines? Anyone who has taken a look into the factory halls of an automobile manufacturer, replete with robots yet nearly bereft of humans, is enduringly impressed, and finds himself feeling sympathy for those who stormed the machines a century ago in order to escape their job-destructive effect.

But sometimes impressions are deceptive. Until 400 years ago, almost no one was able to believe that we're all sitting on a large sphere that revolves around the sun, held in place by the mysterious force of gravity, because the visual impression made on us by the rising and setting sun is so incredibly formative for our normal comprehension. The mechanism by which wealth is created from capital, from machines that displace human workers, seems almost as mysterious as the force of gravity, and is as central to our complex economy as the force of gravity is to the complex natural processes on Earth.

Because this mechanism is complex, we must explain it in simple terms to make it understandable. Let's imagine Robinson Crusoe on his desert island. He feeds himself, with difficulty, by catching fish by hand. In order not to have to catch fish by hand for the rest of his life, he crafts a fishing rod, which makes fishing much easier than trying to catch fish with his hands. What has he done? He has invested in capital stock. Why has he done that? So that he can laze about for a few more hours a day without working, assuming his fishing rod design actually works. Or, alternatively, he could use the extra few hours available to him each day to build a cabin. Or he could do a bit of both: some combination of lazing about and cabin-building. His goal is to improve his lifestyle, to achieve a gain in prosperity. Whether he uses the time saved by the investment in a fishing-rod for more leisure time or for the production of additional goods or production machinery is up to him. In any case, Robinson will not consider himself unemployed, as he will either gain new goods (e.g. a hut) and/or more leisure time by catching fish faster (increasing his labour productivity). (Flassbeck & Spiecker, 2016, p. 27 f.)

In other words: When people go about producing something more intelligently and efficiently than previously, and making their lives easier with the help of machines (capital), that does not result in a rise in unemployment. The increase in productivity can increase the real income of society as a whole. It is therefore possible for everyone to afford more goods or more leisure time. The only bottleneck is the question of distribution of purchasing power. In order to generate additional effective demand for goods, it is necessary to ensure that those who will be the main generators of consumer demand in an economy — i.e. those who do not yet have everything they would like to have, from the palette of goods and services available on the market — must receive the income they need to buy the additional production made possible by more efficient production machinery and processes.

The question of whether to provide an increase in free time is somewhat more complicated, because it is not clear whether a reduction in working hours is really desired by the majority of workers. If this turns out to be the case, however, then it is important to ensure that everyone benefits equally from this possibility. Moreover, any reduction in working hours must be organised in such a way as to prevent consumer demand from collapsing and unused capacities from arising at companies (see Spiecker, 2014).

Now the question remains to be answered as to how to achieve rising incomes and rising demand in tandem with increasing labour productivity. This is absolutely necessary to avoid unemployment due to rationalisation. In the *FAZ* columnist's position referred to above, there is only one way to achieve this — namely falling prices caused by rising productivity. In principle, this approach is indeed feasible. If competitive pressure in the corporate sector is strong enough, rationalisation leads companies that successfully implement it to lower prices, or at least to increase them less than their competitors. If this causes a general reduction in price level, then real wages (purchasing power) rise even as nominal wages remain constant. Rising real wages will generally lead (given an unchanged propensity to save) to rising demand for goods and services, which will lead to a positive employment impulse that can offset the negative job effect of rationalisation of production processes.

Let us assume that an increase in productivity occurs. The *FAZ* columnist assumes in his above-mentioned article that prices (or the price level) must correspondingly fall in absolute terms, in order to generate the increase in real wages necessary for aggregate demand, in turn, to increase by an amount

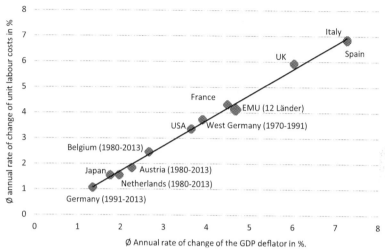

Figure 1: Inflation and unit labour cost growth during the period 1970–2013 in different countries

Source: AMECO, OECD.

that makes it possible to sell the increased production volume, while keeping the same number of workers employed. Is this correct?

The answer is: Not necessarily. Whether or not the price level falls depends on the development of nominal wages; these may be falling, remaining constant, or rising slightly. The latter condition would correspond to the positive inflation targets that Western societies have set themselves.

The crucial empirical relationship is easy to understand (Figure 1). Real wages increase exactly as much as productivity if nominal wages increase year-on-year at the rate of real productivity increase plus the inflation rate or inflation target (measured here as the GDP deflator). If such a rate of nominal wage growth can be implemented, society can durably achieve a slightly positive, stable inflation rate in the long term.

Germany, for example, had an inflation rate of around 3.5% between 1970 and 1991, i.e. until German unification. However, during the prolonged era of wage restraint since the mid-1990s, nominal wage increases were curtailed so sharply that the interplay of nominal wages and productivity resulted in an inflation rate of only 1%. The result of this was the deflationary trend of recent years in Europe. It originated in Germany.

Over long time-frames such as those considered here, competitive pressures on goods markets generally cause inflation rates to fall, if wages are not increased in line with what we have long called the "golden rule": Wages should rise by the sum of the average increase in productivity plus the inflation target.

The result of long-term pressure to restrain nominal wages (i.e. to hold wage increases lower than the general rate of increase in productivity) is therefore a low rate of inflation, or even deflation (as in Japan since the early 1990s). However, a lag in real wages (wages as measured by purchasing power) behind productivity growth is much less likely. Consequently, it is entirely rational to refrain from attempts at redistribution via downward pressure on nominal wages; instead, it would make sense to increase nominal wages in line with the sum of the productivity trend line and the target inflation rate.

This is a message that a newspaper like the neoliberally inclined *FAZ* does not like to hear. Their stance emphasises wage flexibility, which of course means flexibility in real wages. Basically, it amounts to a call for increases in real wages to fall short of productivity growth. But if real wage increases fall short of productivity increases, as has been the case in Germany over the last 15 years, then the domestic population would not be able to afford to buy the increase in the quantity of goods that could potentially be produced. Unemployment is the inevitable consequence, unless foreign demand compensates for weakened domestic demand.

If a country allows average wages to rise more slowly than average productivity, then in order to maintain output and employment, it must rely on foreign countries' willingness to live beyond their means — i.e. for its trading partners to enable the net-exporting country's current account surplus through their own current account deficits. This was the recipe that Germany applied so "successfully" within the framework of European monetary union. It worked because the other countries in the Eurozone could no longer defend themselves by devaluing their currency.

Whether the analysis is applied to the whole world, or to a relatively closed economy such as the US or Europe, the result of such a policy is easily predictable: Falling real wages, or wages lagging behind increases in productivity, will result in increased unemployment. Workers are not merely workers — they are also consumers. If the enhanced production possibilities created by robots (resulting in increases in labour productivity) are not met by additional effective demand, the net result will be that companies dismiss workers.

Because this causal relationship is perfectly clear, there is no need to wait for very imperfect market processes to result — eventually — in price cuts for goods and services, ultimately resulting in real wage increases for those people who still have a job. Instead, it is better to ensure from the outset that nominal wages rise as strongly as the trend increase in labour productivity plus the inflation target. This can be done during sectoral wage negotiations between unions and employers' associations, or if necessary, it can be imposed by the state. Anyone who believes that it is reasonable for the central bank to set an inflation target should logically be in favour of managing nominal wages in this way.

Why is Productivity so Low?

If robots are job killers, then the productivity of labour should go through the roof as more robots are deployed. If robots are actually going to replace people to an unprecedented extent, then labour productivity should in future increase far faster than it has in the past.

Empirical data show that this is not happening — not yet, at least. Figure 2 shows the evolution of hourly labour productivity (with 1991 as the base year) in the five largest industrialised countries. This reveals that productivity growth has dramatically slowed in recent years. Especially since the end of the great financial crisis (GFC) of 2008/09, productivity has stagnated in almost all the countries that many observers believe to be at the forefront of technological progress.

Even in the USA, where economic growth remains relatively robust, productivity growth has come to a standstill.[4] The development is particularly striking in Italy, where a dramatic break in productivity development has occurred since the beginning of this century (which, not coincidentally, is the same year Italy joined the European Monetary Union).

Figure 3 shows the same data as a growth rate compared to the previous year, reflecting the slowdown even more clearly. Productivity growth was at

---

[4] However, the USA numbers show a surprising jump upwards in labour productivity from 2008 to 2009, which is hard to explain — because in a recession, productivity normally declines, given that more workers than needed are kept on staff by companies in the short term.

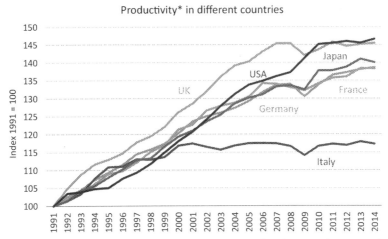

*Real gross domestic product in national currency per hour of employment; index 1991 = 100

Figure 2:   Productivity in different countries

Source: AMECO.

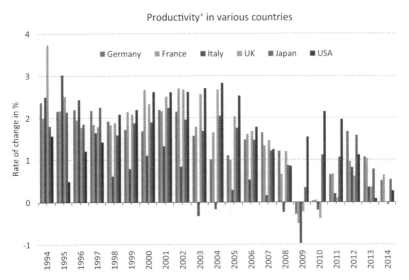

+ Real gross domestic product in national currency per hour of employment; moving 3-year average of annual growth rates

Figure 3:   Productivity in different countries

Source: AMECO.

about 2% in the 1990s. It has been falling since the beginning of the new century, and has recently been well below 1% in all countries.

This certainly cannot be explained solely by a huge overestimation of the effects of the information technology revolution. There is no doubt that this revolution is underway. And there is likewise no doubt that the effects of this revolution on specific workplaces will be as severe as those of earlier technical revolutions.

Today, the implementation of changes that are technologically possible does not seem to be occurring at a pace comparable to that of previous investment cycles driven by major evolutions in technology. The idea that robots are "job killers" is mistaken in any case, because there are countervailing forces that generate additional demand, as described above. Moreover, the idea that robots directly generate higher productivity applies to a much lesser extent than most people believe.

Why are Investments not Increasing?

Figure 4 shows the development of all investments (i.e. investments in machinery and equipment as well as construction investments). Investment activity has been very moderate since the beginning of the 1990s, with the exception of the USA, where construction investments expanded very strongly in the course of the housing bubble in the early 2000s. Germany and Japan, in particular, largely decoupled themselves from a positive development in investment trends since 1991 — in contrast to France, where investment has remained relatively strong. Since the great financial crisis, however, investment activity has only picked up significantly in the USA (and to some extent in Great Britain). Italy, on the other hand, has been crashing since the mid-2000s.

This is also reflected in gross investment rates as a percentage of gross domestic product (GDP) (Figure 5). Japan has experienced a major decline; the USA is catching up from a very low level in the 1990s; Great Britain is historically weak; and Germany too has been experiencing a slow but steady decline for over 20 years. On a long-term basis, France looks in comparatively good shape, but is currently having difficulty emerging from the crisis. Italy is the weakest of the large countries by this measure as well, and it is not surprising that more and more Italian economists have come to associate the country's economic crash directly with membership in the Eurozone.

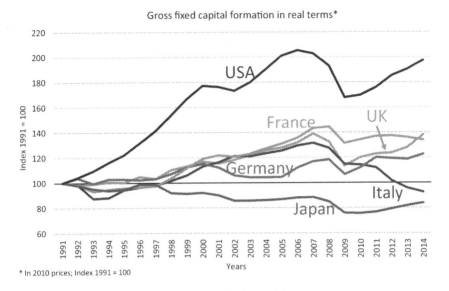

Figure 4:   Real gross fixed capital formation

Source: AMECO.

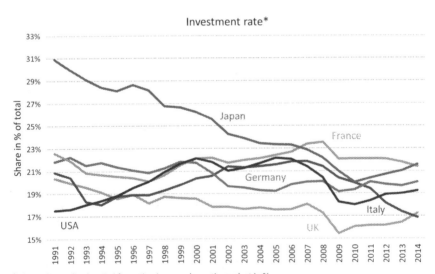

Figure 5:   Investment ratio

Source: AMECO.

The fact that Germany is doing so poorly in terms of capital investment should be seen as a political scandal of the first order, given the massive tax cuts over the past two decades that were justified in the name of "investment promotion." This has been pointed out many times among specialists (cf. Flassbeck & Spiecker, 2013), but there is very little discussion of it in public or political discourse. When it is written about (cf. Fratzscher, 2016; Flassbeck, 2014), the decisive connection to weak demand is generally not mentioned.

Berlin's DIW and Munich's ifo Institute are two of the most prominent economic think-tanks in Germany. The economists at both of these institutions appear unable to recognise, or at any rate openly say, that domestic demand has been extremely weak for years; ifo economists even speak of a "mystery." According to *FAZ*, the newspaper of record in Germany's banking capital, Frankfurt, economist Klaus Wohlrabe of ifo said: "General economic conditions have been very good for years" (Reuters, 2015). In his assessment, Wohlrabe pointed to low oil prices, low interest rates, and good financing conditions for companies, and comes to the conclusion: "Every year, you think it [a domestic investment boom] will get started now, but then it doesn't really."

That's what happens when you impose ideological thought-prohibitions on your assessment framework: your "scientific" explanations do not work out very well. When mainstream economists refer to "good framework conditions," they tend to forget that low taxes for companies and low wages for workers were two key factors introduced in the early 2000s in an attempt to stimulate a high and stable level of investment activity. We have explained how too-low wage increases are responsible for the fact that domestic investment levels are so weak. Yet for a mainstream economist, this proposition is, of course, completely absurd.

From a macroeconomic perspective, the weakness in Europe's productivity growth is the result of a weakness in investment, and the talk of robots displacing people is chimeric. Recognising this eliminates the need to put forward policy proposals in response to robotisation. It is particularly absurd to call for a tax on new machines, as some on the left now consider opportune (cf. Seidl, 2016).

The only "machine tax" urgently needed all over the world is rising real wages. If it is ensured that real wages rise in tandem with productivity, so that employees can participate fully in the economic progress their work has made possible, then the central prerequisite for successful rationalisation of production processes through automation is met. If the products that can be created by means of increasingly efficient production processes are to be sold, then obviously people must have the financial means to purchase them. And as we have explained, this must be achieved through a process that is not dependent on falling prices.

Liberalism's Fake Answers

We have shown that the majority of economists describe and explain the problems of globalisation and digitisation completely inappropriately, with faulty assumptions and analysis. Nevertheless, their analyses remain the basis of economic policy in many countries around the world.

Why are the misconceptions of economic liberalism so persistent? It is because liberalism offers an extremely seductive promise: the promise that a "free" market economy makes it possible to combine maximum individual freedom with maximum economic efficiency. Indeed, it is even promised, as Bernard Mandeville wrote as long ago as 1714 in his *Fable of The Bees* (Mandeville, 1714), that in a market economy, even "private vices" are transformed into "public advantages."

If the work of the "invisible hand" really did make it possible to channel even morally highly questionable actions in a way that ensures they redound to the benefit of all, then a market society would undoubtedly be an unbeatably attractive model of society. The great problem of moral philosophy, namely how to get people to do what contradicts the pursuit of their own selfish interests, would be resolved. In the context of a market society, morality would simply become, as Andreas Suchanek writes, an "investment for one's own benefit." The market economy would therefore be a moral order that does not require moral behaviour at the level of the individual:

> In other words, the moral preferability of the market economy is that it encourages people to invest in the (conditions of) cooperation for mutual benefit and thus to behave according to the Golden Rule. (Suchanek, 2012)

Marvellous! The only problem is that no such social order can arise with real people in the context of real macroeconomic relationships that are not apparent to individual economic actors. In other words, liberalism, as a comprehensive philosophy of society that encompasses both economic liberalism and the various variants of political liberalism, makes promises that cannot be kept.

The Ordering Principles of Economic Liberalism

Hans-Werner Sinn, the recently retired long-time head of Munich's ifo Institute for Economic Research, demonstrated some time ago in the *Süddeutsche Zeitung* how absurd it is to try to align the world with the ideal of a normative theory of the market economy. He first describes the task of economists as follows: "Like sniffer dogs, economists search the economy for market failures and consider how these failures can be corrected by clever state intervention" (Sinn, 2014).

Modern economic liberals apparently see no fundamental contradiction between the state and the market. They are in favour of the state using its power when it comes to correcting "market failures." However, in order to identify market failures, economists are needed who have been suitably trained for this sleuthing task, in the manner of sniffer dogs. In the view of Sinn and his colleagues, this task requires economists who have understood "neoclassical economic theory" and recognised that this theory has identified the necessary and sufficient conditions that must be met for an economic order to be "efficient."

An economic order is efficient, according to liberal icon Ludwig von Mises, "when it points the way for individual action and directs it to where it can be most useful for the purposes of fellow citizens" (cf. Mises, 1940, p. 250 f.). This conviction is common to all liberal economic theories. The market economy is efficient principally because it guarantees a distribution of goods in which nobody is put in a worse position so that another can be put in a better position. All trades are voluntary, and everyone calibrates their trades for their own benefit, given their own priorities and resources. The market economy is therefore regarded from the outset as a just social order.

From this perspective, "market failures" are not actually errors of the market, but rather, they are all those facts that are incompatible with the assumptions and logical derivations of neoclassical economic theory. Eliminating market errors is thus also a matter of establishing justice.

When an economist, in assessing the real existing economy, has identified deviations from the neoclassical master plan, it is his task to propose how to eliminate those deviations. The sniffer dog will, according to Sinn, now assume the role of a doctor:

> A doctor must know what a healthy body looks like, otherwise he cannot diagnose and heal diseases. A good doctor does not intervene arbitrarily in the processes of the body, but only if he can objectively diagnose a disease in the sense of a deviation from the norm, and has an effective therapy available. (Sinn, 2014)

Facts that contradict the requirements of neoclassical theory are therefore diseases that the neoclassically trained economist can recognise and treat.

For example, the French economist Gerard Debreu, using the incorruptible means of mathematics, was awarded the so-called Nobel Prize in Economics[5] in 1983 for proving that there can be no unemployment in a market economy. In a market economy system, those who are without work are not involuntarily unemployed. Rather, they have chosen not to work for the market wage, which always corresponds exactly to the marginal benefit of labour as a factor of production. They prefer instead to wait for better opportunities or to enjoy their leisure time. Anyone who is unemployed has therefore decided not to work on the basis of individual benefit considerations.

In the real world, there are many people who are not waiting for better opportunities, and have not opted for more free time, but actually cannot find paid work. However, rather than acknowledge this as a problem in need of solutions, liberal economic orthodoxy simply reinterprets it as the result of individual behavioural choices. It isn't the real-world behaviour of the individual that is decisive; rather, it is his or her imputed behaviour within the artificial construct of the imaginary perfect market.

Since the market economy guarantees full employment, according to the "logic of the market," it follows that involuntary unemployment can only

---

[5] The Nobel Prize in Economics was not endowed by Alfred Nobel; instead, it was established by the Swedish central bank many decades after Nobel's death. Its prizes are awarded by committees dominated by neoclassical economists.

occur if people do not act appropriately, or if the state has failed to create the conditions that are indispensable for the functioning of market mechanisms. In reality, as we will show below, there are conditions in every real market economy that prevent individuals from improving their situation through their own behaviour; but this fact is simply ignored.

For liberal economic theorists, the market economy is clearly a normative ideal to which reality must be aligned. They therefore call for the privatisation of public services, the liberalisation of trade, the dismantling of all state rules hindering market processes, the reduction of taxes, the dismantling of the welfare state, and the intensification of competition at all levels.

When one examines the meagre foundations of this theory,[6] as outlined briefly below, it is truly astonishing how submissively politicians have followed the policy proposals of neoliberal thinkers over the last 40 years.

Bartering

Adam Smith was of the opinion that anthropological characteristics of human beings explain the existence of barter. Today, perhaps, liberal economists would hesitate to make such a bold statement, but they nevertheless regard the exchange of goods as the outstanding and individual welfare-optimising characteristic of a market economy (Smith, 1979[1776], p. 13 f.).

But if people do not exchange assets simply because they are driven to do so and cannot do otherwise, then what is the reason for this behaviour? Obviously, one must have something that a counterparty would like, and vice versa. But how can it be explained that different people have control of different goods, and therefore have a reason to exchange them?

Ludwig von Mises, who can undoubtedly be regarded as one of the pioneers of neoliberalism, gave the following answer:

> If the surface of the earth were such that the conditions of production were the same at all its points, and if one man were as similar to the rest of mankind as a circle is to any other circle of the same diameter in Euclidean geometry, then the division of labour would offer no advantages to those involved. (Mises, 1940, p. 125)

---

[6] For more details, see Steinhardt (2015, pp. 97–169); the following explanations also refer to that text.

Barter makes it possible to obtain goods that one is not in a position to produce oneself. Someone who barters away a good that had been in his possession is implicitly valuing that good less highly than the good he intends to acquire through exchange. The exchange thus makes it possible for everyone involved to increase their individual net benefit. According to this story, value in a market economy is created not only by production of goods but also by their trade.

For economic liberals, prices are the numerical expression of subjective expectations of utility. For consumer goods, then, these utility expectations must ultimately impact the prices of production factors. In a market economy, according to this concept, goods are always exchanged for goods, and the use of money only disguises this fact. The phrase conventionally used by neoclassical economists to express this notion is "money is merely a veil over barter."

Even the most complex and apparently sophisticated neoclassical economic models attempt to explain the functioning of the market economy on the basis of bartering of goods. They implicitly assume that economic subjects can bring all conceivable goods into a ranked-order list of preferences, and on this basis decide which goods they want to exchange under which circumstances. People have, it is assumed, a definite and knowable set of preferences.

In the 19th century, the Frenchman Léon Walras was the first to use mathematics to show what a completely static economic system could look like if one made certain assumptions about people and their wishes, and about the macroeconomic framework. Of particular relevance is the assumption that perfect information prevails, which means that all economic subjects are aware of all the alternatives for action available to them, and also those of all other economic subjects.

In other words, the class of model initiated by Walras — descendants of which are still in use today — suggests that a market economy could guarantee full employment if all market participants were omniscient.

Moreover, the market economy is not only efficient. Even better, it is also a voluntary association of free people, as Milton Friedman assures us:

> The political principle that underlies the market mechanism is unanimity.
> In an ideal free market resting on private property, no individual can coerce

any other, all cooperation is voluntary, all parties to such cooperation benefit or they need not participate. There are not values, no "social" responsibilities in any sense other than the shared values and responsibilities of individuals. Society is a collection of individuals and of the various groups they voluntarily form. (Friedman, 1970, essay, "The social responsibility of business is to increase its profits.")

But how is it possible for people who act solely in their own interest to maximise the common good? According to economic liberals, it is competition that guides their actions in the right direction.

Competition and Its Enemies

According to economic liberals, in a market economy, several providers must typically compete for the favour of customers in any given product category. Precisely because everyone wants to maximise their profit, yet faces the risk of losing customers to a competitor, competition ensures that goods are produced in the desired quantity and quality with the least possible effort.

Surprisingly, many left-wing politicians see it the same way. The German Left Party co-leader Sahra Wagenknecht, for example, considers the current economic order, which she calls "capitalism," to be problematic. But she distinguishes this "capitalism" from the market economy, which she sees as a good thing. She is convinced that the existing capitalist system's problems are due in large measure to a lack of competition between companies (Wagenknecht, 2011, p. 20).

Competition is good, according to Wagenknecht, because where it occurs, there is "no reason why an entrepreneur should get paid more than his own entrepreneurial contribution." For Wagenknecht, "competition" is to be assessed as unreservedly positive from an ethical point of view, because it excludes so-called "unearned income from capital ownership," which is based on exploitation of workers.

If it is true that unearned income is based on the ethically unjustifiable "exploitation" of employees, one naturally wonders why one then does not simply put a stop to the activities of "yield hunters." The reason, according to Wagenknecht, is that "the calculation of prospective returns is a strong incentive to use labour-saving technologies and to bring new products and services onto the market." Greed on the one hand and fear on the other seem to combine here to produce good results. Greed for the highest possible (non-market) returns and fear of otherwise losing customers to competitors create incentives for producers to offer potential customers the best products at the lowest price.

In her song of praise for competition, Wagenknecht refers to representatives of German Ordoliberalism such as Walter Eucken, Wilhelm Röpke, and Alexander Rüstow. But even Röpke saw that competition is a double-edged sword. The "continuing struggle for self-assertion," he said, "has a worrying tendency to produce effects that cannot leave us indifferent from a moral point of view." He feared that "politeness, friendliness and comradeship" will be deprived of their moral content, since behaviours to which these attributes can be ascribed will degenerate into a mere "means of increasing sales" under conditions of economic competition. While competition cannot be "intense" enough for Wagenknecht, Röpke, by contrast, on the basis of his moral concerns, proposed that competition be softened or "muted" (quoted from Thielemann, 2010, p. 18).

Competition Between Whom and for What?

However, both the song of praise for competition and concerns about its negative consequences are based on a false understanding of what distinguishes entrepreneurial competition. Competition is often seen as a situation where companies can do whatever they want. Or it is even thought that competition prevails when it is not only companies that compete with each other, but nation-states as well. The latter compete to offer the best so-called framework conditions for companies. Nowadays, hardly anyone seems to understand that such ideas are a perversion of the idea of entrepreneurial competition.

Such misconceptions of "competition" should not, however, lead anyone to call into question the usefulness of the competitive dynamics characteristic of market economies. Competition has undoubtedly raised people's standard of living enormously. But this "good" competition is about the technological and organisational market leadership of individual companies. That is not at all the same thing as the ordoliberals' theoretical concept of competition.

For ordoliberals, competition is a situation in which it is impossible for individual companies to make so-called monopoly profits. In other words, they claim that under competitive conditions, companies can only achieve identical profit margins. But this is not competition as it exists in reality.

Entrepreneurial competition for market leadership — competition in the sense of Joseph Schumpeter — does exist in the real world, and it is indispensable for the functioning of a market economy. In this type of competition, companies try to achieve cost advantages by applying technological innovation, without abusing their market power to push wages downward.

However, the investment dynamics that can be generated as a result of innovation must be guided by the state. This guidance must encompass both the provision of a functioning monetary system and the management of income distributions between economic actors. That is because, as we will show later, the market left to its own devices is incapable of providing a distribution of income consistent with full employment — or with social justice.

As Schumpeter first pointed out, innovation competition requires a suitable macroeconomic framework and process conditions comprising many distinct elements. It is a mistake to apply the concept of competition to advocate wage cost-cutting competitions between companies, or attempts by states to reduce business costs in ways that culminate in races to the bottom (for example, by failing to enforce environmental protection laws).

Decades ago, post-Keynesian Cambridge economist Joan Robinson provided the following analogy to show why such races are counterproductive: If a single spectator stands up in a crowded cinema, she can improve her situation because she then has a better view than those that remain seated. If everyone stands up, however, their situation obviously does not improve; compared to the *status quo ante*, it worsens, because no one can see any better, and everyone's feet will soon hurt. So the question arises: Does one cinema-goer's standing up count as an innovation in the Schumpeterian sense? Or is it merely a miserable attempt to gain a short-term advantage for oneself by massively violating an unwritten rule — an advantage that cannot be sustained in the long term in any case, as the system ends up with everyone having to stand?

This question can be answered easily if the central criterion for successful entrepreneurial competition is understood: Competition in the Schumpeterian sense is focussed on innovation, and it can only be considered successful if it has the potential to lead to generally rising incomes. To put it another way: In an innovation-centric competition, there is always an additional net benefit at the end of the process, in the form of a third-party winner whose gains are not made at the expense of any corresponding loser. As a rule, the main winner is the consumer, because the entrepreneur must ultimately pass on his competitive advantage to the consumer in the form of falling prices. In contrast, no one wins in a cinema when one person stands up and consequently forces the others to stand up as well.

Entrepreneurial practice of recent years illustrates this argument. If a company lowers its costs by reducing wages, it may improve its own competitive situation in the short term, and gain market share. However, the collective situation of companies as a whole will not improve through that company's wage-cutting, because its employees (who are always also consumers) will have less money to spend, and therefore demand fewer goods produced by other companies. Where is the third-party winner? There isn't one. The first company lowers its prices, which brings it additional orders. But other companies consequently have fewer orders. The overall situation of companies does not improve. It is a win–lose rather than a win–win game.

It is different when a company tries to reduce its costs not with wage cuts, but rather through organisational and technical innovations. In this case, productivity rises, and consequently, incomes across the economy as a whole may also rise. There is indeed a third-party winner, namely the consumer, including the employee in her role as consumer, because now she can buy more goods than before the productivity-enhancing innovation took place. Either the prices of the innovating company's products have fallen, or wages have risen more strongly without worsening the unit cost situation of companies.

We can see from this exposition that cost reductions are by no means always innovative. Cost reductions that occur in the absence of innovation (i.e. cost reductions achieved simply by paying less for factors of production — in particular, for wages) are of no benefit to society, because one economic actor's costs are always another economic actor's income. Often, such cost reductions are just a desperate attempt by a single company to save its skin. From the point of view of the company's manager, this is by no means irrational. However, it is irrational for a policymaker to want to turn cost-cutting in the absence of innovation into an economic policy strategy.

So, what does this say about economic competition between nations? Does it have the features of Schumpeterian innovation competition, or is it a beggar-thy-neighbour cost-reduction race that is a net negative from a macroeconomic point of view? Is it innovative for states to take part in tax- and cost-cutting competitions, for example, and thereby deprive those members of society who can at least defend themselves of their support? Is it innovative for a government to reduce corporate taxes and consequently be forced to reduce investment in infrastructure and education?

The fact that competitive tax-cutting is essentially ideologically motivated is demonstrated by the unequal treatment of tax cuts and state subsidies, although the boundaries between these measures are in reality blurred. Tax-cutting competitions between nations do not, in the opinion of many market fundamentalists, contravene rules against "dumping" practices that have been established through the World Trade Organisation or the relevant EU competition bodies. Subsidy competitions, in contrast, are understood to be strictly against the rules. The latter are considered bad, because they entail the "danger" of an expansion of state activity, whereas the former are considered good, because restrictions of state activity are "always necessary" in the view of neoliberal theorists.

Left to itself, the market cannot prevent dynamics from arising that undermine productivity-focussed competition. The economic incentives operating on individual entrepreneurs tend to ensure that they will want to do exactly the opposite of that which makes sense for the economy as a whole — i.e. to cut wages and costs, in order to be able to reduce prices and grab market share, or increase short-run profit margins. Entrepreneurs' immediate short-term incentive is to be the first to stand up in the cinema.

The Knowledge Problem and Its Apparent Solution

In view of the aforementioned points, an assertion that a society based on division of labour and free exchange of goods and services is always preferable to other possible forms of society would seem to be on somewhat shaky ground. Liberals such as Friedrich August von Hayek, another winner of the Nobel Prize in economics, would disagree, and claim that this impression arises only when actually existing forms of society are compared with idealised conceptions of possible forms of society. Instead, Hayek said that one must ask why the market economy has established itself as a preeminent mode of social organisation worldwide (Hayek, 1988, p. 38 ff.). Hayek argued that this has occurred because only a market economy allows the so-called "knowledge problem" to be satisfactorily solved.

Hayek begins his evolutionary narrative with his claim of a naturally unequal distribution of knowledge among people. In his opinion, this unequal distribution cannot be eliminated, since there exists something he calls "tactical knowledge," or "how-to knowledge," which he believes cannot be communicated. Hayek assumes that decisions are normally made under conditions of uncertainty, and that the coordination of economic plans between different market participants therefore cannot arise on the basis of their subjective knowledge of the needs or desires of others for their goods.

Just like the neoclassical economists, Hayek assumed that people try to maximise their utility through their actions. Unlike neoclassical economists, however, he saw people as social beings who can learn from each other. In his opinion, people observed that producers who specialised in the production of certain goods, and then covered their needs for other goods by trading, were better off. This observation inspired imitation.

In due course, a generally accepted means of exchange, which we call money, became established as a solution to circumvent the problem of directly comparing benefits of product-pairs and finding exchange partners whose goods were needed. In a market economy, every good has a cash price. The price mechanism characteristic of free markets makes it possible to coordinate the plans of economic entities as if they had the necessary knowledge to compare product-pair benefits.

But this is where a crucial problem arises. Economic liberals like Hayek and his successors have refused to address it, because they intuit that it could debunk their beautiful neoliberal/neoclassical dreamworld. The problem is that there are situations in which the price mechanism is completely misleading. If, for example, the demand for raw materials, land, and other assets only increases because the prices of these assets are rising in a self-reinforcing speculative spiral, and not because people want to own these goods in order to satisfy their "preferences," then the market economy has a fundamental problem: Instead of stabilising prices, the market mechanism destabilises them.

To take another example, if downward pressure on wages can be observed on the labour market, even though existing unemployment has nothing to do with "too high wages," then the market mechanism is fundamentally failing, and the state has to intervene. And if corporations fail to fulfil their most important task — that of using the savings of private households to make productive investments — because there is no price mechanism in operation that would encourage them to do so, then there is an information problem that can only be solved by an economic actor who has insight into (and influence over) macroeconomic relationships that are wholly independent of any individual firm's or investor's benefit-maximisation calculation. That economic actor is undoubtedly none other than the state.

Political Liberalism

Political liberalism focuses on the freedom of people as expressed in individual self-determination. Everyone can think and do whatever they believe to be right. Everyone may — indeed should — pursue happiness according to their own priorities and preferences, and concomitantly, everyone is forbidden to hinder other individuals in their pursuit of personal happiness.

The state must accordingly be neutral in regards to diverse conceptions of what is good and right. The activities of the state are only legitimate insofar as their purpose is to prevent individuals from restricting the freedoms of other citizens.

According to liberal theorists, "freedom" is to be understood as the absence of personal compulsion. In this sense, it must be understood as a negative freedom. One of the most important proponents of classical liberalism, John Stuart Mill, summed up this credo:

> The perfection both of social arrangements and of practical morality would be, to secure to all persons complete independence and freedom of action, subject to no restriction but that of not doing injury to others. (Mill, Principles of Political Economy, Book II, Chapter I.)

Political liberalism is thus a normative theory that deals with the relationship between a state and its citizens. It attempts to answer the question: To what extent, and under what conditions, may people or groups that can be regarded as representatives of the state, rule over other people? The answer offered by liberals is that rulership is legitimised if and only if it is approved by all those over whom the state exercises its rule.

However, the reality is that liberalism cannot really find a satisfactory answer to this question, because, as shown above, it ignores a whole dimension of problems that need to be solved — the macroeconomic dimension — for purely ideological reasons. Liberalism is at best a two-dimensional solution hypothesis in a space that is at least three-dimensional.

Freedom and Coercion

To understand liberalism, one has to keep the ideology's model of human nature in mind. For liberals, people are beings who are distinguished in particular by their ability to take action. Action, in turn, is seen in liberalism as behavior that is subject to human control and decision-making. So when people take action, they do what they do because they want a certain consequence to occur, or a particular situation to arise, and because they believe that their action will cause the desired result. He who acts knows what he is doing and why he is doing it, and he does what he wills.

Moreover, according to liberals, people are not only beings who take action; they are beings who have the ability to act in a self-determined manner. Furthermore, liberals postulate that all people have the desire to live out this ability to as unlimited a degree as possible. According to liberals, people even have the ability and desire to become the people they would like to become.

One can only speak of an "action" if the actor has decided to do something, but not all actions meet liberals' ideal of liberty. For example, if a bank robber says to a bank employee, "give me your money or I'll shoot," the cashier could in principle decide not to hand over the money; yet if she decides to give the money in her till to the bank robber, then she certainly has not done so of her own free will. The action she took was forced on her by the coercive options the bank robber presented. Freedom prevails only where people are not forced by a threat from a third party to take an action they would rather not have taken.

Ideally, people should be able to do what they want to do on the basis of their own concept of a good life, free from any compulsion. Freedom is a circumstance in which people can use their knowledge and skills in whichever ways are to their liking, as long as they do not restrict the freedom of others in doing so.

Liberalism is, on the one hand, a revolutionary doctrine that calls for the elimination of all circumstances that prevent human beings from exercising self-determination. On the other hand, liberalism is also an excellent way of defending oneself against the demands of others, especially when the other is represented by state organisations and has the power to enforce or coerce certain actions. It is no coincidence that liberals have always called for the protection of minority rights, and warned against abuse of power by the majority. The principles of liberalism and of democracy are thus in some degree of mutual tension. "Freedom" is indispensable in order to lead a self-determined life, but the democratic state must, in order to serve the public interest, undoubtedly set limits on the freedoms of individuals.

As already mentioned, liberals only deem state actions as legitimate if they would receive the consent of those affected under somewhat "idealised" epistemic conditions (Bratu, 2014, p. 21). The actions of a liberal state must not express a preference for a certain conception of the good or right life; rather, the state must behave neutrally. Politics must therefore renounce any ambitions to achieve a "better" society through its actions.

But how can the fact that the majority of people in a market economy have to earn their living through dependent employment be reconciled with the right to self-determination? Are such employment relationships not characterised by employers' rights of instruction and control, and does this reality not contradict the ideal of individual self-determination?

For most liberals, the question of the legitimacy of wage labour does not arise, because in their discourse, it is the result of a "capitalistic act between consenting adults" (Nozick, 1974, p. 163). People have the right to dispose of their labour freely, and can therefore make it available to third parties as they see fit. Taking this to its logical extreme, Robert Nozick even sees no problem in people giving up their right to self-determination completely and for the rest of their lives — that is, practically enslaving themselves.

In Nozick's view, a social relationship can be described as "fair" if it has been established on the basis of a contract. Liberals must therefore strictly reject any redistribution of income or wealth, insofar as these are the result of market relations. In their opinion, any such intervention would ultimately be tantamount to a ban on free negotiation of contracts.

Social liberals, on the other hand, recognise that a self-determined life is contingent on material prerequisites. They may see it as legitimate for the state to ensure that all people who are morally innocent of wrongdoing have, at a minimum, their basic needs met. But in adopting this position, social liberals are departing from strict liberalism, because they are accepting that situations exist in which individual freedom is trumped by another value.

John Rawls, arguably the most influential political philosopher of the 20th century, does justice to this intuition with his so-called "difference principle." According to this principle, a social order that allows divergences from strict equality is acceptable only insofar as the inequalities in question tend to make the least advantaged in society materially better off than they would be under strict equality (Rawls, 2017[1971], p.104). In order for this principle to pass the liberal litmus test of consent, Rawls, in a famous thought experiment, imagined that citizens whose consent is required for the construction of a social order characterised by the "difference principle" were required to step behind a so-called "veil of ignorance" (*Ibid.*, p. 159 ff.). Behind this veil, people have no information about their physical or social characteristics; they have no conception of the good; indeed, they do not even know in what historical era or in what kind of society they will be living in. These fictitious individuals then apply razor-sharp logic to infer that under the fictitious circumstances on which Rawls' scenario is based, they may happen to be among the most naturally disadvantaged, born into poor circumstances, with little talent or means. They will therefore agree to all laws designed to ensure that the "difference principle" is respected.

By formulating the difference principle as a condition of a legitimate system of rule, Rawls precisely specified what economists call "Pareto optimality" and regard as the characteristic hallmark of a market economy. Rawls thus makes it clear that political and economic liberalism are mutually supportive. Liberals are committed to human emancipation, and want to see compulsion — whether generated by the force of tradition, or by the state — replaced by free association of free people. It is no coincidence that they mutate into economic liberals in political practice.

The Greens in the German state of Baden-Württemberg are paradigmatic examples of this. The Green Party premier of Baden-Württemberg, Winfried Kretschmann, has openly said that we live in an era marked by "insecurity and crises" (quoted from Feldenkirchen, 2016). In such a time, according to

Kretschmann, "it is important to secure the cohesion of society." However, he is not at all of the opinion that the state is called upon to pursue an economic policy aimed at removing people's fears for their jobs, or that guarantees the cohesion of society through a further development of the welfare state.

Rather, what is needed are "freedom," "individualism," and "security." Since Kretschmann believes the Greens represent the first two values and the third is represented by his political partners in the state's governing coalition, the conservative Christian Democratic Union (CDU) party, it becomes clear that even "progressive" liberals have long since made their peace with the neoliberal *status quo*. This verdict is impressively confirmed in the coalition agreement concluded at state level between the Green Party and the CDU:

> We align our political action with the values consensus of a social and eco-logical market economy [...]. We only use regulatory law instruments where they are really necessary. (Bündnis 90/Die Grünen Baden-Württemberg & CDU Baden-Württemberg, 2016, p. 13)

The highest value to which this coalition of left-wing and right-wing liberals is committed is the market economy. The adjectives "social" and "ecological" are presumably meant to calm the conscience, but can also easily be understood to mean that the management of social and ecological problems should be left to the wisdom of the markets, by means of mechanisms like "emissions trading" or tax-advantaged private savings accounts.

Legislation is the core mechanism of authority of a democratically organised society. Legislation is written by elected representatives of the citizens who are meant to look after the people's interests. Under coalitions of left- and right-wing liberals, it seems the legitimate scope for legislative action is limited to ensuring an orderly functioning of the market economy.

The French philosopher Jean-Claude Michéa sums up the liberal conception of human beings on which statements like the Green–CDU coalition agreement are based as follows:

> In other words, a properly liberal society sees itself as a peaceful collection of abstract individuals who — provided they respect the laws — apparently have nothing in common (neither language, culture nor history) other than their desire to participate in economic growth as producers and/or consumers. (Michéa, 2014, p. 102)

In the context of economic discourse, this abstract individual is called *homo oeconomicus*. The idea of a market economy as a self-controlling social system that is capable of informally coordinating the actions of quasi-autonomous benefit-maximising individual agents is a perfect fit if people are, in fact, *homines oeconomici*. Then, but only then, it is plausible to make the legitimacy of state actions dependent on the consent of all its citizens.

Homo oeconomicus is a being with truly astonishing abilities. For example, individuals of this species can form ranked preferences that cover their entire life spans. They can weigh up all logically possible alternatives for action, and assign probabilities to them. Finally, they are not only capable of defining their personal, self-chosen utility functions; they are also capable of easily choosing and executing actions that maximize them.

But anyone who criticises neoclassical economics for its completely unrealistic assumptions about the abilities of flesh-and-blood people has thoroughly misunderstood the methodology of the discipline, according to economics Nobel Prize winner Robert E. Lucas Jr. (1988):

> By the problem of economic development I mean simply the problem of accounting for the observed pattern, across countries and across time, in levels and rates of growth of per capita income…
>
> I prefer to use the term 'theory' in a very narrow sense, to refer to an explicit dynamic system, something that can be put on a computer and run. This is what I mean by the 'mechanics' of economic development — the construction of a mechanical, artificial world, populated by the interacting robots that economics typically studies, that is capable of exhibiting behavior the gross features of which resemble those of the actual world that I have just described.

In short, liberalism is built on a mere fiction. As soon as one leaves this fictional world behind, one must recognise that (1) real existing market economies require a competent system operator called "the state," and (2) those state actions are legitimate which are oriented towards the optimisation of the common good.

II

The Democratic State and the Economy as a Whole

In Part I, we argued that prevailing theories of political and economic liberalism are mutually supportive, but their policy recommendations are based on two fundamental errors: A false conception of the autonomous individual, and a false conception of the market economy. It has become clear that the liberal worldview does not allow for the necessary role of the state in ensuring the proper functioning of the overall economy in the interest of the common good.

By blocking out the macroeconomic dimension, liberalism has made itself blind from the outset to the unavoidable question of who should play the role of the system operator of the market economy. Clearly defining this role is centrally important in a system characterised by webs of macroeconomic cause-and-effect relationships whose existence cannot be perceived by microeconomic actors like households or companies.

Obviously this is the case with the provision of money, a function which, as we will show, is properly a task of the state. The same applies to the regulation of financial markets and international monetary relations. But it also applies to labour markets, where some economic actions that are rational for individual actors like companies can, in aggregate, have negative macroeconomic consequences, such as weak growth and high unemployment.

What is needed is a new economics — an economics which diagnoses economic realities unbiased by preconceptions or dogmas. The new economics must recognise the need for the state to play a comprehensive role in shaping and managing the real economy, despite liberalism's vehement opposition to the government having such a role. Modern policy concepts must not be based on naive faith in market-fundamentalist dogmas; instead, it must originate in the concrete and empirically confirmed processes of a global economy shaped by the interaction of market and state.

We use the term "state" to refer to today's nation-states. There is simply no other level of policymaking that can be expected to create the conditions for successful and orderly international cooperation. A new order is badly needed in light of the failure of disordered globalisation. It is exactly here where macroeconomics must enter the field and inform policy by setting rules for thinking and acting that are fundamentally different from those appropriate at the level of an individual private household, company, or municipality.

Many people today who are attached to the doctrines of political liberalism dream of total decentralisation, in which binding state regulations no longer exist. Unfortunately, these people generally do not understand that complex societies need state institutions to ensure that minimum standards of economic efficiency and a fair distribution of material goods are achieved. For logically compelling reasons, organisations that take on this function must, as we will show using many examples, behave differently from microeconomic actors concerned with their individual economic performance. Regulatory institutions must be placed at a different decision-making level than the microeconomic level. The only widely accepted system that people have devised so far which meets these requirements is democracy within a defined geographical area.

So we are talking about a democratically organised nation-state. In principle, the name one gives to such a system is of little importance. However, it is easy to understand why many people are reluctant to continue using the terms "nation-state" or "nation," in view of the terrible historical expressions of xenophobia and racist madness that have originated at the nation-state level. Suspicions arise that those who use the term "nation" could be motivated by a covert agenda guided by a nationalist ideology. In our case, nothing could be further from the truth.

But there is no world-state in existence, and the emergence of a world-state is at least as far from realisation as a totally decentralised organisation of society. As long as that remains the case, policy decisions must be made at a level between these two extremes. We refer here to decisions that arise not from an individual economic interest, but rather from the insight that an economic system based on division of labour can function well only if macroeconomic relationships are adequately taken into account in decision-making.

Given the current state of the world, this intermediate level of governance is the nation-state. This applies even to Europe: Despite the existence of the European Union, in Europe, the key economic decisions continue to be made at the nation-state level. There are a few exceptions to this, of which money (the euro monetary system) is by far the most important. Unfortunately the euro system does not work well, for reasons that will be explained next.

Money, Capital and Labour

Money as a state institution

Money — and by this we mean fiat money in the form of bank deposits, banknotes and coins — is undoubtedly a state institution; it arises through the actions of state institutions relating to a clearly defined geographical area.

This also applies to multi-country regional currency unions such as the European Monetary Union. The European Central Bank (ECB) is the central bank of each Member State. When one of its member states gets into economic difficulty, then in order to fulfill its economic policy role appropriately, the ECB must act as if it were a national central bank. This remains the case despite the fact that the ECB blatantly failed to meet its obligations in the early years of the euro crisis.

The issuance of national or supranational fiat money by a state institution created for this purpose, i.e. by the Central Bank, creates uniquely favourable conditions for economic development. Obviously, its role as money issuer obliges the Central Bank to defend the usability of the money it creates. However, neoclassical theory has so far provided grossly misleading advice about what specific tasks accrue to the central bank in consequence of its role as the issuer of money. To understand why this is this the case, we must first clarify the concept of money.

John Maynard Keynes rightly pointed out that the term "money" refers to two distinct things, and that a strict distinction must be made between the two (Keynes, 1930, p. 4 f): it refers to a unit of account, and it refers to a means of payment. Keynes correctly said that the existence of a unit of account, such as "euro" or "dollar," does not by itself determine what the buyer of an asset valuated in that currency, marked with a certain price, must transfer to the asset's seller, in order for the transfer of ownership of the asset to be legally effective.

For example, imagine a farmer wants to buy a dinner table made by a furniture-maker, and the table is valued at €200. In order to pay for the dinner table, the farmer could give the furniture-maker four sheepskins valued, in euro currency terms, at €50 each (if the furniture-maker were willing to accept sheepskins in payment). The four sheepskins are not "money" — they just happen to have the same total euro valuation as the table.

In practice, modern civilisation has developed a more elegant solution: The farmer pays for the table with legal documents we think of as "cash" or "transfers of money between bank accounts."

We must distinguish between "money" as a means of valuating goods and "money" in the sense of a means of payment. In the former case we can speak of a "currency," but only in the latter case can we speak of "money." But what exactly is "money" in this narrow sense?

Clearly, we can pay for economic goods with very different means of payment. In the supermarket, for example, we often take a bill from our wallet and hand it over to the cashier. Sometimes, however, we instead insert a bank card (in Europe, an "EC card") into a machine and transfer euros to the supermarket. And sometimes we pay for an asset by making an electronic transfer from our bank account. In the latter two cases, the transfer of euros is achieved by debiting our account at a bank with a certain number of euros, and crediting the same amount to the seller's account at his or her bank.

What makes all these different "things" money? The German economist Georg Friedrich Knapp wrote at the beginning of the 20th century that money must be regarded as a social phenomenon that has parallels to other social phenomena:

> When we hand our coats to the coat-check staff when we enter the theatre, we receive in return a brass plate of a certain shape that bears a sign, such as a number. Nothing else is written on it, but this "voucher" or "claim tag" has a legal meaning: it is proof that I have the right to demand the return

of my coat. When we send letters, we affix a "stamp" to them, which proves that we have acquired the right to have this letter sent through the post office by having paid postage. (Knapp, 1905, p. 26)

Money is therefore a type of documented claim or title to a "good," which can be exercised by a subject in relation to a counterparty (another subject). Small brass plates with a number on them document a claim by a coat's owner against the theatre cloakroom attendant for the return of the good we call a "coat." A postage stamp documents a claim on a "good" or, in standard parlance, "service" that can be described as: "mail a letter to the specified recipient." By what means such claims on a good or service are documented is, as these examples show, unimportant. The main thing is that someone has determined what a specific voucher, tag, or token means, i.e. it must unambiguously document who has the right to obtain what specific good or service, and under what clearly specified circumstances.

All such tokens document claims of the token's owner for a good or service, in relation to a counterparty. However, not all claims documented in this way are means of payment. According to Knapp, one can speak of "means of payment" only if the document (token or voucher) that gives evidence of one's claim to a good or service is valuated in a currency, and is legally permitted to be used as means of payment.

"Means of payment," then, are documents with which their holder may settle debts denominated in currency — Debts resulting, for example, from purchase contracts, or contracts that transfer usufructuary rights, or employment contracts, or loan contracts. Such "money debts" can be repaid by a debtor's transfer of a suitable "document" to the "money creditor." For example, when shopping in a grocery store, the debt owed by the shopper for removal of goods from the store can be settled by a 20-euro-denominated banknote, if the total currency-valuated price of the food purchased adds up to 20 euros or less.

Going back to the example of the farmer looking to acquire a dinner table: if he pays the furniture-maker with two 100-euro banknotes, rather than four sheepskins, he is paying with money. If instead he offers to pay with sheepskins, he is merely trying to barter. A key difference is that the furniture-maker is legally obliged to take euro money in payment, but would not have been obligated to accept sheepskins in payment.

Money and taxes

In the euro area, banknotes are designated by the legislator as a means of payment that empowers their holders to pay their debts. A means of payment that authorises a debtor to settle his currency-denominated debts, and legally obliges a creditor to accept this means of payment to settle a claim, is called money.

It is worth taking a closer look at some additional properties that can be attributed to banknotes issued by Eurozone central banks like the Bundesbank or Banque de France.

Banknotes (1) by operation of law, authorise a debtor to settle all debts owed to a money-creditor, (2) legally oblige a creditor to accept them to settle a money-denominated debt, and (3) are issued by a state organization.

In accordance with Knapp, we will argue in this book that conditions (2) and (3) do not necessarily represent constitutive characteristics of money. In other words, while banknotes are definitely money, some other documents that do not share characteristics (2) and (3) can also be considered money, as we will explain further in the following.

What definitely distinguishes "money" from all other means of payment, however, is the fact that money is accepted by the state as a means of payment for the settlement of compulsory payments — such as transaction taxes, levies, fees, and income tax debts or value-added-tax debts.

According to this definition, means of payment are "money" only if they can be used to pay tax debts to the state. At the end of the day, it is this characteristic that secures the general acceptance of a means of payment for the settlement of all monetary debts in a given currency area. Assuming that a state can levy taxes and the tax rates are sufficiently high, there can be no doubt that the means of payment accepted by the state in payment of tax obligations will then also be used for the processing of commercial transactions.

Money is thus the documentation of a promise by a state to all holders of this documentation that they can use it to settle tax debts imposed on them by the state, denominated in that state's currency. Money primarily has a value because it can be used to settle tax liabilities denominated in the currency specified by the state.

Capital and productivity

The average productivity of labour (i.e. whole-economy income in relation to total hours worked) is the decisive quantity for any economy. This quantity can only be defined within national borders, because its foundation is the historical accumulation of capital ("capital" in the sense of production machinery, equipment, buildings, and the processes, skills, and organisation needed to build, operate, and maintain these).

Capital accumulation, as we have known since Joseph Schumpeter's pioneering work on economic development (Schumpeter, 2006[1912]), is the result of dynamic economic processes that vary from country to country. Economic cultures and traditions exist that are specific to particular nation-states. The process of capital accumulation reflects many factors and influences that result from national policies, preferences, and goals.

At every moment in historical time, this process gives rise to a unique product: the national capital stock. It is this capital stock, in combination with the historically equally unique potential of the workforce, that makes it possible to generate an income shared in the form of profits and wages by all who are directly involved in the production process. The capital stock also benefits those who are indirectly engaged in production (e.g. government administrators), as well as dependents (e.g. children, retired people).

For economic development to be successful, a realistic combination of sensible policies is needed. This begins with monetary policy, which provides the production process with the means without which it cannot function: namely financial capital in the form of fiat money, which economic actors use to acquire the inputs needed to produce "real capital" in the form of buildings, machines, and equipment (i.e. tangible assets).

How intensively and successfully this process unfolds varies widely. For a variety of reasons, there are considerable regional differences in the dynamism of economic development, even within nation-states. Recognising this, the nation-state has, in the past, set itself the task of equilibrating, to some degree, the living conditions of the people living within its borders, so as to avoid too great a discrepancy between regions. This has involved fiscal measures — for example, the federal government may spend more money, per capita, on infrastructure or job creation measures in some federal states or provinces than in others.

Such measures have had some degree of success. However, by far the most important policy mechanism that has made the diverse production efforts of millions of people, working at very different locations and jobs, into a successful economic model for the nation as a whole, has been the process of negotiating national wage rates for each industry or service sector. This process is described in the next section.

Work and pay

Because capital has a national history, industrial relations, including the incomes of employees, must likewise be determined at national level. Economic conditions are, as economists say, path-dependent, and the specifics of a country's historical economic development path are crucial for workers. How many hours a week people are expected to work; the arrangements for employee participation in company decision-making; workplace safety standards; the key question of what salary level employees receive — All of these depend on the history of the nation's capital stock accumulation process. And this history takes place within a clearly defined geographical area in which democratic political decision-making takes place.

This history is the crucial factor that makes it possible for countries with very different levels of productivity and wages (i.e. countries with very different capital stocks) to trade with each other, without it necessarily being the case that one of the countries is at a systemic disadvantage from the outset. Countries with a large and efficient capital stock and high labour productivity can pay high (real) wages, and countries with a small capital stock and lower productivity can only pay lower (real) wages. In other words, the capital stock level that has been attained determines the level of remuneration prevalent in a country, and its general standard of living.

In the long run, the relationship between the rate of change in nominal wages to the rate of change in productivity (changes in labour costs per unit output) is reflected in price inflation rates in each country. What this means is that the decisive differences that determine "competitiveness" between nations are not differences in productivity or wages, as is usually believed, but rather, differences in the trajectory of inflation or unit labour costs over time.

This connection is unavoidable, because as we have already shown above, no country can live permanently above or below its means. Countries that try to live above their circumstances will sooner or later end up with inflation (always assuming that there is no neighbouring country that is prepared to make up for the gap in the long term), and those who live permanently below their circumstances will end up experiencing deflation.

Countries implicitly choose inflation targets in consequence of policy decisions about how to develop wages in relation to their own productivity trends. Regardless of the details, one thing is clear: Differences in inflation rates between nations which have significant trade relations must be minimised, in order to avoid massive economic and political shocks in the form of the loss of competitiveness of entire nations. Equalisation of inflation rates is precisely what an efficient monetary system has to deliver. This is its core task. Different levels of competitiveness between countries simply cannot be maintained for long periods of time without generating crises.

For this reason, the politically organised geographical area within which wage increases are agreed between representatives of employers and employees must be the same as the area whose productivity level is used as the basis for wage negotiations. Given two nations or regions with significantly different levels of productivity, it is not possible to split the difference, calculate an average, and pay the same wages to workers in both. Doing so would cause enormous damage in both countries.

An even more extreme idea that was at one point pursued by European Union policymakers in Brussels was that workers should take their wage rates with them when moving from a low-productivity area to a high-productivity area (what we have described above as the "country of origin" principle). This is an absurd proposition. Migration of workers can only take place according to the "country of destination" principle, i.e. workers must always be paid the standard wage of the country in which they are working, no matter where they have come from. (This principle was ultimately accepted by Brussels through an amendment of the so-called Posting of Workers Directive, or PWD.) Even then, however, labour migration does not automatically lead to a balance in the economic situation of the two countries.

Despite its internationalist aspirations, the trade union movement has remained an enterprise largely confined to limited national territories. This undoubtedly applies to Europe, where trade unions regularly issue joint statements and invoke common goals, but in reality, as the German example of wage dumping in monetary union shows, no real international solidarity or genuine cooperation exists across national borders.

However, it must be recognised that the work of Europe's trade unions has been highly path-dependent, i.e. dependent on historical developments that have nearly all taken place at the national level. This can be clearly seen in the blanket collective agreement, a wage-bargaining practice which shaped the German economic landscape for many decades and was only largely destroyed at the beginning of the 1990s under massive political pressure from a red–green federal government (a governing coalition of the German Social Democratic Party and the Green Party). Unfortunately, to this day, only a few people have understood how important this national institution was for Germany's past economic success. We will come back to that in Chapter 5 of this book.

Many believe that the economic importance of national borders, especially in Europe, can be made irrelevant simply by encouraging labour migration between high-wage and low-wage countries. But this is an erroneous idea, which in turn is based on the errors of neoclassical economic theory. In nearly all realistic cases, as we explained in Part 1, it is impossible for the market to strike a balance between different wage levels without causing huge distortions.

Democracy and the Nation-state

The state is considered obsolete not only by neo-liberals, but also by many of their critics. It is one thing to dream of overcoming the nation-state, but it is quite another to have a clear understanding of the political reality of our societies and to develop realistic policy strategies based on that understanding. As soon as one faces up to political reality, one recognises that "the nation state, despite undeniable partial loss of sovereignty due to globalisation and transfers of sovereignty through EU integration, will remain the dominant form of socialisation for the foreseeable future." (Wahl, 2016)

As already mentioned above, we recognise that many states — certainly Germany, but also others — have abused their monopoly on domestic use of force in the name of "great ideals." And it cannot be denied that the cause of interstate conflicts can be traced back to an "exaggeration of the distinction between 'us' and 'them'" (*Ibid.*).

It must also be conceded that many deplorable social conditions in today's Europe — such as the catastrophic economic and social situation in many Eurozone countries, or the low-wage sector and the Hartz IV welfare regulatory regime in Germany — are clearly attributable to national measures, especially national laws. Nor can it be denied that the functioning of a modern economy characterised by diverse cross-border interdependencies requires the political and legal coordination of all countries participating in it.

It is more than understandable, given this context, that doubts might arise about the wisdom of a position proposing that strengthening the nation-state is the right way to promote a more social and more democratic world. However, despite these doubts, we must ask whether a democratically organised community may need the institutional framework of a nation-state to be properly realised.

The State

Liberals' desire to free themselves from state paternalism goes so far that the existence of states is sometimes simply denied. Although it is admitted that there are individual state actors, such as a government, the many organisations subsumed under the name "state" often have such different functions and interests that any talk of "the state" as a single actor is, liberals claim, completely mistaken. For liberals, the state is at best an arena for action defined by certain rules in which different actors try to assert their interests (e.g. Claus Offe makes this argument [Offe, 1987]).

If that were the case, then it would also be wrong to regard Deutsche Bank as a single actor. After all, Deutsche Bank is likewise constituted of a large number of different organizations that perform very different functions. But the fact that a local bank branch's credit department has a different function than its corporate clients credit department, and that conflicts sometimes arise between these departments, for example, is no reason why Deutsche Bank should not be seen as a single actor. It was undoubtedly Deutsche Bank that made questionable loans in the USA for which it later had to present itself in court. Deutsche Bank is certainly not (or not only) an arena for action; it is also an actor in its own right, characterised by the fact that the actions of a large number of individuals are coordinated to achieve specific goals, by means of an organisational structure designed for that purpose.

In the same way, notwithstanding the separation of powers typical of liberal democracies, it cannot be concluded that a state of this type is not an organisation. Rather, a state is to be regarded as an organisation if the actions of different state bodies, such as those of governments, parliaments, courts, central banks, etc., are functionally so interrelated and coordinated that they allow a state goal to be defined and achieved.

In our opinion, the renowned state theorist Hermann Heller correctly described the defining goal or function of a state as follows: "The function of the state consists [...] in the independent organization and activation of social interaction within a territory, based on the historical necessity of a common *status vivendi* for all conflicting interests on a territory that encompasses all of them [...]" (Heller, 1934, p. 230).

If a state is an organisation whose function can be defined in this way, then the question naturally arises whether particular political measures should be excluded from the spectrum of all possibilities merely because neoliberalism systematically ignores them on the basis of its naive market theory.

In the course of this book, we will work out, on the basis of a realistic economic theory, what role a state must assume if its goal is to achieve a fair balance between conflicting interests. The renaissance of the state we are calling for is not motivated by a faith-driven statist agenda; rather, it is based on insight into macroeconomic and global causalities and realities.

Democracy

According to the German constitution — the *Grundgesetz* ("Basic Law"), as it is known in Germany — the state is the representative of the people in a democratically organised community. The state is responsible for ensuring that the rules of conduct desired by the people are followed by all. The first question to address is what conditions must be met for a state to be legitimised as the rules-establishing representative of its people.

A "representative" is someone who acts in the interest of third parties. In order for the state to be able to represent the interests of the people, as required by Article 20 of Germany's Basic Law, it is by no means necessary to begin by searching for a people bereft of a state. Analogously, there are no children who do not have (or at some point in time have had) parents. Nor is there reason to doubt that parents can act in the interests of their children.

Liberal critics of the state, in particular, will be pleased by the reference to the relationship between parents and their children. It enables them to criticise the state as potentially paternalistic, and therefore to suggest that its sphere of influence should be limited as much as possible. What is correct about this criticism is that states are not akin to voluntary associations or clubs, in which one has decided to become a member, and from which one can withdraw at any time. A citizen is born into a state in the same sense that one is born into a family. And if the accusation of paternalistic treatment of citizens by their state is aimed at expressing the fact that states often act against the explicitly expressed interests of their citizens, then a valid concern has been raised.

But is the principle that not everyone should always get what they want really to be criticised? Is it not the case that a citizen sometimes wants something socially undesirable, sometimes even something that is against his or her own best interest? And when one bears responsibility towards a group of people, is it not the case that one must sometimes weigh up their incompatible interests? It is only when a state acts against the declared interests of its citizens that the question arises to what extent such actions are justified.

Suppose, on the other hand, that a state is legitimised only to take actions which each citizen would agree to on the basis of his or her known personal interests. Under that circumstance, the issue of coercive rulership, the question in response to which the concept of democracy arose, goes away. The position of many liberal democracy theorists is thus paradoxical: it says that the only state actions that can be considered legitimate are those that do not require any legitimation at all.

But if it is true that a state is an actor with abilities that citizens do not possess, and if it can even pursue goals that deviate from the declared interests of its citizens, then it is absurd to demand that the state should only carry out actions that every citizen would carry out himself on the basis of his "slightly idealized" epistemic position. This criterion for the legitimacy of state actions makes no sense, because it excludes actions that might be taken on the basis of macroeconomic relationships that "the people," looking at the world from their individual microeconomic perspectives, can neither perceive nor comprehend.

Let us take the example of public debt. When citizens are asked about this topic, they regularly give answers that are understandable given the point of view of the individual economic actor, but which show that they do not understand the relevant interrelationships. They fear that future generations will be burdened by higher debts, but do not understand that creditors' claims against the state will also be passed along to future generations, so that the net asset position of future generations remains absolutely unchanged with higher debts. Does the fact that most people misunderstand macroeconomic relationships imply that an elected representative of the people should be able to evade responsibility for macroeconomic policy, even if he has an insight which is not available to the citizens and which, moreover, is difficult to communicate to them? Hardly.

Since in a political community there are not only many different interests, but also many such macroeconomic relationships, the usual mechanism of freely electing representatives of the people to a parliament is by no means sufficient to ensure that majority decisions are used to pass laws representing the will of the people. Rather, a democratically elected government needs a mandate that allows it to decide even those issues on which there exists no "popular opinion" or where the "popular opinion" collides with the assured findings of the experts.

This category of questions is largely ignored by many theorists of democracy. In their eyes, the only matter of importance is that the people's representatives must be chosen by the electorate — directly or at least indirectly — in universal, free, equal, and secret elections (Müller, 2016, p. 19). If the representatives have thus been authorized to represent the interests of the people, and must regularly stand for re-election, and in this sense are accountable to the people, then in the opinion of many democracy theorists, it is unnecessary to ask whether a state's actions really represent the "will of the people."

The common good

But which actions are then legitimately within the purview of a democratic state, and which are not? Merely pointing to a postulated "popular will" cannot be a satisfactory answer. There is no doubt that the people who constitute the nation have different and sometimes conflicting interests. However, interests can only be meaningfully attributed to individuals. After all, one "has interests" if he can regard certain facts or prospective outcomes as "good" for himself. The individual people who constitute the citizenry of the state at a given moment in time have their diverse interests, but this does not add up to the People's interest, where "the People" is understood as a collective or community. In this view, it appears as if the requirement of Germany's Basic Law that the state should represent the interests of its people, in the sense of its community, is unfulfillable. But this appearance is deceptive.

Let us call conditions, outcomes, or facts that are in the interest of an individual "goods." It is certainly rational for all of us to aim our actions at the "acquisition" of goods. In today's social science contexts, it is often concluded from this that people always act on the basis of their subjective preferences, or at least should so act. It is doubtless true that we sometimes have to choose between different options for action, and therefore have to think about which goods are of greater or lesser importance to us. So sometimes we are forced to rank our interests according to how relatively important they are to us, i.e. decide on a so-called preference order, in order to be able to decide rationally which action we should take under particular circumstances.

However, we do not always act only for ourselves. Sometimes we act for third parties, or even for a group of third parties. And when we act for such a group, we are often forced to make normatively relevant distinctions between the preferences of the different individuals in that group. In the emergency department of a hospital, for example, doctors must decide which patients should be treated first. As a rule, the seriously injured person will be treated before someone suffering from an itch, because the interest of the seriously injured person weighs more heavily.

So situations exist in which third parties must take actions for a group of people, and must decide what actions they should take under particular circumstances. It cannot be ruled out that no matter what choice they make, at least one person in the group will be negatively affected. However, there can also be no doubt that some such decisions are morally justified.

Liberals insist in this context that individual preferences of third parties cannot be appraised or assessed, and that in the case of conflicts of interest between individuals, no rational decision can be made as to which options for action a state organisation should implement. The state must remain neutral towards the many different conceptions of what constitutes a good life, since these are ultimately based on subjective preferences.

But why should the argument we used in the example of the hospital emergency room not apply to the actions of a state whose task under the Basic Law is to represent the interests of a group of people called "the People"?

As this example shows, making normative and evaluative prioritisation decisions is essential and unavoidable in real life. A suggestion that the state in particular should not do so, or is unable to do so, is simply not rationally comprehensible. What we must insist, however, both for emergency rooms and for the actions of a state, is that when decisions are taken, it must be treated as irrelevant specifically whose personal interests are at stake. In other words, whoever acts in the interest of a group must be impartial in determining which legitimate interests of the group members have priority in which circumstances.

While such questions arise time and again in social contexts in which actions are taken in the interest of third parties, it is obvious that in practice, it is not possible for the preferences of all group members or all alternative courses of action to be considered before actions are taken. Our social life, as we have already pointed out, takes place in and through a multitude of formal and informal institutions into which each of us is born and brought up. The idea that this might somehow be avoidable is not merely utopian, it is absurd.

To openly acknowledge the fact that people often follow rules set by the state, that the necessary arrangements for state action are routinely implemented by third parties through a variety of mechanisms and methods, and that a reasonably stable political order is impossible without a certain degree of "habitual obedience" (John Austin) on the part of citizens, sounds altogether horrible to liberal ears. But one cannot avoid confronting this reality if one wants to analyse the complex relationship between a state and its citizens.

Certainly, norms and laws can be critically reflected upon. Liberals have worked very hard at this, rightly pointing out that many norms and laws are not in harmony with the framework of enlightened self-interest they favour. They have duly called for reforms consistent with that framework, and over the last 40 years, policymakers have proved extremely compliant to their demands.

However, the rankings of interests implied in norms and laws can be viewed not only from the perspectives of self-interested individuals, but also from an impartial perspective, as shown by the example of the hospital emergency department. Reflections from this perspective make it necessary, as Walter Pfannkuche (2016) writes, "to look at things from the position of the other". Such an approach defines the logic of moral thinking; it requires an ability to imagine walking a mile in the shoes of another, or to conceptually switch roles with a counterparty. The aim of this is "to search for rules of conduct that one could accept if one were in someone else's position."

From such a moral perspective we can, for example, criticise our current pension system, because, from an impartial perspective, the interest of pensioners in a materially secure retirement is clearly more important than the interest of insurance companies in opening up another profitable business field. So if a parliament decides on a pension reform that guarantees all pensioners an acceptable standard of living, and the state has the means to do so, then such a reform could be legitimised in terms of the common good.

Of course, one could counter this justification by saying that the description of conflict of interests is wrong, or the belief that the state has the means necessary to provide for pensioners is wrong. Liberals would argue that there is a conflict of interest, but that it is between the old and the young, not between pensioners and insurance companies. And they would likely claim that the state simply cannot afford to feed its elderly citizens using state resources, so everyone must make individual provision for old age.

However, as we will show later in detail, this liberal position is completely wrong, because it ignores the relevant macroeconomic relationships. For the economy as a whole, the simple truth is that it cannot save on a net basis, because every successful new financial saving by an economic party always means a corresponding new debt on the part of a counterparty.

Consequently, in any debate on pensions, the normative and factual questions related to determining the common good must be answered simultaneously. This requires a clear understanding of the relevant macroeconomic facts and their interrelationships — an understanding that can only be demanded from organisations that are commonly referred to as "states." And a state can only be considered democratic if it is oriented towards the common good.

There is no denying that it is often difficult to define the public interest and to identify the appropriate actions to secure it. It is therefore essential to conduct an honest discourse on matters relevant to the public interest, and to ensure this discourse is securely anchored institutionally. And it is also essential that this discourse be conducted openly and publicly as much as possible, because a state that has the task of representing the interests of its citizens is undoubtedly called upon to explain to them why it implements certain measures and refrains from implementing others.

Sovereignty

In light of the foregoing points, a state can be considered democratic if (1) the actions of that state are oriented towards the common good, and (2) the laws it enacts or repeals are explicitly based on decisions of the people or on decisions of the people's representatives. A state that fully meets condition (2) is referred to as a sovereign state.

It is clear that in the EU, the sovereignty of member states is limited in this sense. For example, the former judge of the Federal Constitutional Court, Dieter Grimm, has pointed out that the European Court of Justice (ECJ) can override national law by its interpretation of the provisions of the Lisbon Treaty, and the organs of EU member states would have no prospect of success if they should attempt to contest an ECJ ruling (Grimm, 2016, pp. 51–67). But if, as Article 20 of Germany's Basic Law states, all state authority must emanate from the people, then the ECJ undermines the right of the German people to self-determination as guaranteed by the Basic Law. In other words, without sovereignty in the sense of condition (2), there can be no democracy.

Does this mean, however, that the transfer of sovereign rights from national to European level must be rejected? Grimm suggests that such a transfer can be considered justifiable as long as the constitutional courts of EU member states are able to rule on laws effectively set by a supranational organisation, and retain the authority to strike them down if they find these laws to not be in conformity with the national constitution.

The problem with this proposal is that constitutional principles are so-called general clauses. The content of these principles is so far-reaching that their so-called "interpretation" effectively amounts to legislation by judges.

In a democratic community, however, the law should be set not by judges, but by the people or their representatives.

Since such judge-created law is inevitable, the people, or rather their representatives, must ultimately be able to revise and correct such laws. But this means one must demand either that the rulings of the European Court of Justice or other supranational organisations must either be adopted unanimously by majorities of the representatives of all member states, or that clearly defined veto rights are granted to member states.

Anyone who takes democracy seriously should therefore realize that the question of sovereignty remains active and topical. And of course, saying that a democratic government is sovereign does not mean that such an association is omnipotent. Those who insist on democratic sovereignty do not demand that a state should regulate all relations between its citizens. But the state must be able to decide, on the basis of democratic procedures, which relationships of its citizens it wants to regulate, and which overall societal goals should be achieved.

An entirely different question is what room for manoeuvre a state which is "sovereign" in this sense actually still effectively retains in the context of a capitalistically organised world economy. In the following pages, we will argue that an adequate understanding of how a market economy functions shows that there are many more options for policy action than the neoliberal narrative would have us believe.

Fundamentals of a New Economics

In the ongoing global debate among economists over doctrine and interpretive frameworks, a distinction is very often made between supply-side and demand-side orientations. Supply theorists are usually characterised as tending to rely on the market to solve economic problems, while demand theorists ("Keynesians") rely more on government to steer the economy.

This suggests that the demand side of an economy is not really a market phenomenon, which is obviously wrong. In reality, there exists no *a priori* basis at all that might determine what is more important for economic processes: supply or demand. Neoliberals have evaded serious debate on this issue by postulating one particular doctrine or "law" as "true": Say's Law, proclaimed by French economist Jean Baptiste Say in the 18th century, which posits that supply creates consequent demand. As has been shown many times (e.g. Flassbeck, 1982), this is not always wrong, but the opposite is just as true: Demand creates consequent supply.

One might just as well argue whether player A or player B is the "real source of the game" in a game of tennis. It is not possible to find a solution to the challenge of understanding economic systems in this way; any such attempt is doomed to failure from the outset. Developing an adequate understanding of the functioning of an economy is not essentially a matter of focusing either on supply or on demand. The key, instead, is to distinguish between theories in which macroeconomic income is predetermined, as is the case in the neoclassical model, and those in which it is not. Theoretical systems that take the latter position are usually called Keynesian models.

It is one thing to ask oneself how best to distribute an existing income, an existing cake. But it is a completely different matter to ask yourself what conditions must be met in order to generate a sufficiently high income (i.e. bake a large enough cake), and how to further increase its size. The difference between neoclassical and Keynesian models is about statics versus dynamics. Or, as Paul Davidson put it (Davidson, 2011), whether one makes an ergodic or a nonergodic system the research object of economics, i.e. a system whose laws of motion are invariant in time, or one that can change at any time.

In non-ergodic systems, humans act under "objective uncertainty about the future," as Keynes put it; in ergodic systems, by contrast, they know the process characteristics that govern their own actions and, like robots, run through the single and only program that they have at their disposal. Economists must decide from the outset whether they want to analyse robots or humans. If they want to analyse and understand systems composed of people, not robots, then they must try to understand people's actions under conditions of uncertainty, and take into account their limited insight into and information about the contexts and relationships within which they act.

Moreover, one should not overlook the fact that in a market economy, "in addition to consequences and connections that depend on human behaviour," there are also those that "would remain unchanged even if people behaved in the most unusual ways" (Stützel, 2011, p. 1 ff.). The connections that Wolfgang Stützel has in mind are consequences of the fact that market economies are monetary economies. For monetary economies, there can be no income without expenditure. It follows logically from this extremely trivial observation that the existence of one economic sector with revenue surpluses necessarily entails a counterparty sector with revenue deficits. If the private sector, as is the case in Germany, "saves," i.e. achieves surpluses, then the state and/or foreign countries must necessarily "suffer" deficits. Such relationships are analysed under the name "balance-sheet mechanics," and we will continue to be concerned with these in what follows.

Keynesian and neoclassical economics as antipodes?

Again and again, one meets people who are critical of the economics taught today, but still doubt that real alternatives to the prevailing doctrine of neo-classicism are available. Such people understand that the dominant neoclassical doctrine cannot satisfactorily explain what is happening in the real economy, and they search for better approaches. But they view Keynesianism, which would be an obvious alternative to the prevailing theory, with a similar degree of skepticism, since they assume that it too is fraught with ideological biases.

Consequently, an antipodal picture prevails: On one side, there is neo-classical theory, in which the functioning of markets dominates social relationships, and whose political expression focuses largely on market solutions. On the other side, there is Keynesianism, which places market failures at the centre of its analysis and relies on the state for economic policy. What could be more natural for a critically thinking person than to say: 'I am critical of all traditional positions, and therefore maintain equal distance from both schools; the truth probably lies somewhere in the middle.'

There are many positions that seem to fit perfectly with this antipodal worldview. For the neoclassicists, if the market economy is to function, all prices must react flexibly to changes in supply and demand. Keynesians, on the other hand, tend to build models with rigid wages and prices and to defend the rigidity of wages as normal or even desirable.

Because the caricature of the two theories as antipodes to each other seems so obviously correct, politics often seeks a middle way between the two, or even attempts completely different solutions, the famous "third ways." But this is a mistake. There is neither a center position nor anything outside these two "extremes" that could be aspired to in order to advance our critical understanding of a market economy system.

This is because although the above statements sound like theoretical antipodes, in reality they are the result of two very different systems of conceptual predicates. In our view, there is a decisive characteristic that makes the two "theories" non-comparable even at a methodological level. This characteristic is logical empiricism: The willingness to recognise and incorporate undeniable macroeconomic interrelationships, unavoidable epistemological truths, and empirically verified information into the theoretical system. Keynesianism has that willingness; neoclassicism does not have it.

Saving and investing as a science programme

By coming to the topic of saving and investing, we are reaching the central point of contention in the academic and political controversy which has, for more than 80 years now, left its mark on economic science. It is this issue that has driven the errors and confusions of international and national economic policy like none other. It is exactly here where opinions diverge. And rightly so, because it is here, in the question of how a market economy determines its own future development, that the central weakness of economic liberalism is to be found. Neither Neoclassicism, Ordoliberalism, the Austrian School, Monetarism, nor other variations on the theme of economic liberalism have found an answer to this question.

It is not the case that economists who use liberal economic arguments generally do not consider macroeconomic interrelations; they do sometimes use balance-sheet mechanics, in the broadest sense. Indeed, one could say they use balance-sheet analysis too often, but above all too thoughtlessly: Balance-sheet mechanics is only used insofar as they seem to fit easily into the economic-liberal framework of standard assumptions. The best example of this is the assumption that saving equals investment, which is endlessly emphasised by neoclassical economists. $I = S$ has almost become a battle cry for the fact that market forces always do the right thing and can be relied upon.

But what does this "equation" really mean? The idea that saving money equals investing is correct in the sense that you will always find out afterwards that the portions of your income that were not consumed were invested. This is because there exist only these two categories of expenditure for the world as a whole. However, the decisive question remains hidden from view: How exactly have savings plans connected with investment plans over time, and, most importantly, how has macroeconomic income changed in this process? $I = S$ is not wrong, but it is insufficient, because it says absolutely nothing about this.

In the search for answers to this question, however, a neoclassical economist will behave very differently from a social scientist applying an empirical methodology. A social scientist who does not believe *a priori* that market processes lead to an equilibrium (or does not consider equilibria to be relevant) will ask herself how, i.e. through what sequences of events, the income of an economy is generated. She knows that savings and investment must be equal in size *ex post*, but she also knows that this must not prevent her from thinking about the processes responsible for generating income, and the specifics of the different roles played by private households, public budgets, and companies in saving and investing.

A neoclassical economist takes a completely different approach. He is looking from the outset for a market process that can bring the desire of private households to save for the future into line with the investment desires of companies. Consequently, he is looking for a market process and price mechanism that will guarantee the appropriate adjustment of companies' investment plans, even as the volume of private households' aggregate savings changes. Once he has found such a market process and price, the problem is solved, as far as he is concerned, because the market will always ensure that S and I are the same. In the market for savings and capital, the interest rate was "identified" as the key price; it falls when households save more, thereby incentivising companies to invest more.

How the aggregate income of the economy develops within that context is of little importance for neoclassicist economists, because the income development trajectory as such (the growth path) is predetermined in the ergodic system (by technical progress and other circumstances), and the capital market is responsible for all other adjustments.

For a neoclassical economist, the idea that the state might be needed in order to ensure a sensible economic development trajectory seems completely outlandish. A biologist looking for symbiotic relationships between ants and tree frogs in the deepest jungle would not even think of problematising the role of humans. The "natural order" is one that does without the state; therefore, problems that require state intervention for their solution cannot exist.

Once the natural order has been found — in our case, a regional capital market that regulates everything — there is no need to further explore the system's laws of motion. The only thing that can go wrong now is the restriction of capital markets' freedom through government intervention, which restricts price flexibility and thereby prevents the market from ensuring efficient implementation of savings desires into investments at all times.

Can this alleged capital market interest rate mechanism even exist under realistic conditions? Can it exist, in a fiat money economy, in the absence of a state? These are questions that neoclassical economics never asks itself. It does not ask such questions because it does not want to find any answers to them. The theory-building effort is only aimed at confirming (or rather inventing) the possibility of a solution to the savings-and-investment relationship problem that takes the form of a market process and price mechanism.

Today, it can only be regarded as a major strategic error of Keynesianism to have accepted neoclassical economics as a scientific counterpart, instead of characterising it from the outset as a normative construction that serves no worthwhile social purpose. A science can never win an argument against an artificial theory with a strong ideological superstructure, because it is not important for the artificial theory to make scientific progress. The only aim of the promoters of the ideologised theory is to defend their position at all costs — including the costs of ignoring empirical results and tolerating logical inconsistencies. Neoclassical economics is not a special case of the "general theory" that Keynes tried to establish. Neoclassical theory, unlike Keynes's theory, is not an attempt to understand or model the real economy. It must be understood *a priori* as a normative construct.

Who decides on saving and investing?

Neoclassical theorists see savers as having the leading role in the transformation of saving into investing, because free consumers can decide at any time whether they want to spend their income today or prefer to put it aside, i.e. save up some money now in order to spend it later. This is an absolutely central connection for neoclassical theory, because it is here that the freedom of the individual to decide on his own fate is concentrated like nowhere else. Consuming or investing (saving) is the most important decision that the self-determined individual makes, and in the logic of liberalism and neo-classical theory, it determines the fate of the nation.

Over the past 40 years, the save-or-spend decision has been made the core methodological focus of economics, and the key criterion for assessing whether a given piece of economic theorising was "scientific."

"Microfoundations" was the magic word to which all economists world-wide had to bow, if they wanted to publish in one of the leading academic journals in economics. Only those who based their model on the core assumption that private households make save-or-spend decisions rationally, and that the aggregate of their wishes determines the future development of the macroeconomy, could claim to be doing scientific work and hope to embark on an academic career and earn a living as an economist.

Usually an interest-rate mechanism is cited as proof of this core neoclassical thesis. This mechanism is meant to convert increased savings into investments. In this view, savings do not pose a problem for growth and full employment, as they directly induce investment. Although saving money (rather than spending it on consumer goods) lowers consumer demand, and thereby causes reduced employment in consumer goods industries, the increased supply of money collected in savings pools offered to borrowers via financial capital markets puts downward pressure on interest rates, thereby stimulating borrowing and consequent investments in real production capital. This not only offsets the drop in consumer demand; it also increases the economy's future growth potential. However, achieving this outcome requires flexible prices and wages. That, in a nutshell, is the neoclassical thesis about how savings relate to investment and to aggregate economic production.

This argument is wrong, because it fails to properly account for the macroeconomic effects of a sector's attempts to save. If one economic sector saves some amount, other sectors are consequently deprived of the corresponding volume of demand. When private households consume less, consumer goods companies' sales and profits fall, and the state records lower tax revenues. As a result of their decreased income, these companies invest less, which also has a negative impact on the capital goods sector, and on state revenues. If the state is concerned with avoiding increasing its debt burden, then in light of its reduced revenues, it too will spend less; this further reduces demand for goods and services supplied by companies — either directly, through reduced state purchases of goods, or indirectly, if the state reduces transfers to private households and thereby reduces household demand.

Contrary to the assumptions of the neoclassical model, this drop in demand is not offset by an increasing supply of savings-pool financial capital that could lead to falling interest rates. Why? Because some people's attempts to save reduce the incomes of other people. If private households and the state both try to save at the same time, then gross revenues and net incomes of companies will fall. If companies stick to their previous investment plans (which is unlikely, since their capacity utilisation is declining — why expand production capacity if many of your existing machines are idle?), they can now raise less of the necessary financial capital from their own earnings (in other words, the companies' internal supply of investible financial capital has fallen). Companies would therefore have to ask banks for more money in order to make the same volume of investment as what they had previously planned. As a result, an increase in savings on the part of private households leads to a higher demand for borrowing money from companies (assuming their investment plans have not changed). The net effect on the interest rates is zero: more money is offered by saver-lenders, but this is balanced out by more money being demanded by borrowers. Interest rates cannot fall in this scenario, and therefore there is no price-of-money stimulus for an increase in investments. Consequently, there is no automatic demand replacement for the lower consumer demand caused by increased household savings.

But in fact, the effect of increased household savings ratios is actually much worse. The foregoing scenario assumed that company investments in production capacity would remain constant in an environment of increased savings and decreased consumer demand. This is completely unrealistic. Why should companies want to invest as much as before, when demand for their products is falling? Why buy more production machinery when many of the machines you already have are idle?

In reality, companies will tend to invest less and demand less financial capital when combined household and government savings-rates increase, because companies' capacity utilisation rates and financial revenues will be lower. Many companies incur financial losses in such an environment. The reduction in demand for investment money could then lead to a fall in interest rates after all. However, this would be the consequence of lower investment activity, and will not generate a positive impetus for more investments.

Instead, a more likely result would be for lower interest rates and declining investment volumes to occur at the same time.

This is the situation that provokes the Central Bank to use its liquidity to ensure that interest rates continue to fall even further; in other words, to provide a real impetus to borrowers. Sometimes such an impulse works, sometimes not. In recent years, central banks around the world have driven interest rates down close to zero, but investment activity has not been picking up. In such a situation, where interest rates are stuck at the zero lower bound (ZLB), the interest-rate mechanism imagined by neoclassical economists could not function anyway, even if their assumption of a positive investment impulse generated by falling interest rates through more savings was correct.

Neoclassical economic doctrine also misjudges the importance of flexible prices and wages. Its adherents have said, for example, that the economic slump in southern Europe is not the result of austerity policy; rather, the problem has been that the positive effect of very low interest rates has been counteracted by rigid wages and immobile workers (see Mayer, 2013). This is — empirically and theoretically — an astonishing argument. Empirically astonishing because things are particularly bad in countries where unit labour costs have been falling in absolute terms since 2010. The two countries where wages have not fallen in absolute terms, namely France and Italy, have fared less badly in terms of recession than the other southern European economies. How then can rigid wages and prices be blamed for the recession?

The obvious explanation for the failure of austerity policy is that wage reductions have directly caused domestic demand to collapse. Since the demand side of the private sector is in a downward spiral, the interest rate stimulus provided by loose monetary policy is no longer effective. Some businesses refrain from investing due to lack of demand, and others cannot get money from the banks. Austerity measures are exacerbating the crisis not because they encounter rigid prices and wages, but because their negative impact on the economy is exacerbated by the downward adjustment of prices and wages.

Income as a compensation mechanism

Why is it so difficult for adherents of neoclassical theory to recognise that interest rate adjustments cannot fulfil the function their theory attributes to them? The reason is that they have refused to describe the process that purportedly would generate a return to economic "equilibrium" after an austerity drive. Instead, they simply argue that there is an *ex post* end-point of the process at which saving and investment are equal, and this must be the equilibrium state. There is a price (the interest rate) in a highly efficient market (the capital market), and we can observe that companies usually invest. Consequently, there is no reason to worry about whether and how the process works in detail.

The issue that actually matters, namely the question of whether the overall result $S = I$ emerges because the interest rate plays the role expected by their theory, or whether something completely different happens, is simply ignored — because their theory says that it cannot be the case that the capital market does not fulfil its task efficiently.

But there is another factor that reconciles saving and investment (*ex post*), even if the interest mechanism fails completely: Total macroeconomic income. If private households and the state both cut back on spending, and the cutbacks taken together are larger than the investment spending plans of companies, then aggregate income will fall. Accordingly, resources will remain unused, or goods that were produced will sit unsold in warehouses, which sends a signal to companies that they should reduce their investment activities and lay off workers.

In countries whose governments adopted austerity programmes, the state had intended to reduce its debt in relation to its originally expected income. But the unexpected decline in macroeconomic income instead caused the government's debt to rise in relation to the actually realised lower macroeconomic income (i.e. the public debt to GDP ratio increased). Corporate debt ratios are also likely to be higher, due to unexpectedly lower revenues and incomes. Private households will find that their savings ratios are higher than expected, again in relation to their lower income. $S = I$ remains true, i.e. savings remain equal to investment, but everyone has become poorer (and some have become unemployed) because the mechanism that neoclassical theory said should have turned an increased desire to save into larger total investment volumes has not worked.

If one ignores, from the outset, the change in income caused by this dynamic process, as many neoclassical economists do, then one simply cannot understand what is happening in reality, and obviously one cannot give sensible economic policy advice either. If a policy advisor sticks to the theory and insists that the state must under no circumstances allow its debt to rise in relation to income, then he will prescribe that the spending cutback plans should be revised upwards again in response to an emerging recession, without being sure that corporate investment plans are going in the same direction, namely upwards. If instead they are going downwards, because the demand and income situation for companies is constantly deteriorating, then the state's attempt to cut costs will strengthen the recessionary trend and worsen the overall loss of income and jobs.

In the current global situation, even a massive interest rate cut initiated by central banks worldwide has not been sufficient to offset companies' pessimistic expectations regarding their future business prospects. Not even a zero interest rate has caused businesses to increase their investment levels. Even if, as some say, companies had previously invested far too much (which can be ruled out for the majority of countries anyway), one would have to take note of the fact that even a programme of extremely low interest rates maintained by a central bank literally for decades can fail to increase investment levels, as has been the case in Japan since the early 1990s. This observation should profoundly shake the belief that a process of interest rate cuts left to the market alone will always suffice to stabilise an economy. Given these facts, for economists to recommend to states in recession (or experiencing very low growth) that they can continue their austerity programmes, or make even deeper expenditure cuts, is outrageous and irresponsible.

The net result of the great controversy between neoclassical economics and Keynesianism is therefore simple to express: Cutbacks and savings worsen business conditions for companies. The paradox of saving, often called the "paradox of thrift," applies at the whole-economy level, and that is why austerity is wrong and dangerous. However, this can only be recognised if one leaves the micro-level and includes macroeconomic relationships in economic analysis. Anyone who tries to understand the market economy, but for ideological reasons fails to take a genuinely macroeconomic view, will never be able to explain the economy's real processes, or prescribe policy mechanisms that could improve their trajectories.

Neoclassical economic theory is an unsuitable basis for economic policy. It does not even recognise corporate profits as a source of financing — instead, it assumes a kind of "pseudo-profit" in terms of favourable interest rates in the context of a posited long-term competitive equilibrium.

The current account and national savings

Keynesian and neoclassical economics also appear to go in precisely opposite directions on the matter of national current account surpluses. A surplus in a country's current account is analogous to domestic saving (rather than spending). In explaining how such surpluses arise, neoclassical economists emphasize the importance of capital flows. Here, too, the autonomous decisions of consumers to save more or save less are in the foreground. Proper Keynesians see it the other way round: Capital flows adapt to the flows of goods, which are determined by (among other things) the competitiveness of a country (which is, at its core, a consequence of the undervaluation or overvaluation of its currency).

Let us look at the current account balances of some major economies and their causes, which are currently the most important political cases. A clear understanding of the relevant interrelationships is needed in order to reach reasonable conclusions. So-called balance-sheet mechanics (a set of logically indisputable macroeconomic relationships) are an unavoidable component of the analysis, but by themselves they cannot suffice to answer the really decisive question: that of cause and effect.

Even economists who are considered relatively enlightened are often unable to distinguish the logic of balance-sheet accounting identities from "real" theoretical insights. Jeffrey Sachs, Martin Wolf, and Barry Eichengreen, for example, support Hans-Werner Sinn's thesis that the emergence of current account balances (i.e. whether they are in surplus or in deficit) depends on an economy's "propensity to save," i.e. a high propensity to save equals a current account surplus, and vice versa (Wolf, 2017; Sachs, 2017; Eichengreen, 2017).

This apparently means that economies with a high propensity to save live below their means, i.e. earn more than they spend, while economies with current account deficits live above their means, because they spend more than they earn. Barry Eichengreen, for example, says the following in an article about Germany's current account surpluses:

> Back in the real world, the explanation for Germany's external surplus is not that it manipulates its currency or discriminates against imports, but that it saves more than it invests. The correspondence of savings minus investment with exports minus imports is not an economic theory; it's an

accounting identity. Germans collectively spend less than they produce, and the difference necessarily shows up as net exports. (Eichengreen, 2017, translation by the authors)

This shows that even a world-renowned economic historian can make the mistake of interpreting an accounting identity (a statement of definition) as a statement of content. Eichengreen appears not to understand that there is a flexible macroeconomic income (national income) that stands behind the identity. The movements of this income (and their causes) are what determine the identity's quantities. The entire core of the Keynesian revolution in economic theory has been completely misunderstood here.

The Deutsche Bundesbank, Germany's central bank, also stumbled into this conceptual trap. On the one hand, it cannot avoid recognising indisputable macroeconomic relationships, but at the same time, it does not want to call the neoliberal agenda into question under any circumstances. This is evident in the Bundesbank's comments on the development of Germany's current account surpluses and their counterparts in the so-called German savings balances.

A special publication from 2017 on the financial balances of Germany's broad economic sectors correctly says:

The system of double-entry bookkeeping in the financial accounts results from creditor-debtor relationships. All receivables are equally matched by liabilities, broken out by instrument and sector, and further into transactions and portfolios: The financial assets of one party are the financial debts of a counterparty. This results in a necessary consistency of the data: The totals of the respective balance sheet items of instruments and sectors must agree in their values. The necessary requirement for consistency applies to the outcome of the financial statement, as well as to the sources and procedures used, and ensuring this consistency is a particular challenge. (German Bundesbank, 2017c)

It follows, however, that the content of the following paragraph from the same publication is incorrect:

Germany's current account surplus can also be analysed from the perspective of investment and savings decisions by domestic economic agents. This is because the macroeconomic lending/borrowing balance, which largely corresponds to the current account balance, results from the difference between savings and investment in the national accounts. (...) According to this view, the current account surplus did not increase further in 2016 because the total volume of savings in the German economy as a whole, which had increased sharply in the two previous years, had shrunk slightly relative to GDP. This largely offset the decline in the volume of investments.

The fact that there is an arithmetic identity of domestic financial assets accumulation on the one hand, and an increasing debtor position of foreigners *vis-à-vis* Germany on the other, does not justify viewing these balances as emerging from the savings decisions of domestic economic entities.

This is because, as the Bundesbank itself has stated, the banks' decision to grant loans to domestic or foreign borrowers does not depend on the existence of depositors' savings in the accounts of those banks, nor, therefore, on domestic savings decisions. Given this fact, there is no possibility of explaining domestic lending via "savings decisions." Lending to foreign borrowers, which is actually what a current account surplus is all about, has nothing at all to do with the savings decisions of German residents.

In the latter paragraph quoted above, the Bundesbank made inappropriate use of a convention in accounting terminology according to which the domestic macroeconomic balance is referred to as national "savings," even though, as the Bundesbank is well aware, this has nothing to do with the future-oriented decisions of private households or companies to retain some proportion of their "given" annual income in savings accounts (i.e. to save rather than spend). In reality, there is no "given" income; there is always uncertainty about how much income can be generated in a certain period. This applies to companies especially.

The fact that the Bundesbank knows this is shown at another point in the same document, where it writes, again correctly, the following:

Favourable interest rates are not by themselves sufficient for companies to significantly expand their production capacities. Rather, expectations of financial returns on investment based on general economic conditions and longer-term sales prospects are the factors most relevant for investment decisions. (German Central Bank, 2017a)

The decisive factor for companies' investment and savings decisions is thus their expectations of future demand for their products, i.e. on (uncertain) estimates of how the incomes of consumers (private households) are likely to develop, and of households' propensity to save. The less the income of private households increases and the higher their propensity to save, the lower the demand for the products and services of companies, and thus the lower companies' demand for capital goods (production equipment).

If this is the case, then it is also true that money-saving in itself, i.e. the decision of private households (and companies) to retain in their savings accounts some part of their income, represents a brake on investment activity. Unless there are autonomous investments by businesses — which is to say, investments that are independent of household demand, investments that fall magically out of a clear blue sky — any attempt by any sector to spend less than it receives in income will act as a brake on investment.

By admitting that it is not interest rates, but rather aggregate demand that is decisive for investment activity, the Bundesbank directly disproves its own claim that savings decisions are responsible for investment activity. According to the neoclassical view, savings decisions can only influence investment activity via interest rates. However, if interest rates are basically not suitable for regulating investment levels up or down, and if even extremely (artificially!) low interest rates produced by central bank action have not sufficed to stimulate investment activity, the consequences are clear. We can infer that savings decisions do not play a role in stimulating investment activity (by influencing domestic debt), nor in putting foreigners into net debt *vis-à-vis* Germany, i.e. in creating current account surpluses.

Precisely because the accounting identities of balance-sheet mechanics are indisputable, the following question must be asked: If it is correct that by definition, economies with surpluses earn more than they spend, and if we call this behaviour "saving," then the statement that "economies that save have surpluses and those that do not save have deficits" has no content. For this statement is nothing more than a tautological repetition of the logic of balance-sheet mechanics using the word "saving." Consequently, the statement (and any empirical evidence based on it) is completely empty.

However, at the same logical level, "as Keynesians" one can only say that economies that export more than they import have surpluses, and vice versa. This statement can of course be dismissed as trivial; yet the first, neoclassical statement is repeatedly used and acknowledged as a statement of content, although it has exactly the same content as the second — i.e. it has no additional content at all; it is simply a restatement of a definition. Apparently, the word "saving" creates a fictional conception of a presumed behavior of private households and public budget managers that people believe can be inferred from balance-sheet mechanics. However, the above-mentioned macroeconomic "saving" has nothing to do with the concrete behaviour of any of these actors.

Price ratios in an international context

One can easily check this by asking how the savings behaviour of the world's various countries can be reconciled on the basis of microeconomic foundations. After all, we know from balance-sheet mechanics (and common sense) that there is no way for the world as a whole to "save" in the sense defined above, i.e. to spend less than it takes in. The net savings of the world as a whole are always exactly equal to zero.

This has a clear and fatal consequence for attempts to provide a microeconomic foundation ("micro-foundation") for macroeconomic prediction systems. If all countries in the world wanted to be net savers in order to prepare for the future (as is stated in Germany in all seriousness as the reason for the nation's surpluses), our ability to think logically would unfortunately force us to tell the world that this is impossible. All the squirrels in the world can stash nuts to prepare for winter, but all countries cannot provide for the future by achieving net surpluses in their current accounts.

The microfoundations approach is driven *ad absurdum* here, at a crucial point. For a correct economic analysis, we obviously need a macro-foundation much more urgently than a micro-foundation. Neoclassical economics again proves to be simply inconsistent, on logical grounds.

If all countries in the world have identical austerity plans, and all of them desire to save more money to provide for the future, there must exist one or more mechanisms to ensure that these inconsistent austerity plans are brought into line with the logical need to achieve an absolutely balanced current account for the whole world. There is a crucial logical category to take note of here: The competition to achieve current account surpluses is (unlike the sum of all trade) a zero-sum game for all countries of the world taken together. It is therefore imperative that some countries must abandon the goal of creating current account surpluses. But how do you get them to do that — against their declared will?

Neoclassical economics has no answer. It ignores this obvious problem, and thus excludes itself from any claim to belong to the category of serious economic theories, even at this early stage, because the capital flows controlled by national austerity plans do not, in neoclassical theory, have a zero-sum character.

But the analytical approaches of many Keynesians also show one large or several small gaps at this point, and fail to provide a logically compelling explanation of how to deal with the zero-sum current-accounts game. Many different factors that can lead to positive or negative current account balances are discussed, such as changes in the terms of trade, differences in GDP growth rates, or differences in competitiveness of countries, which are reflected in an undervaluation or overvaluation of currencies.

Yet even if the GDP growth rates of all countries were the same, a mechanism to bring the world's current account balance to zero would still be required. Logically, this can only be a mechanism that itself has zero-sum character, i.e. always takes away from one party what it gives to a counterparty. The two most important mechanisms of this kind are (i) changes in the terms of trade, i.e. changes in the ratio of import prices to export prices; and (ii) closely related, but not the same: changes in export price ratios (expressed in international currency), i.e. what are called "real exchange rate" changes (changes in the competitiveness of countries).

What this boils down to is that, in a consistent analysis, only price ratios can be responsible for current account balances. Where there are changes in the terms of trade, changes in price ratios may reflect real changes in scarcity (of raw materials in particular), which all countries will be willing to accept. In the case of "real exchange rate" changes, however, price ratio changes do not reflect the changing preferences of countries for real goods or services. Instead, the changes are an expression of a process that in some way regulates the conflict that occurs when countries have similar desires. How this happens and whether it occurs in a rational or chaotic way is a completely open question.

The only sensible prescription that economic theory can offer in response to the question of how best to determine real exchange rate changes is very simple: Since international relations do not allow any country to simply impose its "wishes" on other countries with any legitimacy, the only rule that independent and equal states can hope to agree on is that the real exchange rates and competitive relations between countries should not change at all. This entails a wonderful micro-foundation, because it is only under these conditions that competition between companies on the global level can take place in the same way that it does within nation-states (Flassbeck, 1988).

Constant real exchange rates

If a rule requiring constant real exchange rates applies, then nominal currency exchange rate changes must precisely compensate for the inflation differences between countries. If this happens, the international system will have done what it feasibly can do to make the process of balancing current accounts as conflict-free as possible.

This rule was and remains the entirely valid and indisputable core idea behind the global monetary system agreed at Bretton Woods in July 1944. It was this core idea, apart from any specific design details, that was the crucial contribution which John Maynard Keynes brought to the table at that time.

The acceptance of this rule has enormous consequences for the coexistence of nations, because it prevents, from the outset, any attempt to start a competition between nation-states. With this mechanism, every country is always made to rely on its own means and circumstances. A country can make an effort to increase its productivity, but it must use its successes in this domain to increase domestic incomes, because a strategy of undervaluation is excluded. If the rule is followed, price reductions made possible by achieving higher productivity yet keeping nominal wages constant cannot have an impact on a country's international competitiveness, because its currency will appreciate in compensation.

Applied in the context of a monetary union or a currency board with fixed exchange rates, this rule means that no country would be allowed to pursue an undervaluation strategy in the form of a wage restraint policy (i.e. wage increases less than productivity increases). Wages must always increase in tandem with national productivity and with the common inflation target agreed by the member states. Without this minimum standard of rational behaviour on the part of individual member states, a monetary union or a system of fixed exchange rates can never work.

It is well known by now that Germany violated this rule from the outset within the framework of the European Monetary Union (EMU). The logic set out in these pages demonstrates how questionable — even nonsensical — it is to cook up all kinds of arguments to attempt to justify a behaviour which is inconsistent with peaceful cooperation between EMU nation-states.

It follows from these considerations that monetary policy cooperation is necessary and unavoidable between nation-states that wish to trade with each other. The simplest form of cooperation would be to leave the adjustment of currency exchange rates to a foreign exchange market that always finds the right exchange rate, i.e. a currency market that consistently ensures real exchange rates remain constant. But this foreign exchange market does not exist, as we will show in Chapter 3 of this book. Consequently, there is no way around the creation of an institutional mechanism for the determination of exchange rates based on intergovernmental cooperation, if we want to fulfil the minimum requirement for beneficial international trade. This is all the more true in a globalised economy.

In a multi-currency management system or currency board in which exchange rates are meant, in principle, to be fixed, the degree to which they can stay constant in practice will depend on the degree to which member states are prepared to recognise the principle of a constant real exchange rate even in the absence of nominal exchange rate fluctuations. In other words, to what extent are member states willing and able to coordinate national wage policies? If the ability or propensity to do so is weak, then currency exchange rates must be adapted as early and smoothly as possible to differences between member nations' domestic inflation rates, as these arise (UNCTAD, 2009, chapter IV).

III

Neoliberalism as Regression

When neoliberalism began its triumphal procession at the end of the 1970s, many believed that for many decades to come, no dogma would arise to challenge that of a dynamic business sector freed from state shackles, driven by entrepreneurial investment, missing no opportunity to exploit and increase the economic potential of all states.

But things have turned out very differently. It is not just that countless crises have shaken the liberated economy and repeatedly set its progress back by years. Beyond this, there have been long-term changes that not only are failing to move the world directly toward a free-enterprise paradise, but are in fact causing millions to call the neoliberal economic system as such into question. The most important of these changes is usually discussed today under the rubric of "inequality," i.e. the fact that many people are being systematically uncoupled from the prosperity train and left behind, as what Keynes once called "poverty in the midst of plenty" has arisen.

The importance of this fact cannot be overestimated. The historian and publicist Sebastian Haffner wrote the following remarkable sentences in his book *From Bismarck to Hitler*, published in 1987:

> It is true that during the early 1900s, the great discovery of later times had not yet been made that workers were not only a cost factor, but were also a mass of consumers, and that it was therefore in the interest of industry to allow ever higher wages, albeit after engaging in some sham battles over wage rates with trade unions. But it was the case, even before this

understanding emerged, that workers had become scarcer, that trade unions had begun to play a certain role, and that employers slowly diverged or were dissuaded from the old "iron wage law" of paying as low wages as possible. This meant a certain social peace, and this social peace also had a political impact, mainly in the development of German social democracy. (Haffner, 1987, p. 85)

And a little later in the same book he wrote: "All classes were doing better all the time." (Haffner, 1987, p. 88; we are obliged to Friederike Spiecker for the reference.)

In other words, Haffner understood that people's participation in the progress of capitalism through higher wages is one of the basic prerequisites for social peace and for a flourishing social democracy. But even more important was his clear statement of the "great discovery" of the working class as a "consumer mass" to which higher wages were conceded precisely because it was very much in industry's own interest to grant them. In that light, neoliberalism is exposed as a regression: It emerged in the mid-1970s with the principal goal of making labour markets more flexible and enabling entrepreneurs to reduce rather than increase wages. Neoliberalism is thus revealed to be a step backward into the economic misunderstandings of the 19th century — a pathological regression to the childhood of economics.

The global economy is suffering more from this misunderstanding than from any other development. Only a radical rethinking of the functioning of the "labour market" and the causes and consequences of "inequality," as we present it in the following sections, can overcome this great regression.

The Labour Market is not a Market

In the western industrialised world, since the mid-1970s the great majority of economic power has fallen into the hands of corporations. Given the enormous task of dealing with the consequences of oil price explosions, inflation, and unemployment, the governments of most countries more or less capitulated and left it to global corporations to look for solutions. Margaret Thatcher, Ronald Reagan, and Helmut Kohl, who took the helm in three important countries in the early 1980s, were inspired by the ideas of Friedrich August von Hayek, all of whose prescriptions amount to pushing

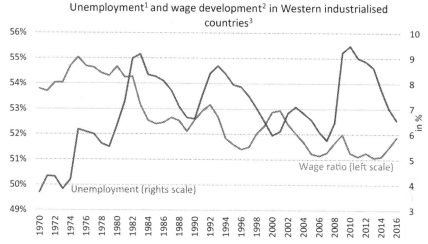

Figure 6:   Unemployment and wage trends in the western industrialized countries
Source: AMECO.

back state influence, giving the "markets" the reins and leaving them in charge of the global economy.

But the Keynesian bastions of economic policy still existed at the time. Why was it so easy for the neoliberal counterrevolutionaries to take them by storm? The explanation for this lies exactly where the counterrevolution began, namely in the unresolved and misunderstood events of those years. Figure 6 shows that two phenomena occurred during this decade, the combination of which channelled an incredible amount of water onto the mill-wheels of the neoclassical-monetarist paradigm. Initially, in the early 1970s, the proportion of national income going to wages rose in all major industrialised countries, because trade unions overreached after the OPEC-organised oil price explosions. In the context of full employment achieved almost everywhere, they were able to obtain double-digit wage-growth rates for their members.

After some delay, as Figure 6 shows, unemployment rose throughout the Western world. What could have seemed more obvious than to resurrect the old neoclassical doctrine, which had long been thought dead, claiming a connection between real wages and unemployment — and in the light of the apparently irrefutable evidence of higher wages being followed by higher unemployment in the 1970s, discarding Keynesianism as a false doctrine?

The relationship between wage levels and the unemployment rate looks unequivocal in Figure 6, yet in fact, it is anything but. Along with high wage increases (see Flassbeck, Horn & Zwiener, 1989) and high oil prices, inflation also reached unexpected levels. Monetary policymakers around the world reacted to this with interest rate hikes, thereby adding a further demand-dampening factor to the original negative demand shock of the OPEC oil price increases. The outcome was a collapse in investment activity. This suggests that it was a completely different nexus (a demand-side Keynesian one) that came into play in the 1970s and caused unemployment to skyrocket.

However, the neoclassical nexus had simple and seemingly unbeatable evidence on its side. Subtleties of economic analysis no longer played a role in the ideological battles between the defenders on the demand side and the attackers on the supply side. The obvious narrative prevailed: That of a failure of "Keynesianism" to deal with the new phenomenon of stagflation, that is, the combination of stagnation and inflation, which shaped large parts of the 1970s and 1980s. The supply-side attackers' victory was a total one, and the demand side left the field extremely weakened.

Although the following decades were by no means a success story, the now dominant supply-side mainstream nevertheless succeeded in inventing the story of the "Great Moderation," in which economists persuaded themselves that the two decades between the beginning of the 1980s and the end of the century had been very successful, because there had been neither major crises nor major tensions between inflation and unemployment.

When the death knell for this transfiguration story rang in 2008/09, one might have expected that enough Keynesians would be ready to finally throw the neoclassical doctrine into the dustbin of history, and to take over the levers of macroeconomic policy. The reality was far from it. Monetarism, i.e. the hope that the money system could be technocratically controlled, had been discredited, yet even the obvious failure of neoclassical orthodoxy to explain the dramatic rise in unemployment and subsequent deflation in the wake of the great financial crisis did not suffice to awaken the Keynesians from their hibernation. In addition, they lacked political momentum because in nearly all countries, social democratic parties, driven by an extreme and irrational phobia against public debt, had completely renounced Keynesianism.

So, what the picture above clearly shows simply went unseen and unrecognised: In the 2008/09 crisis, unemployment rose to its highest level since the Second World War, even though the wage share of national income at the outbreak of the crisis was low, not high — indeed it was the lowest it had been since the Second World War. If unemployment rises in an environment of already low wages, the result can only be that wages will increase even less than before, because the balance of power on the labour market has shifted further in favour of employers. The result is deflation, or at least a deflationary trend that can be observed almost everywhere in the world since 2008.

Academic Keynesianism overlooked this clear evidence, and missed a golden opportunity to score points in the contest for policy influence. Keynesians failed to make the point that growing unemployment, in an environment of low wage increases and a very low wage share of national income, empirically disproves the neoclassical model of how labour markets function. Keynesians have also failed to draw attention to the fact that three fundamental theoretical pillars of neoclassical economics and other liberal economic theories — monetarism, efficient financial markets, and the liberal model of the labour market — have all been disproven by logic and empirical evidence, and that liberal theorists can therefore no longer claim to make credible economic policy evaluations or recommendations.

Slim pickings

A few years ago, *The Financial Times* published an excellent article about how an economic upswing in the US apparently can either result in higher wages — or not (Politi, 2014). The FT reported on an upscale retail cookware business in Charlottesville, Virginia, that had increased its employees' wages in recent months because its owners felt that "there were less people out there, there was less to pick from," and they feared losing staff. Later in the same article, the newspaper reported on a "staffing and recruiting company" in Charlottesville whose founder said, "I am not seeing a huge demand for increased wages," because "I am still seeing a lot of people who are thankful to get a job."

Jason Furman, who was then chairman of the Council of Economic Advisers, said that "growing their wages" was the biggest challenge for many

Americans. A full seven years after the end of the financial crisis and the economic upheaval it brought, in USA in 2014, nominal wages were rising by barely more than two percent, which means they were very nearly stagnant in real terms.

At this point, professional economists will object that in an environment of high unemployment, it is not possible to push through substantial wage increases. It is only after the economy has caught up and the demand for labour is growing strongly that the American employee can credibly threaten her boss that she will quit unless her wages are significantly increased. However, it turns out that this situation may never arise, because, as the same FT rightly points out, the US Federal Reserve will quickly swing into action and raise interest rates in the event of strong wage increases, because "wages are tightly linked to inflation."

Even under normal economic conditions, it is an open question whether employees in a liberalised, "flexible" labour market can get their money's worth, in the sense of seeing their wages rise in tandem with rising productivity. Whether real wages in the upswing phase rise sufficiently strongly or for a sufficient period of time to compensate for losses experienced during the downturn phase depends on so many factors that there is no guarantee of a symmetrical distribution of real wage gains and losses over the course of the economic cycle.

There are many arguments against this symmetry being achieved. For one thing, central banks tend to raise interest rates immediately if the average rate of wage increases exceeds productivity gains or inflation targets — yet wage rates might well have to exceed productivity gains for a period, if workers are to be compensated for the real wage losses they incurred during a preceding recession.

When central banks raise rates quickly at the first sign of wage rises outpacing inflation targets, this tends to slow or halt an economic upswing at an early stage. Yet in an economy such as North America or Europe (i.e. in large closed economies with low global trade integration), real wage increases at the rate of productivity growth are needed in order to generate the demand necessary to fully utilise the capacities of the economy over the economic cycle.

The real problem with this story, however, is that current economic circumstances are by no means normal. It seems that no one is prepared to acknowledge that the wave of unemployment in the industrialised world which arose after the 2007–2008 financial crisis had nothing at all to do with high wages or a wage-related risk of inflation. On the contrary, it was the bursting of a huge financial bubble that caused unemployment to rise, even though the wage ratio (i.e. the wage share of total national income) was low prior to 2008, and a pattern of great inequality in the distribution of income had already been established.

Under such conditions, downward pressure on wages is simply counter-productive. It destabilises the economy, because domestic demand cannot pick up. Yet a boost in demand is precisely what is needed to reduce unemployment. By reacting to a demand shock by depressing wages, the labour market is doing exactly the opposite of what is necessary to put the economy back on a path where new jobs can be created. Downward pressure on wages reduces employment and new job creation.

Another thing that too many Keynesians fail to understand is that recognising the fact that wages determine prices ("wages are tightly linked to inflation") means recognising that the labour market does not function in accordance with the neoclassical model, in which real wages are thought to be inversely related to employment. A deep fear of calling into question the received idea of the labour market that has been taught for so many years now in undergraduate economics courses seems to be blocking this recognition.

And yet inequality — the great social challenge of our time — can only be addressed through a correct understanding of the labour market. The decisive issue is how the balance of power on the "labour market" shapes the development of incomes. The question is how a further decline of the wage share of national income can be prevented politically, and how to convey to policymakers the recognition that it must be prevented for economic reasons.

Eugen von Böhm-Bawerk and the power of the market

The neoclassical narrative mistakenly claiming that the "labour market" is a market like any other has a long history. A significant milestone in this discourse was a long essay published in 1914 by Eugen von Böhm-Bawerk, one of the founders of the so-called Austrian School, who at least tried to take the aspect of political power into account. In 1962, at a time when Germany still had a tradition of reality-based economics, the *Verein für Sozialpolitik* (Social Policy Association), a leading national association of economists, dedicated an annual conference and several essays to this topic.

The original dispute, as can be read, for example, in Wilhelm Krelle's essay at the association's 1962 conference, revolved around the question of whether workers' wages are above all the result of the existing balance of power between employers and employees, or whether they obey economic law, i.e. whether wages are determined anonymously on a functioning market in accordance with supply and demand. Böhm-Bawerk, whose theoretical edifice was based on the neoclassical theory of marginal productivity, ascribed the upper hand to economic law. He was later to be declared the "winner" in this debate. He remains the winner to this day, at least when the prevailing doctrine in academic economics is taken as a benchmark.

However, in recent decades we have learned quite a lot about the labour market and its problems, especially about the macroeconomic feedback of wage levels on demand for goods and thus on employment. We know much more about this than Böhm-Bawerk or other 19th-century economists did. We are in a position to know that in the case of the labour market, supply and demand are not independent of each other, and therefore the neoclassical assumption of independent supply and demand functions must lead economic theory completely astray, with devastating consequences for its policy relevance. But this fact is systematically and consciously ignored. That is why it makes sense to take up this issue once again, and examine it in detail in light of recent developments.

Increasing inequality is an embarrassment to the prevailing doctrine, because under the assumption of a balance of power in the labour market, it is difficult to understand, in the context of the neoclassical model, why income and wealth inequality are increasing. That is why liberal economists always cite various external factors, or "shocks," in an effort to explain away what their model cannot actually explain.

Some time ago, the Austrian newspaper *Standard* published a long article on the question of why the share of wages in national income has decreased (Moser, 2016). As is often the case with newspaper articles, it got some things right, such as its recognition of changed power structures favouring employers over employees (on this issue, the article cited a relevant study by the

Austrian Chamber of Labour). But to "compensate" for this element of pro-labour analysis, however, other explanatory elements were also brought into play — technological changes, or the impacts of globalisation. As is almost always the case when it comes to topics that are central to the Zeitgeist and engage with its prevailing doctrines, newspaper readers end up in a swamp of confusion, unable to draw a conclusion, because the article's writer has developed no convincing and well-argued position.

The technology argument can also be found in an assessment report of the German Council of Economic Experts (Bofinger *et al.*, 2016) published in 2016. Paragraph 819 states: "The increase in wage inequality between 1999 and 2005 in the upper half of the wage distribution is explained not least by technological progress, which has put highly qualified workers in a disproportionately better position than low-skilled workers."

It is doubtless very pleasant for representatives of the ruling doctrine to find reasons — like technology and globalisation — which seemingly objectively ensure that inequality must increase, because by citing such explanations, critical questions can be fended off and "the market" can be defended as the appropriate mechanism for finding the right wages.

Empirical findings

Despite varying assessments and reports on the temporal development of income distribution in Germany, there is broad consensus that over the past two decades, the share of total income going to salaried employees has declined, and the incomes of low-wage workers have fallen behind particularly sharply. In this text, we use the so-called "real wage position" to describe the functional distribution of income between labour and capital. It shows real hourly wages per hour lagging behind hourly productivity (Figure 7).

In this graph, the real wage position is inverted; i.e. a rising curve means an improvement for the capital side. As expected, in the first years of the new century, the distribution of national income (share of GDP) moved very strongly in favour of capital in Germany, in contrast to the relatively flat trend in France. In the wake of the global financial crisis of 2007–2008, during the global recession, the workers saw a relative gain for a short time, but as soon as the post-recession upswing took hold, the long-term trend in

Figure 7:   Real wage position (invested)

Source: AMECO, OECD.

Germany for a significant redistribution in favour of employers took hold once again.

The graph comparing income trends of different income groups looks almost exactly the same (Figure 8). A rising Gini coefficient denotes rising inequality. Figure 8 shows a clear long-term rising trend in the Gini coefficient for Germany. The distribution position of lower incomes deteriorated especially markedly between 2000 and 2005. Here too, the changes in France are much less pronounced. In the mid-1990s, France had a higher Gini coefficient than Germany, i.e. greater inequality; Germany has since caught up.

In regard to these findings, public commentators from neoliberal circles such as the German Council of Economic Experts like to point out that the situation has not changed significantly since 2005. But what does that mean? Despite falling unemployment in Germany and massive changes in secondary distribution (via the state) in favour of companies, the distribution of

Figure 8:   Gini coefficient

Source: OECD, Eurostat.

national income has deteriorated only slightly since 2005. That is to say: Germany's income distribution has remained as extremely one-sided as it was driven by political pressure to become, in the first years of the present century.

There can be no doubt that this lopsided distribution was a deliberate policy choice. It is no coincidence that functional and personal income distribution has been developing in a very similar way. Both are the result of massive state intervention in the balance of power on the labour market and thus in the distribution of incomes. One wonders why so many observers still deny or relativise this finding. The change in distribution was the declared aim of the state's policy efforts. They wanted more inequality, and they got it.

Why would one expect all of the many attempts to change income and wealth distribution in favour of businesses and the well-off have failed? Over the past 20 years, the state has halved corporate taxes in Germany, abolished the wealth tax, and reduced the capital gains tax. At the same time, corporate profits have been good because the export channel was wide open. A big low-wage sector was created and social support was drastically reduced. It is perfectly clear, given these measures, that the distribution should have changed in favour of employers and the better-off in general — and so it has. Why should this be denied or downplayed? Instead, we must ask whether this was a sensible policy, and what can be done to renormalise the situation.

There is no individual productivity

When Eugen von Böhm-Bawerk wrote his famous essay on power and economic law, he probably could not have guessed how clearly it would be possible, years later, to show on the basis of empirical data that his view was untenable. Figures 9 and 10 illustrate once again the development of real wages and productivity per hour in Germany and France since the start of the European Monetary Union.

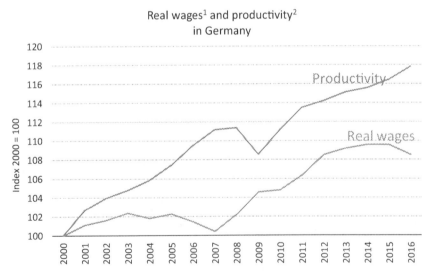

Real wages[1] and productivity[2] in Germany

[1] Gross income from employee labour, price adjusted with GDP deflator, per hour worked by employees, 2000 = 100; value for 2016 of average hours worked by employees: own estimation
[2] Real gross domestic product in national currency per hour of employment, 2000 = 100

Figure 9:   Real wages and productivity in Germany

Source: AMECO, OECD.

Figure 10:   Real wages and productivity in France

Source: AMECO, OECD.

Germany and France had approximately the same level of unemployment at the beginning of the century in both countries. Political power was exercised in Germany to ensure that real wages have not followed productivity — in contrast to France, where they remained closely correlated. And thus, many sectoral wages in Germany have remained below the marginal productivity of the workplace (i.e. the productivity that the most recently hired worker still generates), i.e. below what the market is meant to assign as wages to each individual, according to the neoclassical view. The "economic law" relating wages to marginal productivity was therefore not impervious to being undercut through the exercise of political power.

Eugen von Böhm-Bawerk described this "economic law" as follows:

> According to the formula of the economic school that develops a wage theory based on the modern theory of marginal utility, we find that given free and fully effective competition on both sides, the wage level should be

determined by the "marginal productivity of labour," i.e. by the value of additional production which the "last," most dispensable worker in the industry still generates for his employer. The wage could not be any higher than this value, because otherwise the entrepreneur would gain no advantage, but rather, would suffer a loss from the employment of the "last" worker, and would therefore prefer to reduce his number of workers by one head. But under the condition of fully effective mutual competition, the wage could not be significantly lower either, because otherwise the employment of the "last" worker would be linked to a noticeable extra profit. As long as this remains the case, there would be an incentive for a further expansion of the enterprises in the industry, resulting in the employment of even more workers, and in an environment of fully effective competition between enterprises, this opportunity would be exploited. The competition could not fail to eat up the existing margin between the value of the marginal product and the wage, from two sides: on one side, by increasing wages as a result of the demand for more workers, and on the other side, by quietly reducing the value of additional product by increasing the supply of goods produced to even larger quantities. These impulses would not only "constrict" the wage level, but, due to the proximity of the limiting barriers, virtually determine it; e.g. with the amount of 5K 50h [Kronen/Heller] for the working day. (Böhm-Bawerk, 1914, p. 225 f.)

What is remarkable is that he writes several times that the prerequisite for this process is *free and fully effective competition on both sides.* This of course excludes a significant part of the real-world power problem from the outset, because whether and in what way there is fully effective competition among sellers and buyers of labour depends above all on the employment situation in an economy, and additionally on the social security of employees in the event of unemployment.

In jurisdictions where there exists substantial underemployment and unemployment (and this is the situation that characterises most of the world most of the time), fully effective competition between employers does not exist, because all companies can get workers who are prepared to work for less than the fictitious marginal product if the alternative is unemployment with little social security rather than another job. The weaker the level of social security, the less effective the competition between employers for employees.

Böhm-Bawerk's position is microeconomically untenable, too, even if one assumes full employment. Even at the level of microeconomics, there is usually no such thing as "marginal productivity." Given absolutely standardised processes on the assembly line, one may be able to calculate by how much production costs increase when an additional worker is employed. In the vast majority of activities, however, this is not known.

Then there is the question of whether the products produced can also be sold, because only then is the work employed for their production truly productive. In the biggest sectors of the economy, such as services (including industrial production-related services), the entrepreneur cannot estimate how much he can earn additionally by hiring a worker or employee. That is why he has no choice: He pays the going market wage when full employment prevails, and tries to stay below it when he is in a favourable negotiating position because of widespread unemployment. He puts employees to work where he can use them right at the moment. He may find over time that a new employee can be deployed much more usefully and productively in some other task than that for which he was originally hired, without necessarily having to change his salary in consequence. An employee can have many different productivities, depending on where he is used in the production process. There is no market process that would prevent a company from putting an employee to work at a task at which he generates far more production (and earnings) than reflected by his wage, because the underlying cost and earnings structures are simply non-transparent, or the costs of obtaining the necessary information are too high.

The reality is that neither marginal productivity nor marginal revenues can reliably be calculated in the real world. These notional quantities are not the basis for real-world business decisions.

But where does the going market wage come from? Is it not the result of labour productivity after all, at the end of the day? Indeed, we have repeatedly shown that average wages in an economy are closely related to productivity. The dynamics of real wages over time, i.e. year-on-year changes, are fairly closely linked to productivity in most developed countries (this can be completely otherwise in developing countries; we will deal with that topic later). But these are productivity developments that have absolutely nothing to do with individual productivity. This is shown indisputably by the annual adjustment of wages in the service sectors, where, as a rule, the economy's average increase in productivity is used as a component of wage determination in negotiations, even though service occupations have very little to do with the development of overall productivity — the latter depends predominantly on the manufacturing sector.

Incidentally, this also applies in the event that competition among companies is functional, but trade unions are extremely weak. Even then, real wages in all sectors would tend to increase, completely independently of the sectors' productivity development, because prices in the most productive sectors will be falling, and hence real wages effectively increasing — including the real wages of workers who themselves have not become more productive at all.

Over many years, the connection between individual productivity and wages completely disappears with such a growth dynamic. This dynamic simply does not appear in the static picture painted by Böhm-Bawerk. Occupational groups such as primary school teachers or nurses, whose job description and individual "productivity" remain unchanged over decades, nevertheless experience real wage increases in line with overall economic productivity. Other professions disappear completely, because they are no longer needed in the wake of changes in the structures of demand or after the emergence of new technologies. But even on the way out the door, practitioners of these vanishing professions are neither willing nor able (at least under conditions of full employment) to prevent the disappearance of their activities by adjusting their wages downwards. In contrast, workers whose competencies are favoured by structural change — such as experts in new technologies — can increase their wages not because their personal, individual productivity is especially high or increasing rapidly, but because their skills are scarce.

The idea of individual marginal productivity is untenable, because what "productivity" ultimately means depends on the wages themselves. As a result, the supply and demand functions in the so-called labour market are not independent of one another. Only if wages rise can demand for work increase sufficiently (cf. Flassbeck & Spiecker, 2016, p. 77 ff.).

The wage dynamics in a closed system such as the world as a whole is therefore quite different from those predicted by the neoclassical model. A reduction in nominal average wages can either lead immediately to a price reduction (which eliminates the neoclassical economists' hoped-for effect of a real wage reduction), or it can achieve a real wage reduction if prices do not react immediately. However, a reduction in real wages certainly will lead to a rapid reduction in demand, which destroys the hoped-for positive employment effect the neoclassical model expects will result from substitution of capital by labour (cf. Flassbeck, 2000). Once again, "marginal productivity" cannot provide any indication of what is happening on the "labour market" (or rather, in terms of employment).

Because its model of the labour market is wrong, it is irresponsible to work with the simple neoclassical supply-and-demand apparatus when addressing questions about the causes of unemployment. Joachim Möller, Director of the German government employment agency's Institute for Employment Research, speaks of red lines on minimum wages. In an interview with *Zeit* newspaper, he said: "If you significantly increase the minimum wage, it is to be feared that jobs will be lost in consequence. There's a red line somewhere that one mustn't cross." (*Zeit* Online, 2016)

In his conceptual world, this red line seems to be the marginal productivity of the lower wage groups, which cannot be exceeded without causing increased unemployment as a result. But such a position is pure fantasy.

The German Council of Economic Experts also states in its new annual report, published slightly more than a year after a federal minimum wage in Germany took effect in January 2015 after decades of resistance and objections by employers' federations and centre-right politicians:

> The effects of a minimum wage cannot be unequivocally determined by theory, since they depend among other things on the productivity of the labour force and the market power of employers. But not least because of this, the overall very positive labour market development [in Germany in recent years] should not lead to the conclusion that there is no employment effect of the minimum wage. The minimum wage significantly constrains the wage-formation process in the low-wage sector. (Bofinger *et al.*, 2016, paragraph 770)

This statement too is clearly shaped by the idea of individual marginal productivity. However, the productivity quantity assumed here for the lower qualification levels does not really exist. Productivity itself is the result of a complex process of interplay of supply and demand on goods markets at home and abroad. If the minimum wage is increased, the prices of those goods and services whose production has mainly involved minimum-wage workers may increase. However, overall demand will also certainly rise as a consequence of the minimum-wage increase, since few companies immediately or directly link employment adjustments with wage increases. Since aggregate demand for goods has risen, then overall production will also rise, and a presumed ratio of wages to a given, fixed level of productivity (i.e. a given GDP), as assumed by marginal productivity theory, clearly no longer exists.

The export channel

In an economy such as Germany's, where foreign demand, especially for industrial products, is now larger and more important than domestic demand, the trade unions face a different situation in collective bargaining (even abstracting from the loss of bargaining power caused by unemployment and the Agenda 2010 wage-suppression policy) than do unions in countries in which domestic demand dominates. It is undeniable that individual companies or an entire industry can gain an advantage in foreign trade, at least temporarily, through lower wage agreements. It is also undeniable that companies often threaten to migrate to lower-wage countries if their cost-cutting demands are not met.

In such a situation, the trade union side's purchasing-power argument collapses completely, because the negotiating trade unionists and the works councils of large export-oriented companies both know that it does not apply in their case. But where is the power of the theory of marginal productivity here, the theory in which almost all economists allegedly believe, the force of which supposedly nearly always forces wages to the right value?

If, as has been the case in Germany for 15 years now, even the trade unions bow to this foreign trade argument, all other lifelines that might justify a rational income distribution and wage policy will be tenuous. Moreover, if you are in a monetary union in which a country's wage moderation is not punished with an appreciation of its own currency, what happens is what we have shown above: In one country (Germany), trends in real wages are completely decoupled from trends in productivity for several years, while in a neighbouring country (in this case France), they remain closely linked to productivity. On the demand side, this remains unpunished at first, because the country manipulating wages can more than gain in increased exports that which it loses in domestic market demand.

Inequality without Function

Inequality is the subject of intense discussion and debate around the world today. A big problem is that almost everyone uses the term differently. There is no coherence or agreement on which specific issues are under discussion, no clarity about which income or wealth classes, regions, or time periods are being talked about. Consequently, empirical data are also not comparable. While one discussant reviews global inequality and lauds eastern Asia's successes in catching up with developed countries and reducing poverty, another is outraged at the increasing relative poverty within rich countries, and a third talks about the inequality inherent in a capitalist system because of the self-reinforcing dynamics of wealth ownership and accumulation.

It is therefore essential to sort out the interrelationships involved in different aspects of inequality, and to get to the bottom of some of its phenomena. We must try to make the discussion more objective by systematically asking which forms of inequality are unavoidable in a capitalist system, and which can be eliminated or at least reduced. The choice of words used to refer to the system we are examining is not important. Whether one calls the economic system in which we live the "market economy" or "capitalism," what matters is not the name; it is to develop as comprehensive an understanding as possible of how this system works.

Natural inequality?

In their search for the causes of material inequality, fervent defenders of liberalism have always quickly found what they were looking for: It is the "natural inequality of people." Because human beings are inherently unequal, liberals say, they cannot be forced into personal or even merely material equality without completely destroying human freedom and creativity.

Now there is certainly no denying that people are born unequal. They have different talents that they inherited from their parents. But starting immediately after birth, it becomes increasingly difficult to give a purely "natural" explanation for inequality. The quality and quantity of food intake in the first days of life can already decide whether or not a child grows up healthy. The social conditions and family context a child experiences in the first few years of life can determine which possibilities and opportunities that exist in a society a child will be able to access and make use of.

Consequently, "natural inequality" does not go very far as a justification for human material inequality. At the latest, when children enter school, their parents' material resources play a massive role in deciding whether and how successfully a child can make a living later on. This means that a society that wants all its children to get a comparable start in life must intervene in the material distribution of goods, and provide extra support for poorer families.

But even if, as intelligent liberals would admit, it makes sense to ensure that all children's opportunities are reasonably equal, it is not possible to fully prevent material and personal inequalities between people in any society or in any type of economy. That which is called luck, chance, or fate inevitably comes into play. One young person finds himself in the right place at the right time, and meets early success; another is unlucky, falls ill early in life and cannot use his potential. One has a brilliant idea, but cannot realise it because he is too far ahead of his time; another borrows a simple idea that fits with the spirit of the times, acts on it, and is incredibly successful. One is the best athlete in the world in a discipline that is unattractive to the masses and therefore has no material benefit; another is merely very good at a sport whose expert players are worshipped as heroes, and becomes rich.

All this happens in complex societies, and hardly anyone would doubt that the result is material inequality. But one can already see from these examples that the oversimple liberal idea that "everyone is the architect of his own fortune, and must be rewarded accordingly" no longer applies — at least not if you take off the liberal blinkers. Everything that comes immediately after birth already depends on the social position of the parents, which no newborn child has "earned." The good things provided to someone by life are not automatically provided in proportion to the "merit" or "achievement" of the individual. For the most part, they are owed to social circumstances, and cannot easily be attributed primarily to the individual and his or her "ability" or "will," because he or she cannot achieve anything at all without being embedded in society.

The greater the division of labour in society, the less its overall output can be attributed to individual performance. The division of labour means that the individual only gives the impetus for something; its eventual provision is the result of the interaction of more and more individuals. As the division of labour increases, the "right" of individuals to call a certain social position or income their "own" and to defend it tooth and nail against redistributive measures of the state diminishes.

At this point, liberals will be tempted to resort to a simple mental trick to avoid the unpleasant discussion that should now follow. They say that precisely because the world is so complex, it is impossible to give people real justice. Material justice is not something that can be provided or even specified. The state is therefore the wrong addressee for people to approach with demands for material justice. The only thing the state can do is to ensure that formal justice prevails, i.e. that all people are treated equally before the law.

But why should the state confine itself to this assignment? After all, in all modern societies, we have a common yardstick for success and failure: The income that each person earns. Many of the complex processes described above are reflected in individual income, which individuals cannot simply claim as their property, because it was only possible to earn their income within the framework of an economy based on the division of labour.

Formal or material tax justice?

This raises the central question of how each individual's income, obtained from "the market," should be taxed by the state. What speaks for formal justice, and what for material justice?

Formal justice would apparently already be served if the state were to demand from everyone an absolutely equal amount of money to pay for the services the state provides to society. A poll tax would therefore be appropriate, insofar as people use the broad services of the state (e.g. provision of security) quantitatively in the same way.

But what sensible person would really consider a poll tax to be an appropriate taxation system? As soon as one goes beyond the idea of a pure remuneration of the state for its services, and introduces notions of solidarity or willingness to make sacrifices and, derived from this, differences in ability to contribute, one must move to proportional taxation. This is because the level of sacrifice that someone makes for society can only be reasonably measured in relation to his or her income. This does not contradict the principle of equal treatment, because citizens are asked to provide to the state in equal proportion to their income.

Society can also go one step further, and decide on progressive taxation. This means that the services provided collectively by society, and which complement the output of the individual, are weighted so highly that society decides to charge a price for its services that is progressively higher the higher an individual's income.

In order to justify a higher tax contribution from wealthy citizens than from the less fortunate, it is possible to make an argument that excessive material inequality is a danger to an economy based on division of labour. Too much inequality can destroy the motivation of those lagging behind. How taxation is organised, i.e. whether purely as a progressive income tax or as a combination of a progressive income tax with inheritance and wealth taxes, is ultimately not decisive, even if there are good reasons to impose taxes on assets (i.e. inheritance or wealth taxes) in order to move economic conditions a small distance back in the direction of a level playing field of equal starting conditions.

How far one can go with taxation is a difficult question to answer. "Quite far, measured against the current low level of taxation in most industrialised countries," is certainly a good answer, because in recent decades we have been persuaded that "too high taxes" are the biggest obstacle to growth and progress. That is not true, as is known today and as we will explain in some detail later. But anyone who experienced how, in Germany in the 1980s and 1990s, a powerful lobby of business associations and liberal parties fought and "successfully" eliminated wealth taxes (taxation of assets) knows that the systemic ability of a representative democracy to defend itself against this type of intensive special-interest lobbying is very weak.

The industry and business association lobbyists' demands for massive tax cuts were explicitly justified at the time by the impact of taxes on the "willingness of the elite achievers to perform," which they claimed was diminished if too large a piece of the cake was taken away from them. However, in retrospect, it turns out that no measurable indicator has evidenced any sign that after the "achievers'" tax rates went down, their performance went up. Perhaps the theorists of lower taxation forgot to include in their model the possibility that the less well-paid colleagues and employees of the top performers might develop a declining willingness to work very hard as a result of the state's having allowed inequality to become too extreme.

But there are probably quite different reasons for the grandiose failure of the supply-side policy (the attempt to durably stimulate the economy by relieving the elites and companies of much of their burden of taxation). It seems likely that the postulated negative impact of progressive taxation and redistribution by the state on the private sector's willingness to invest and produce has been greatly overestimated. The loud howling of lobbyists tends to be misinterpreted as a sign of real pain, when in reality it is largely theatre and fakery.

This suggests that the state has a wide scope to ensure that the highly unequal results of market processes generated by the primary distribution channel (i.e. the distribution of earned income through wages and rents) are corrected through the secondary distribution channel (redistribution of a part of national income through taxation, public spending and transfers). Of course, this does not mean that the state can or should collect taxes and redistribute income without limit. But wherever the reasonable limit may be, it is certain that today we are very far away from it.

Global inequality is decreasing

The decline in global inequality, as measured by comparing average incomes in different world regions, is frequently cited as proof of the thesis that even in a market economy, inequality can decline without massive state intervention in secondary distribution. The claim is made that the fact that some developing countries are catching up to the industrialised world in terms of living standards shows that the market system does not need inequality to function.

But this statement does not hold up under scrutiny, because the unfolding of developing countries' catching-up is a completely different process from the normal course of economic development, and because the catching-up process tends to create massive new inequalities in the developing countries themselves. Take China, the country that has been the dominant player in this game in purely quantitative terms over the past 30 years. In China, the decades-long catching-up process, with growth rates of up to ten percent per year, has led a very large number of very poor people (an estimated 300 to 500 million Chinese) to rise very quickly from absolute global poverty (say from an income of one dollar a day) to earning ten or twenty dollars a day today.

Looking at global income distribution, the effect of poverty reduction in China, a result of the catching-up process in that one very large country, has been so strong that global income distribution measures have improved, even though domestic income distributions within all countries, including China, have become more unequal.

Let us take a rough-cut look at how the catching-up process on the one hand, and the process of normal economic development on the other, each function. Normal economic development takes place when Schumpeter's famous pioneering entrepreneur has an idea for improving production processes or products, or launches a completely new product onto the market. This means that this entrepreneur increases his productivity in comparison to his competitors, and — assuming all other things are equal, including input costs — he makes a higher profit, or grabs market share away from his competitors, by being able to offer lower prices.

The principle here is that the Schumpeterian entrepreneur combines individually higher productivity with the same wage rates everyone else pays, and thereby achieves success. Inequality is likely to increase as a result of technical innovations and their implementation, and, in fact, this is indeed the most important way in which the market economy continues to produce new inequalities. The newly produced inequality will only disappear if a competitive process succeeds in breaking the pioneer's temporary monopoly profit, triggering general price cuts in line with the higher productivity the innovation has made possible. It is this increase in productivity that eventually causes an increase in real wages across the entire breadth of the economy.

A nation's catching-up process usually works the other way round, which is why the results of catching-up should not simply be compared or thrown together with normal domestic economic development. Because developing countries have lower wages than industrialised countries, entrepreneurs can achieve monopoly profits by relocating highly technologised, high-productivity production to a developing country. One simply combines a given set of high-productivity machinery and processes with low wages anywhere in the world. Because there is no new idea or innovation involved, this process always is a displacement competition for market share, fought against equally technically advanced companies that have remained at their old, higher-wage location, and also against the established domestic companies in the developing country that may not have state-of-the-art machinery or processes. Because this is not about new ideas, but about existing technologies, implementation can take place very quickly and on a large scale. In China, this occurred primarily through direct investment by foreign companies. In Japan and Korea, the implementation of catching-up (by copying and/or importing Western technologies) was organised or at least orchestrated by the state.

This process generates high profits for the companies that use it (profits which the host state, were it sufficiently brave, could tax away a considerable portion of, which it generally refrains from doing, because it is in competition with other low-wage countries). In addition, it creates enormous income opportunities for a poor population, due to the rapid increase in productivity that the catching-up process involves (rapid because only well-known, tried-and-tested machines and processes are installed and implemented).

In China over the past 20 years, productivity in the economy as a whole has increased by almost ten percent each year, and real wages have risen just as sharply (not least because of massive government support, particularly through increases in the minimum wage). This catching-up phenomenon has unfolded at the same time that real wages in the rich countries have stagnated. The confluence of these two phenomena shows up in global data as decreasing inequality, even though the decrease has nothing to do with the process of market economy development, since this confluence is a unique phenomenon.

In China itself, of course, this enormous growth in productivity has not only eliminated much poverty, it has also created a great deal of absolute new wealth, because the catching-up process, although strongly controlled and managed by the state, was implemented predominantly by private (domestic and foreign) companies. Here, too, inequality has very probably increased in significant part because even the nominally communist Chinese government did not dare to intervene as courageously in secondary distribution as would have been necessary to maintain a constant level of internal inequality.

The indispensable principle of equal distribution of income growth

Comparing economic development in a developing country such as China with the normal growth process in an industrialised country brings up an important principle that should be taken into account when discussing inequality. Inequality at the micro-level, which arises again and again in the context of the Schumpeterian entrepreneurial processes, has an important function which should not be underestimated: It creates an important incentive for economic development to be set in motion in the first place. In this respect, representatives of liberal ideas are right to argue that neither the state nor trade unions should suppress these processes by immediately taxing away the pioneer entrepreneur's monopoly profit.

If we consider this position to be correct, we must recognise that it has decisive consequences: It entails taking a position that wages should not be negotiated at company level, but rather at industry level or even at the macroeconomic level, because only then will the right microeconomic incentives be operational. Wages should not be negotiated at the individual firm level, as is often done today, because under that circumstance, it is indeed possible for workers to collect the innovative company's monopoly rents (or part of it) for themselves — and that would mean the company's innovation would no longer benefit other workers in the form of price reductions.

It also follows that there is no justification for allowing wages to lag behind productivity increases at the macroeconomic level, i.e. for allowing the emergence of functional inequality (inequality between labour and capital) on a large scale. The pioneering entrepreneur still gets his temporary monopoly profit even when his workers' wages fully adapt to the macroeconomy's average productivity development. Since all other arguments for general wage restraint are untenable (cf. Flassbeck & Spiecker, 2016), there is absolutely no justification for demanding wage restraint in primary distribution and imposing it with political force, as happened in Germany at the beginning of the present century.

The bottom line is that increasing inequality can scarcely be justified. The fact that people are unequal and are also unequally remunerated is one thing. To systematically increase inequality by favouring the better-paid, as has been the case in many countries over the last 30 years, is a completely different matter. Nothing can justify the latter.

Those who say that a market economy creates inequality deliberately blur the boundaries between the two phenomena, because they pretend that the increasing inequality of recent decades is just one particular type of the general and inevitable phenomenon of inequality. This is wrong and dangerous. Precisely because there is plenty of inequality anyway, additional inequality promoted by government policy choices and by one-sided power relations in the labour market should be strictly avoided.

In general, German economists pay little attention to such considerations. Clemens Fuest of Munich's ifo Institute, for example, wrote an op-ed in the *FAZ* newspaper on the topic of inequality in Germany (Fuest, 2017), but did not get to the heart of the problem. While acknowledging that rising inequality in Germany arose primarily at the time of Agenda 2010 policy and that its roots are to be found in the labour market, he evaded drawing the appropriate conclusions by means of a simple trick.

He wrote that "the distribution of income in Germany has remained practically unchanged over the past ten years," and one could have the impression that "the representatives of the injustice thesis are ten years too late." But why should a drastic shift in income distribution not be corrected when the balance of power "in the labour market" (or better "in industrial relations") is, for whatever reason, normalising? Why not make up lost ground? To this objection, which he explicitly mentions, he answered as follows:

> That would be the right thing to do if the previously lost employment opportunities for low-skilled workers had returned. But that is not the case. The factors mentioned at the beginning, which favour more highly qualified work, have by no means disappeared. An important reason for the falling unemployment of recent years is that wage costs, especially in the lower wage groups, have risen only very moderately during those years. At the same time, Agenda 2010 labour market reforms have ensured that the unemployed are placed into new jobs more quickly, but are also under greater pressure to take available jobs, even if the pay is not high. (Fuest, 2017)

This is not an argument, it is a diversion. He is just trying to rationalise what is irrational. He pretends that it was only a "wrong" wage structure that was responsible for the high unemployment, while the political imposition of the "right" wage structure provided for the reduction of unemployment. However, the increase in inequality between income groups can be observed precisely during the period (in particular 2000 to 2005) during which the inequality between labour and capital in Germany changed particularly strongly in favour of capital.

This clearly speaks against Fuest's thesis that it was above all changes in the remuneration of qualified and unqualified workers that are responsible for today's level of inequality. Anyone who talks about inequality in the first decade of this century must not ignore the increasingly unequal functional distribution between labour and capital. Moreover, the change in wage structure cannot in principle explain general unemployment, and simply assuming the existence of a functioning neoclassical labour market as a given is not justified in any case.

Even in Germany, even after the Agenda 2010 "reforms" of the Red–Green coalition, after the change in wage structure and the massive reduction in wage levels, new unemployment arose. Anyone who ignores this, and also ignores the fact that Germany has exported a considerable part of its unemployment to its trading partners by reducing its wage level relative to those partners (again, it is the overall wage level that is relevant here, not the wage structure), does not really want to understand, but rather distract.

An appropriate assessment of increasing inequality, whether it is observed only for a limited stretch of time or continues to this day, is difficult even for most good-faith authors, because within the conceptual framework of the fictitious neoclassical labour market, inequality (including increasing inequality) has, as a rule, positive effects. It allegedly leads to more employment and offers greater opportunities for the future. It is only after recognising that such a labour market does not actually exist that one can adequately assess material inequality. It then becomes clear that neither the bulk of existing absolute inequality nor the increase in inequality that has developed over the last 30 years has a positive function in a market economy.

Functionless Profits

For any well-trained economist, the title of this section sounds like a contradiction in terms. Have we not learned that profits are only generated by companies when they successfully hold their own against the competition?

Then profit automatically has a function, namely to direct the efforts of companies to where they expect the highest profits.

If one were to write "functionless rents," however, one would get approval from all sides, because for centuries the term "rent" has subsumed functionless income. Income like the famous "ground rent," which the beneficiary has not earned, but which comes to him anyway, for example because land he happens to own in a particular region becomes more valuable due to events for which he is not responsible, such as the construction of a train station nearby.

But of course, things are not as simple as classical theory would have them. What about the profits that fall to a German car manufacturing company because it benefits from the wage dumping staged by the German state by enforcing national wage-restraint policies, at the expense of the other member countries in the European Monetary Union? Is that profit or is it rent? What about the profit that only comes to a company because the managing director of its most important competitor dies in an automobile accident, and the company cannot find a suitable successor? What about the incredible profits a company like Google makes over decades just because nobody found a similarly good search algorithm early in the development of the Internet, and so Google was able to lock in first-mover network effects?

Finally, what about the famous pioneer rents accruing to the Schumpeterian entrepreneur, i.e. the rents that arise because he combines higher productivity from an innovation with existing wage levels? Are they justified, and if yes, for how long a time period? Does this also apply to the completely different types of rents that arise for companies that successfully relocate their production to low-wage countries, which combine existing high-productivity machinery and processes with the low wages prevalent in another country?

As one can see, many questions quickly arise about the distinction between profit and rent, but few answers. Since in reality there is never full competition and never an economic equilibrium, the distinction between profit and rent is in practice not very useful. Everything we call "profit" is really a mixture of profit and rent, and no one can clearly separate what is the one and what is the other, or what part has a useful economic function and what part does not.

Nevertheless, we can and must ask whether companies as a whole have dealt sensibly with the undreamt-of power they have acquired in the course of the neoliberal revolution, in terms of their function in the macroeconomy. After all, everyone expected companies newly freed from state constraints, and blessed with much lower taxes, to create new demand by expanding supply with the help of massively increased investment activity. In this respect, four decades on, the net outcome of the neoliberal turn can only be described as catastrophic.

Investments in tangible assets: the Achilles' heel of the neoclassical revolution

Anyone who believes what they read in the nation's leading news media knows that the German economy is chugging along splendidly. The rude health of German companies can be verified daily in reports about record profits and rising share prices. Yet surprisingly, there is very little talk about the central thing that economic activity is really principally about, namely investment — which is to say, investment in the creation of new plants and equipment.

If the numerous cheerleaders and spin-doctors of German business and their assistants in various institutes and foundations remain silent on such an important topic, this may be due to the fact that the investment activities of German companies can more aptly be described as modest than glorious.

Indeed, the level of investment can be considered disastrously low. If one considers how much money German companies have earned in recent years, and continue to earn now, the silence of the stakeholders, media, and politicians on this matter is a massive scandal. Perhaps it can even be considered the largest scandal in a country in which everyone pretends every day to want to provide for the future through prudent decisions and sound long-term investments. Granted, one need not say many words on this subject — one can simply let the facts speak for themselves.

Figure 11 shows gross fixed capital formation, i.e. equipment and buildings, in relation to gross domestic product. Between 1970 and German unification in 1989, the investment rate in Germany pointed in only one direction — downwards. Only German unification, which is clearly visible

Investment ratio[1]

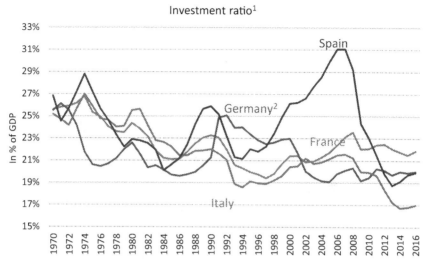

1. Gross fixed capital formation as % of GDP
2. until 1991 West Germany

Figure 11:   Investment ratio

Source: AMECO.

as a break in the series, brought an improvement for several years. After that, interrupted only by a small upturn at the end of the 1990s and another just before the financial bubble burst in 2008, there is a relentless downward trend throughout. And what of the celebrated upswing after the recession of 2009?

The massive slump of almost ten percent in investment in equipment and commercial buildings in 2009 was followed by a brief upswing in 2010 and 2011, but after that, investment activity flatlined. It was still not picking up as of 2016. It is a remarkable fact that five years into the so-called upswing, the investment rate has not budged, even as the public is daily enjoined to celebrate the marvellous state of the German economy (AMECO, 2017b).

If one looks only at the data for private sector investment (Figure 12), the picture does not look much different over the same time series. Here, too, the French curve has been above the German curve since about 2004.

Public investment in Germany has developed particularly catastrophi-cally (Figure 13). With its rate of public investment stuck at the absurdly low

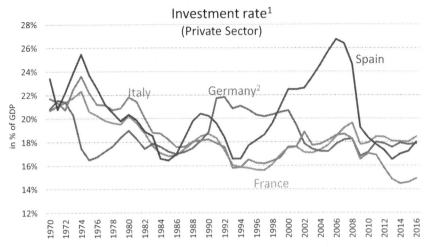

¹· Gross fixed capital formation as % of GDP
²· until 1991 West Germany

Figure 12:   Investment rate (Private sector)

Source: AMECO.

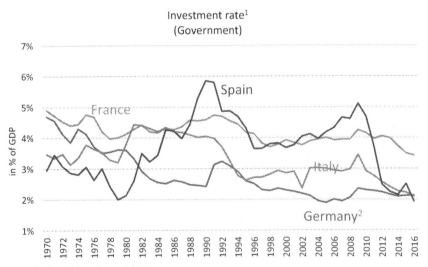

¹· Gross fixed capital formation as % of GDP
²· until 1991 West Germany

Figure 13:   Investment rate (Government)

Source: AMECO.

value of two percent of GDP despite the fact that the public sector budget situation is outstandingly favourable, with tax revenues pouring in, moderate cumulative debt, and the government able to borrow money at an interest rate very close to zero, Germany is showing that it when it comes to economic policy, its decision-makers elevate ideology above everything else.

The repeated assertion that Germany underwent a painful adjustment process at the beginning of the European Monetary Union and emerged stronger from this reform phase cannot be seen from the investment data. The meagre performance of German companies is certainly surprising to many observers who have a critical view of Germany's role in Europe, but continue to believe that it remains in a good position compared to other European nations, not least as a result of the technological leadership positions of many German companies.

What is easily forgotten, however, is the incredibly weak development of the German domestic economy over the past 15 years. Companies in export-oriented industries have certainly invested heavily in Germany and abroad, but as far as the domestic economy was concerned, there was little incentive to build up new production capacities, because demand barely increased in real terms.

Seen from this perspective, Germany's wage-dumping of recent years, which brought domestic companies high profits in a simple manner (namely without investment under uncertainty), has proved fatal. On the one hand, it led companies to be complacent, because they were able to do good business on foreign markets. On the other hand, given structurally weak cost pressures and weak domestic demand, they did not invest as much as would otherwise have been the case. In addition, the government has done everything it could to design its tax policies so as to relieve companies as much as possible, without even linking this relief to the crucial contribution companies are meant to make in a market economy, namely productive investment. It is in this sense that companies can be said to have made non-functional profits; for years they have behaved less like innovation-driven production companies than like mutual funds, collecting money for distribution to shareholders.

The European crisis shows that this economic model has no future. A change must be initiated by the state. If the state does not want to get further into debt, then it must ensure that companies increase their investment ratios. To do this, the state must exert pressure on companies to accept higher wage increases over a long period of time, and it must also systematically raise corporate taxes, in order to absorb functionless profits. Unfortunately, both of these measures are considered taboo by almost all participants in the political discussion.

Companies' behaving as savers shakes the foundations of liberalism

It is difficult to understand why such radical intervention by the state is considered taboo. Neither liberalism, nor conservatism, nor social democracy in Germany have been able (or willing) to recognise the fundamental changes that have occurred in corporate behaviour since the glorious era of the post-war German economic miracle.

One of the most beautiful and beloved stories of economists is that of the always provident state. Neoclassical economists and Keynesians can agree at any time of day or night and within minutes that the state must act anti-cyclically during a crisis or recession, and that the same rule applies to the upswing. Indeed, during the upswing, the government should save and even collect budget surpluses, and use them to reduce its debt in absolute terms, in order to prevent it from recording constantly rising debt levels, which in the long run would entail accumulating unsustainable interest burdens.

This is really a beautiful story, and whenever it came up for discussion, for many decades economists only fought over the question of whether states would in practice actually pay down debt with budget surpluses gained during expansions. The Keynesians tended to be full of confidence in the rationality of the state, but the neoliberals were highly suspicious, because they generally did not trust the state to behave sensibly. In recent years, however, the German Finance Minister has proven, with an achievement that can only be called historic, that the Keynesians were right; the German state is indeed well able to behave symmetrically, that is, to prudently and providentially pay down debt during the good times.

Sadly, as is so often the case with simple, beautiful stories, this one does not quite capture the nature of reality in all its cruel complexity. Unfortunately, the world has recently been changing in some rather fundamental ways, and the conditions of this new world require solutions that demand from adherents of both the leading economic sects that which is hardest for them — a rethink.

What is still not understood today is the fact that the market economy that both neoliberals and traditional Keynesians nurture fond dreams of actually ceased to exist quite a long time ago. This vanished world was one in which companies still fulfilled the most important role assigned to any player in a market economy, namely that of being a debtor and investor at the same time.

In the 1950s and 1960s, enterprises were the natural counterparties to net-saving households (Figures 14 and 15).

In the 1950s, the state afforded itself the "luxury" of collecting extremely high surpluses (over ten percent of GDP in 1953), which went down in history as the "Julius tower" (named after Finance Minister Julius Schäffer). He was able to do this because Germany's foreign trade surplus increased dramatically during the Korean crisis. Although the connection between the foreign trade surplus and state saving is completely clear in the picture, the heroic story of Mr. Schäffer is still told today as if it was only the unbending

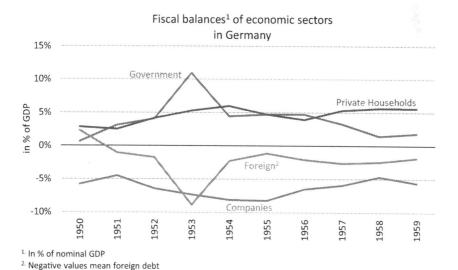

Figure 14:   Financing balances of the economic sectors in Germany (1950–1959)
Source: Federal Statistical Office.

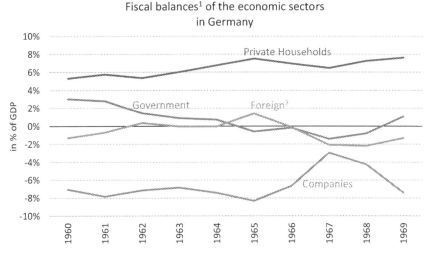

Figure 15:   Fiscal balances of the economic sectors in Germany (1960–1969)

Source: Federal Statistical Office.

will of this remarkable man who managed to make sure that Germany was prepared for the future with the Julius Tower.

Even in the 1960s (Figure 15) it was still easy for the government to achieve a balanced budget, because the general boom led the corporate sector to assume the role of the most important debtor and investor. Remember the accounting identity: For there to be a net saver, someone else has to be a net debtor. In the 1960s, it was Germany's corporate sector that took on net debt.

But when we look at the net lending/borrowing balances of the individual sectors today, it can be seen that Germany's non-financial enterprises are net savers, i.e. show surpluses in their cash flow statement, as illustrated in Figure 16. This has been the case since around the turn of the century. Since German households remain net savers as always, and the state stopped taking on new debt as of 2012, who is left to play the debtor role? Only foreigners. The burden of accumulating debt, from the German point of view, now lies solely with foreign countries.

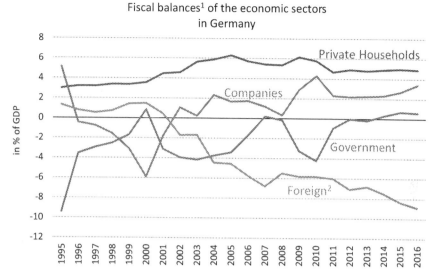

Figure 16: Fiscal balances of the economic sectors in Germany (1995–2016)
Source: AMECO.

The corporate sector as a net saver, and foreign countries as the only debtor, is an undesirable development in our market economy of a significance and seriousness that can hardly be overstated. The whole idea of a market economy across all classical and neoclassical schools of thought was built on the foundation that companies would be assigned the primary responsibility for the profitable use of savings. Now it turns out to be the case not only that the transformation of household savings into investment money through the banking system is a fiction, but also, and much worse, companies no longer systematically compensate for the demand lost through households' savings habit, even though monetary policymakers have been making an extremely generous offer to prospective borrowers with their zero-interest policies all around the world.

The USA (Figure 17) is a key case study of a large relatively closed economy, i.e. an economy in which external relations are not of significant importance. The financial balances of the macroeconomic sectors (i.e. net

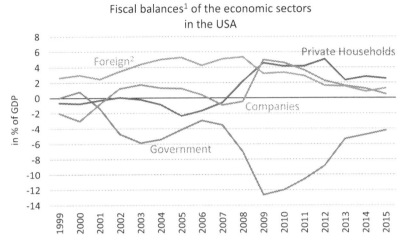

Figure 17:   Financing balances of the economic sectors in the USA

Source: AMECO.

saving on the one hand and net debt on the other, or receipts minus expenditures for the respective sector) clearly show the fundamental change that emerged in the wake of the global financial crisis of 2008/09 — though it had already been developing before that. Here again, all sectors are net savers except the state.

Companies were still on the debtor side until the turn of the century. They have been on the saver side (i.e. above zero) alongside private households since 2008. Since the USA has a current account deficit (it imports more than it exports), the state is necessarily on the debtor side, as otherwise the economy would collapse.

In the euro area, which is also a large, relatively closed economy, the situation is somewhat different, as the 19-nation euro area as a whole has a substantial current account surplus with the rest of the world (Figure 18). But here too, since the early 2000s and especially since the 2008 financial crisis, the corporate sector has abandoned its net debtor role and switched to the savers' side.

If Germany's domestic sectoral balances are arithmetically subtracted from the euro area, and sectoral balances and the foreign trade balance of the

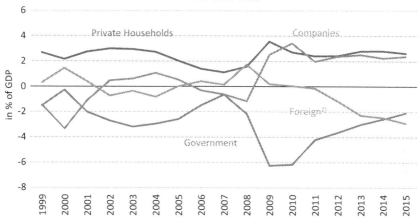

Figure 18:   Net lending/borrowing of euro-area economic sectors

Source: AMECO.

euro area without Germany are calculated, the result looks extremely similar to the USA's sectoral balances (Figure 19).

If foreign trade no longer plays a major role, as is the case for large economic areas such as the USA and Europe, and companies systematically change over to the net-saver side, the fate of public finances is sealed. (For the world as a whole, there is no such thing as 'foreign trade,' and there will not be until we establish colonies on Mars or the Moon.) The government will then have to incur new debts year-on-year forever, no matter how large the cumulative public debt level is. Small mercantilist nations like Germany may for a while evade this compelling logic through even higher current account surpluses, but they are the famous dwarves whose shadow is only so long because the spiritual sun is so low in their country.

Anyone who wants to say something relevant on the question of debt must begin his analysis at exactly this point. We must plead for higher public investment, but we must also say that received notions of the virtue of "consolidating public finances" are fundamentally obsolete. The controversies in

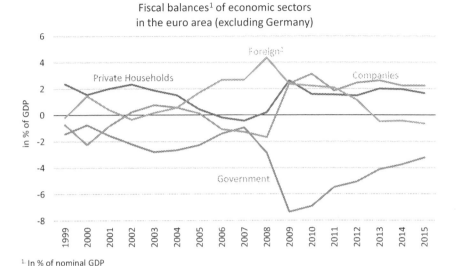

Figure 19:   Net lending/borrowing of euro-area economic sectors (excluding Germany)
Source: AMECO.

many European countries show that the fate of the continent will be decided by this question. The Conservatives are consistently completely wrong on this issue, but the majority of citizens are on their side, because they simply cannot understand the debt problem: They intuitively and mistakenly think that if "saving" is a good and virtuous thing for a private household to do, it's good for the public household as well. If no new progressive political movement dares to take up this issue aggressively, then the seemingly unresolved debt problem will play into the hands of populist nationalist movements, because they are unencumbered from the outset by any impulse towards offering honest analyses or rational solutions.

In this new world, it is no longer appropriate to philosophise about whether and how quickly the state should use "the good times" to run surpluses and pay down its debt. The good times simply no longer exist in this sense because the corporate sector is so strong and so powerful that companies simply can no longer be pushed into the role of the debtor. The power of the corporate sector is a direct result of the neoliberal revolution. The neoliberals and their successful decades-long push for the imposition of a "supply-side policy" are directly responsible for the enormous and continuing rise in global public debt. Congratulations!

Richard Koo, chief economist of Nomura Research Institute in Tokyo, is among the few economists whose understanding of sectoral balance-sheet mechanics leads him to emphasize this issue in his speeches and writings. Koo reminds the state of its role as net debtor and believes that the changed role of companies — their shift toward becoming net savers — has to do with "balance-sheet recessions." His thesis is that after such a recession, companies, burdened by too much accumulated debt, prioritize using their profits to pay down debt in order to repair their balance sheets.

This was perhaps an appropriate explanation immediately after the global crisis, but it is no longer the case today. What we see today has more to do with the secular shift of power in favour of companies on the labour market and *vis-à-vis* the state, a power shift which has been directly promoted by many conservative governments around the world since the 1970s, and is still being promoted today through an agenda of deregulation and tax cuts for corporations.

If this assessment is correct, then the market economy capitalist system worldwide is on a direct road towards collapse. If one combines the power of companies to choose their side of the savings medal with an insistence that the state must reduce its debt, then one is choosing — assuming, as a given, a positive propensity of private households to net-save — a constellation that is impossible for basic arithmetical and logical reasons. Systems confronted with powerful demands to implement impossible scenarios tend to collapse. It does not matter whether it is clueless politicians with no understanding of balance-sheet mechanics who try to do the impossible in the illusion that they are being virtuous, or whether powerful interested parties pushing forward an austerity agenda are the motive force. If all sectors attempt to save at the same time, downfall is inevitable.

Should corporate taxes be increased?

Tax increases are in many respects a taboo topic in neoliberalism in general and in Germany in particular. By far the biggest taboo, however, is around the taxes that companies must and should pay. Although there is talk of international problems such as tax avoidance by large globally operating companies, the modest level of tax burden on domestic companies is seen by all parties as being a given, a closed issue.

This is not justified by any rational analysis; it is due solely to the enormous power of the business lobby. Under great pressure from the lobby, over the past few decades Germany radically reduced taxes on businesses, because it was firmly believed that there was a close and inverse link between the level of corporate taxation and investment activity.

As we have previously noted, the logic of tax relief for the "top performers" and "high achievers" was applied to household incomes as well: The red–green government (a coalition of Social Democratic and Green parties), newly elected in 1998, lowered the top income tax rate, which never went below 56 percent during the post-war "economic miracle" years, down to 42 percent.

Even more dramatically, total taxes for German corporations were cut in half in the first years after the turn of the century (Figure 20).

But as it turns out, none of the wondrous miracles of economic glory the prophets of tax-cutting promised would occur in the aftermath of a significant tax cut have in fact happened. Corporate investment activity has not

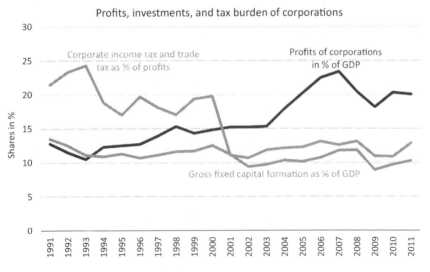

Figure 20:   Profits, investments, and tax burden of corporations

Source: Federal Statistical Office (national accounts).

gone through the roof. Nor have the "top performers" whose motivation it was deemed necessary to stimulate through tax relief gone on a workaholic binge and driven productivity higher in an ecstasy of innovation and creativity. Germany's productivity has not risen any faster than France's, and both have remained nearly equal (though Germany's is slightly lower). Germany's export successes have resulted solely from price-cutting enabled by relative wage cuts; they are not the result of superior productivity development.

So if the massive reduction in tax rates on income and profits was completely unjustified, why not admit the mistake and demand a revision of past tax relief? But no — any and every kind of tax increase proposal is mercilessly badmouthed in large parts of the media. The rejection of new taxes is invariably framed as a defence of the "middle class," because nobody wants to openly defend the rich. And it was indeed a clever move in the tax reforms enacted at the turn of the century to set the top tax rate at such a low income that one can suggest without blushing that the beneficiaries include "middle class" taxpayers. If the taxable income at which the top tax rate applies were twice as high as it is today, it would be a lot more difficult to sell the programme as being about relieving the middle class.

The same ruse was applied in order to sell corporate tax relief. The discussion was framed as being about providing relief to "small and medium-sized companies," "family businesses" and the like — not about enriching the top executives and shareholders of megacorporations.

In the mid-2000s, when Germany's wage restraint policy (resulting in a real relative devaluation of unit costs) began to take hold, improving the competitive position of German corporations *vis-à-vis* competitors in other European countries, the net incomes of German companies exploded, as shown in Figure 20. However, the investment boom expected by everyone in consequence failed to materialise, as the figure also shows. If there had been even a shred of truth in the theory about an excessively high tax burden discouraging corporate investment, then once corporate taxes dropped by half as a result of the red–green tax reform, investment in Germany would have increased and would have supported the economy for many years. However, as shown, the investment rate rose only very slightly from an extremely low base in the first few years of the new century, before dropping to an all-time low after the financial crisis of 2008. Since then, investment activity has remained extremely weak.

It is repeatedly argued that 95 percent of income tax is already paid by only half of the taxpayers (cf. Flassbeck, 2013c). However, this comparison is clearly misleading and intended to manipulate public opinion. It compares a proportion of persons with a proportion of tax revenue, i.e. with a sum of money, which is of course inadmissible (cf. Flassbeck, 2013a). Since taxes are paid from the income of individuals, their total income must be compared with their contribution of taxes. Only then do you know whether they are under a proportionately light or heavy load. If the wealthier half of the tax-payers earns 95 percent of the income, then it is perfectly acceptable and normal that they pay 95 percent of the income tax.

In general, we must be clear about the fact that macroeconomic stagnation is first and foremost a debt problem, not a tax problem. If the state succeeds in inducing companies to take on more debt by increasing corporate taxes, the debt problem described above can be solved. If this is not done, and the corporate sector remains a net saver, then the state must play the role of net debtor instead. There is no way around this. A position such as that of almost all left-wing parties, according to which the state should raise taxes to finance investments in order to keep its debt low, is nonsensical. It ignores the fact that the savings problem must always be solved by increasing some sector's level of debt, regardless of how high or low taxes are.

Secular stagnation?

The puzzling over the causes of the quasi-stagnation of the world economy since the end of the great financial crisis is taking on bizarre traits in some quarters. Because ideological prejudices prevent neoliberals from piercing the fog and perceiving the causes of businesses' macroeconomically dysfunctional low-investment, net-saver behaviour, analysts seek apparently objective external factors that might explain our era's historically atypical weakness of investment.

Robert J. Shiller, Yale University Professor and Nobel Laureate, correctly identifies low interest rates as the best indicator to show that the industrialised part of the world economy is still far from normal recovery and economic development (Shiller, 2017). But Shiller takes up the idea of "secular stagnation," which had been popularised by Alvin Hansen (in 1938) and was revived by Larry Summers a few years ago (as Shiller notes). His explanation of the weakness of private spending (consumption above all, but also investment) is based on the notion of animal spirits, i.e. the degree of pessimism or optimism of economic actors. According to Shiller, it is only if people are optimistic about the future will they be prepared to spend enough money to stimulate the economy: "Barring exceptionally strong stimulus measures, this sense of foreboding [associated with a fear that a crash like 2008 might recur, or that technology change might make them unemployable] will limit their spending."

Is it only our fear that prevents us from "spending enough money"? If you think about it for a moment, you will realise that this is a very odd theory. If Shiller's hypothesis were correct, one would expect to observe that the savings rate of private households rose after the crisis and remained high since. However, in most countries, this has not been the case. The opposite is true; in many countries, the private savings rate has actually fallen. Japan is the classic example here, but in Italy, too, the savings rate is at a historical low.

What Shiller, like many other Nobel Prize–winning economists, apparently cannot understand is the simple fact that the variable that determines the spending behaviour of private households more than any other is the development of household income *per se*, and not the "willingness" to spend more or less from an existing income. Because he remains attached to the conceptual world of neoclassical economics, he obviously assumes that the income of households is a given, is of course correct (since it is determined by the market), and is completely outside the purview of any political influence.

Those who make these assumptions are making a crucial mistake. Shiller, like Paul Krugman (2013a) or Joe Stiglitz (2014), has failed to understand what we explained above, namely that in the course of the financial crisis of 2008/09, unemployment rose massively without any neoclassical reason, i.e. without "too high wages." In the wake of this spike in unemployment, the balance of power in industrial relations, which was already very one-sided, shifted even further in favour of employers. As a result, wages in most developed countries have risen much less after the crisis than they have tended to do during a normal upswing (one that occurs after a normal downturn). This explains deflation and weak demand at the same time. It also explains why inequality has continued to increase in most countries.

This is obviously a very different explanation of the causality of the current stagnation than explanations that focus on the savings rate, or differential savings rates of rich and poor households. The increasing inequality between labour and capital, and increasing inequality between different subgroups of wage-earners, are thus not the original reason for weak GDP growth; they are its consequence. The grossly unequal distribution of national income, for its part, cements the trend of poor macroeconomic development, and this will continue until and unless economic policy opposes growing inequality with all its might. This must include implementing a full employment policy, among other things, to ensure that workers really do become scarce, so that their bargaining power increases.

Why does Shiller not write (at least additionally) about the falling or only slightly rising incomes of non-elite employees as a group? Is it not true that the real incomes of employees in America have risen far less in recent years than would have been justified, given average productivity development? This has had a negative impact on consumption, and it has weakened investment activity and the economy as a whole. The supply of jobs on offer has not been strengthened by downward pressures on wages — it has clearly been weakened. This is the exact opposite of what neoclassical labour market theory predicts.

What is coming to light here is a fundamental weakness in the conceptual framework even of some prominent economists who cannot easily be assigned to the camp of neoclassical orthodoxy. Even most of those who would call themselves Keynesians fundamentally do not question the neoclassical model of the functioning of the labour market. Instead, they mainly preoccupy themselves with the question of who saves how much of their income (which is allocated by the market and thus must be accepted as correct), and consequently how strongly their savings decisions burden or stimulate the economic cycle. They therefore demand only slight government policy corrections of the apparently objective income distribution results, so that a little more aggregate demand is generated by virtue of the low savings rate of the (relatively poor) beneficiaries of government redistribution. Even a direct increase in demand by the state itself is merely an attempt to compensate for the negative impact on demand of temporarily high savings in private households.

Such a position adds nothing to the real explanation, which is that unemployment is caused by falling or insufficiently rising wages. The fact that the labour market, as we saw in the wake of the 2008/09 episode, generates absolutely counterproductive results, is completely ignored. Unemployment rose dramatically after 2008/09, even though wages were historically low rather than high. This is the empirical reality. Only those who take note of this and completely reject neoclassical employment theory can really contribute to a new understanding of economic processes and give useful economic policy advice.

Moreover, at a time when companies are net savers, the old macroeconomic relationships are no longer valid anyway. Why philosophise about savings rate shifts in private households when, at the same time, we observe that corporations, too, have become net savers? This is a complete reversal of the traditional position of businesses, whose role in the system was supposed to be to borrow money from households and invest it.

As shown in the previous section, with all the other sectors intent on net-saving, the state has become the permanently debt-incurring counterparty of the savings-obsessed private sector. Finance ministers will have to throw overboard all their old prejudices regarding sustainable debt levels and new borrowing. This is certainly true if one is smart enough to recognise that current account surpluses and thus mercantilism *à la* Merkel and Schäuble are no solution to the world's savings problem. (Wolfgang Schäuble was Germany's conservative finance minister from 2009 to 2017. He proudly built a reputation on the "black zero," i.e. balancing the federal budget, running modest surpluses from 2014 onward. His successor, Olaf Scholz, nominally a social democratic party politician, has continued this policy.)

Financial Markets Produce the Wrong Prices

Financial markets play a central role in neoclassical theory. They are the flywheel that makes all market participants do their best, because they recognise and exploit any lack of efficiency in other markets. Their incomparable efficiency is a spur to the economy, yet they mercilessly punish any misconduct by providing or denying credit and liquidity, the real lifeblood of the market.

So much for the cartoon. In reality, the biggest distortions in the real economy are generated by the financial sector, which, if not regulated extremely restrictively by the state and the international community, has the potential to do enormous damage. Why major financial crises repeatedly occur remains little understood, because here too, the prevailing neoliberal doctrine refuses to question basic assumptions about the rationality of financial markets. That is why any investigation into the nature and specifics of the regression in macroeconomic conditions triggered by neoliberalism must undoubtedly include the question of what is really going wrong in the financial markets, and a recognition that they are not among the assets of the neoliberal revolution.

In the years following the great financial crisis, there was an interesting worldwide controversy over whether commodity and food prices had been manipulated and driven to new heights by international financial speculators. Neoliberal economists and the "markets" denied this, of course. Amazingly, right after the great financial crisis had demonstrated how absurdly far the prices of internationally traded real estate securities could move away from the "fundamentals," apologists for financial markets hauled the discredited "efficient markets" hypothesis out of the drawer again, in order to deflect calls for increased regulation associated with the discussion over distortions of commodity prices.

It became clear during the discussion of this issue that the key issues of financial markets analysis are still not generally understood. The challenge really is about understanding how these markets work, even if many of those who take part in such discussions are from the outset merely trying to confirm their position that financial markets can do no wrong. The problem, as in other areas, is that rather than approaching economics as a science and attempting a rational, empirically driven analysis, people enter the debate with fixed prejudices and immovable *a priori* assumptions.

Efficient markets?

In a contribution to the discussion on the efficiency of financial markets, David Bicchetti and Nicolas Maystre of UNCTAD presented some convincing evidence (Bicchetti & Maystre, 2012). They showed that especially in high-frequency trading, a fundamental change took place after the financial crisis: The correlations (of five-minute earnings) between an oil price (here WTI) and the Standard & Poor's (S&P) share index systematically went up, and — with one brief exception during the Libyan crisis — remained relatively high until mid-2012. After that, the correlations moved downwards again.

This clearly indicates a driving influence of financial markets. Initially, the financial markets got heavily involved in the commodity markets. This is the phenomenon usually called financialisation. However, after it became apparent that a projected decades-long rally in the commodity markets was an illusion, the financial markets withdrew again.

This also applies to important foodstuffs. For maize, sugar, soybeans, beef, and wheat, it can be shown that the correlation of their (five-minute) yields with the same share index shows a break in 2008, that the correlations subsequently rose and remained quite high until mid-2012, and then declined.

The observed decline in the importance of financialisation for commodity prices (and for earnings from the commodity business, with earnings being the difference between the purchase price and the selling price five minutes later) is consistent with reports from regulators such as Britain's Financial Conduct Authority (FCA) (2014), which found that much smaller amounts of capital had been flowing into the commodity markets in 2014 than a couple of years previously. The recently observed link between declining price correlation and declining speculative financial flows demonstrates, on empirical evidence, that the claim that financialisation (i.e. increasing investment in commodity securities) had massively distorted prices for several years was correct.

One can only speculate, in the truest sense of the word, about the reasons for the withdrawal of these "investors," whose active presence in markets is considered absolutely necessary by defenders of financialisation. It was probably simply that falling profits and lower risk diversification made speculation unattractive. The close correlation of commodity price developments with other financial market products has reduced commodities' value in terms of portfolio diversification. In addition, many participants from the "financial industry" certainly do not like the public exposure and greater attention of regulators associated with the lively discussion about commodity speculation that occurred for a few years after 2008. What was probably decisive, however, was that the speculators' expectation that a "new super-cycle" for raw materials was emerging (i.e. an upcoming decades-long shortage) turned out to be mistaken.

Even if the political significance of commodity markets speculation thus diminishes, it is important to understand what has happened in these markets, and why the prevailing economic orthodoxy was wrong in its diagnosis in this case too. In the end, commodity prices are above all a question of currency relations, which play a much bigger role in generating price distortions than does commodity speculation. We will try once more to explain why the hypothesis of efficient financial markets is fundamentally wrong, and why it is so difficult for many people to understand this fact.

In the commodity markets, just as in currency markets, there are basically three variables with which speculators can make money. Let us start with the foreign exchange markets, where the relevant relationships may be a little easier to understand.

Currency speculation

As a rule, you cannot earn money by exchanging one currency for another, because the currency itself, if we take cash for example, does not yield any profit. Even investing in foreign currencies should not yield any particular return in a functioning currency system, because the basic idea of any sensible currency system is to make short-term speculation with currencies unattractive. That was the idea that once stood behind flexible exchange rates; the premise was that if currency exchanges were left to free markets, an equilibrium would automatically set in, making speculation null and void.

But things have turned out very differently. Flexible exchange rates have become established in many parts of the world, but the system works completely differently from how the protagonists of the market solution had assumed it would. Currency speculation is the rule, not the exception — and it causes enormous damage, because the prevailing doctrine in economics refuses to let go of the idea that only markets can find the right prices on currency markets.

Anyone who wants to make profits by simply exchanging one currency for another (this is the so-called "carry trade") must bear in mind (i) the interest rate of the "funding currency" (i.e. the currency he owns or in which he is in debt), (ii) the interest rate of the target currency (i.e. the currency into which he exchanges his stock of funding currency), and (iii) possible changes in the currency ratio, i.e. the exchange rate between the target currency and funding currency during the time-frame of the investment in foreign currency.

As a rule, a currency speculator will only "invest" in currencies whose interest rate is higher than that of their funding currency. This is relatively simple in the currency markets, because the short-term (nominal) interest rates, which are usually the focus, are largely determined by central banks, and therefore do not fluctuate very much. Once the speculator has chosen a target currency with a relatively high interest rate, he usually makes a profit, because the return only depends on the two currencies' nominal interest rates (the investor does not want to buy anything in the country of the target currency), and these are generally quite predictable.

In such a market, the difference between the price of a currency specified in a currency futures contract (i.e. you sign a contract today agreeing to pay a specific amount six months from now for a specified amount of the currency) and the spot price (i.e. the price valid today) is very stable. The target currency is traded at a discount for the future that exactly corresponds to the interest rate difference between the countries. If this were not the case, risk-free arbitrage gains could be made, which is usually not possible because the market really is efficient in this respect (in regard to completely risk-free transactions).

Risk enters the transaction because the target currency could depreciate, which means that the speculator would receive less of his own currency at the end of the investment period than he originally paid, once the target currency has been converted back into his funding currency. Conversely, if the target currency appreciates in relative value, he then receives the income from the interest differential plus a revaluation premium, because a positive amount is added to the interest difference when the bond is converted back into his own currency.

If this same carry trade is carried out by a large number of "investors" around the world, a phenomenon occurs that characterises all financial markets and ultimately causes the market to fail in its vaunted quest for "efficiency." The problem occurs when many speculators make the same trade, causing the target currency to rise in value. Others notice this, prompting them to join in speculating on a continued rise. Ultimately a large herd of investors piles in, causing the currency to rise further than its fundamentals justify — i.e. more than would be justified in a perfect neoclassical market.

The carry trade in itself causes the market to send a false signal: It generates external demand for a higher-interest currency, driving its value upward, when actually a higher interest rate (and the higher inflation rate causing it) should cause demand for that currency to dampen (as domestic borrowers' willingness to borrow declines), and its relative value to depreciate. This false signal is reinforced when herds of FX speculators plunge into such a transaction and overinflate the currency's value — until speculators get nervous at the obvious overvaluation and a sell-side stampede occurs, causing a sudden crash in the target currency's value.

A case study: This happened to the Brazilian Real between 2003 and 2008. The "FX futures contracts" for the Real pointed in the wrong direction during the entire period, which is to say, the FX futures did not contain any valid information about the future. Because of speculators buying Real futures, the Real continually appreciated over the five years. In the case of Brazil, this was macroeconomically absurd, because the country's currency was rising in value even though the inflation rate was relatively high — which means more dollars were required to buy the same number of Reals year-on-year, even though less goods and services could be bought with those Reals in Brazil. The Brazilian economy appreciated very strongly in real terms and lost international competitiveness. However, an FX "investor" (speculator) does not care about the real-world impact of his carry trade; he is only interested in his net income, which increases when the target currency appreciates.

However, FX speculators are aware that the target currency's appreciation creates a situation in the target country that will eventually become unsustainable and lead to a crisis, because the country is constantly losing market share on international markets, running a current account deficit, and increasing its external debt. As a result, the risk of such currency investments increases over time, and as things get increasingly dodgy, everyone in the target FX market nervously monitors the situation, ready to pull out at short notice. When the reversal happens, it turns into a stampede for the exits, and the currency suddenly devalues. Sages working for the business sections of the newspapers then write long columns listing all the things the target countries have done wrong, thereby provoking the wrath of "the markets."

Commodity speculation

In commodity speculation, the three variables at stake are the current price of the commodity (the spot price), the expected future price (the price of futures contracts, i.e. contracts that have to be serviced not today but in three months, for example), and — often overlooked — the development of the overall market, i.e. the direction in which spot and future prices develop together.

In the case of crude oil, for example, there is usually a difference between spot and futures prices, and there is the broader movement of both prices, which is independent of the difference. The big difference between the foreign exchange and commodities markets is that in commodities markets, the difference between spot and futures prices is not stable, but fluctuates very strongly. Another complicating factor for the commodities "investor" is that this difference varies regionally, and is significantly influenced by many individual events on the various regional commodities markets.

Hedging transactions, which are always mentioned in defense of commodities futures markets and against which no one has any objections, take place between spot and futures prices. If some market participants expect prices to be significantly higher in six months than today — due to regional climate models suggesting a high risk of an unfavourable harvest, for example — then customers of commodity producers (e.g. buyers of soybeans from Argentine farmers) try to buy futures contracts that offer them protection against the risk of rising prices. If farmers or other market participants disagree with these buyers' expectations about soybean price trends (i.e. if they expect prices to fall, remain constant, or rise only slightly), they are happy to sell such futures contracts to hedgers, because with those contracts in hand, they can more securely project their future cash flow (for a given harvest quantity).

Since the farmers, in this example, believe the likelihood of significantly higher prices at harvest-time is low, these contracts serve the interests of both sides of the futures transaction, although one side will eventually lose the bet (if the prices are really high after six months, the farmers have lost because they would have earned more without futures contracts). But perhaps the losing side can accept that because of their lower risk exposure.

If there is strong demand for many futures contracts in a given commodities market, their price increases, i.e. the difference between spot and futures prices increases (the market is then said to be in *contango*). If hardly anyone is looking to buy futures contracts, it can be the other way round, with futures prices below spot prices (the market is then in *backwardation*). However, the differences between futures and spot prices remain relatively small as a rule, because given uncertainty about the future, neither side of the deal dares to place too large a bet.

But what happens in such a market when large numbers of "financial investors" suddenly appear who have no idea of the concrete market conditions but are only united in the expectation of achieving returns by buying derivatives cheaply today (in this case, commodity futures contracts which they want to hold, or "go long in" in market jargon) and selling them later at higher prices? These investors appear to be driven by the expectation that commodity prices will generally rise. For many years, China's development played the key role in sustaining this expectation, because it was expected that the fast-industrialising country would continue to consume enormous amounts of commodity resources, yet produces so little of them itself that raw material prices would only know one direction for many years to come: Upwards. And because there were many players managing very large sums of money who all had this expectation and acted accordingly, this is exactly what happened: Commodity prices went up. As in all financial markets, there are positive feedback loops, self-reinforcing developments that cause prices to rise far beyond what they would have done without financialisation (i.e. in the absence of financial speculators).

And then, just as in the currency market, something can happen that is not meant to happen: Commodity futures prices rise so sharply that the spot price is pulled up too. Every primary producer then says to himself that since the difference between spot and future prices has widened, he can increase his spot prices today to narrow the gap. In light of the considerably higher futures prices driven up by financial investors, everyone will be prepared to pay a higher spot price. In this way, as occurred in 2008, the whole system of spot and future prices can get shifted upwards (although the oil market was constantly in backwardation, i.e. the futures prices were below the spot prices). In the subsequent phase of generally rising prices after the financial crisis, the oil market was in contango, but nevertheless, commodities markets generally went up.

In these phases of generally rising prices, speculators can make profits with futures contracts, even if they are wrong about the difference between spot and futures prices. They just have to find someone willing to buy the contract at a higher price than they bought it for, which is not difficult, because in this environment, the counterparty expects prices to continue to rise. Even if the contract as such generates losses because, for example, the actual future price, contrary to expectation, ends up below the spot price at maturity, a speculator can still make a profit by on-selling the contract before it matures, as long as the general expectation is that commodity prices will continue to rise.

However, the longer such a boom lasts, the greater the likelihood that it will collapse and "investors" will incur losses across the board. An oil price of 150 dollars a barrel will simply become unrealistic if people increasingly realise inventories are full and production is running at full speed, as was the case in the first few years following the crisis. A dying boom, however, means that passive investors such as index funds and money managers, who have gone long in anticipation of further price increases, will incur more and more losses. At some point their expectations change, and they increasingly withdraw from commodities markets due to a lack of positive return expectations. This happened after 2010 because too many concrete indicators showed that the expected commodities super-cycle had not materialised, or had already reached its end.

Distorted prices

The result of all this is clear: over a number of years the prices of raw materials, including many foodstuffs, were massively distorted upwards. And this is more than worrying, because billions of people who have little money depend on these foods from day to day. They cannot wait for the "long run" of economists to return, as in "prices tend to reflect fundamentals in the long run." And Keynes' famous quote that "in the long run we are all dead" is not quite right, in this context. You will be dead in the short run if you do not have enough affordable food available to you.

All this is not discussed in detail in the prevailing economic discourse because many so-called academics take the free-market ideologues' side immediately and without much thought, full-throatedly and reflexively defending everything that happens in markets. This is what is really bad about this development: It is nearly impossible to engage in reasonable discussions about such complex phenomena and the appropriate role of the state in regulating such markets because too many of those who are highly paid to exercise academic freedom in the service of scientific enlightenment do exactly the opposite.

In Switzerland, a referendum drive was initiated by the Young Social Democrats (Jusos) asking voters to approve a ban on food speculation. This example shows how crudely a government led by the perceived interests of business can deal with such a topic in public. The Swiss Jusos were absolutely right with this initiative, but they had no chance against the joint phalanx of government and business, who opposed it.

Opponents of the initiative repeatedly made arguments based on a popular but untenable prejudice. So-called experts claimed that since there are always two sides to every deal on the commodity markets, this somehow meant that prices could not actually rise because one party buys and another sells. Obviously the latter is the case in all markets, yet we see price increases and price reductions. Especially in the financial markets, there are strong price fluctuations, notwithstanding the fact that every transaction involves a buyer and a seller.

The misunderstanding probably comes from the fact that it is difficult to imagine how, for example, a general market dynamic that massively drives up practically all financial market prices (i.e. stocks, commodities, currencies and their derivatives) can come about, and why, in such an environment, any market players then sell their positions at all. If a lot of people want to go long, they can either buy commodity futures contracts that are based on rising prices, or commodity derivatives, which are usually bets designed to win if the commodity boom continues for a long time to come. Of course, anyone who buys a futures contract or bets on rising prices with a derivative must find someone willing to sell that futures contract or bet against rising prices. But here, as in any other market, it depends on the dynamics of both sides.

If long lines form in front of a potato stand at a market because everyone wants a particularly good potato variety, the seller will eventually increase the price. There is still a sale for every transaction, and yet the price rises. If there is a buying hype and consequently a growing price bubble in financialised commodity markets because everyone thinks they have to go long now, perhaps because of a narrative about the rise of China and India, then of course there are still contrarian sellers who think the expectations of the masses are exaggerated, or security-oriented sellers who entered the rally early on, and prefer the certainty of locking in a profit now to the uncertainty of waiting and hoping for an even higher profit.

But if a flood of eager buyers is crowding into the market, the existence of these sellers is not going to prevent a massive price increase. Some of the sellers may even return to the market as buyers shortly after their sale, because they too have become convinced that the price increase will continue.

The demonstrably uniform development of futures prices and spot prices during the commodities boom of the 2000s proves that the type of transactions that drives both prices up at the same time has nothing to do with classical hedging transactions. Some market participants always half-heartedly take positions against the dominant trend, but in this situation there was no great counter-movement of "shorters," i.e. those who bet on falling prices, such that prices would just remain constant.

This kind of dynamic happens frequently in financial markets because there is great uncertainty about the "right" price and there is no such thing as an "equilibrium price" (contrary to what is assumed in some theories of perfectly efficient markets) in relation to which an "investor" could orient his position by means of hedge contracts.

It is worth dwelling for a moment on how unrealistic a theory is which assumes that in a situation where half the world is betting huge sums of money on rising prices, roughly the same number of people will immediately start to build up a counter position with roughly the same amount of money, because they are quite sure the other half of the world is wrong and will not succeed in driving up prices despite investing huge sums.

This is particularly absurd in the commodity markets, where after 2005 it was completely new money that was "invested," and much more money flowed in than had ever been present in these markets before. What really happens when a price bubble gets going in some financial asset is exactly the opposite of what the efficient-markets hypothesis claims will happen. Once such a bubble starts, more and more speculators jump on the bandwagon, and the herd begins to run, because the boosterish story underlying the bubble still sounds totally convincing during its early years. Anyone who opposes the booster narrative loses for a long time, and exits the market.

It is only when speculation on rising prices has taken on completely absurd dimensions after a few years, so that with the benefit of common sense and some research, one can see that the bubble is about to burst, that one can realistically resist and have some prospect of success by speculating against the masses with a short position — for example, by buying an insurance policy in the style of the famous "credit default swaps" (CDS). The film "The Big Short," based on Michael Lewis's 2010 book of the same name, does a marvellous job of showing these dynamics in action. But as a rule, only a few contrarians attempt to short the market in the early phase of a bubble, and as the film shows very well, even they tend to doubt their own judgment for a long time, because they can scarcely bring themselves to believe that most of the investing world is completely wrong. Yet every bubble inflates for a few years, and then stops growing at some point. Prices fall rapidly (as they did on the commodity markets after 2010), because now everyone is counting on falling prices. The bubble bursts.

All these insights should have long been known to science, so that they can be made available to policymakers if and when necessary. But this is not the case. So-called economic science has preached the efficiency of the capital markets for decades, and continues to defend this absurd theory even after the bursting of the ultimate bubble in 2008. The fact that the financial markets systematically generate wrong and dangerous prices, that enormous misallocation of financial capital and gigantic waves of capital destruction routinely result from the operation of "liberalised financial markets," remains a taboo topic, and breaking the taboo is usually punishable by exclusion from the academic community.

Unfortunately, politicians have still not understood (or in some cases do not want to understand) that nothing useful can be done with the traditional "scientific" insights of mainstream academic economics. It is particularly absurd that the Swiss Federal Council (the national government) commissioned an investigation in which speculation with foodstuffs was investigated by means of a meta-study, to determine the "scientific" position on whether speculation drives prices to unrealistic values. In such a meta-study, the number of studies that take pro and contra positions on a given question are counted, and the question is decided by simple majority. The majority is assumed to have the correct position. If 51 out of 100 investigations deem that speculation is harmless, the meta-study approach requires one to take that as the truth.

The strange thing is that if the issue at hand were not foodstuff speculation but rather currency speculation in which Swiss francs were the target quantity, the Swiss Federal Council would not need a study (and certainly not a meta-study) to assess the situation. The council would not believe any study (nor any hundred studies) which claimed that there was no such speculation, or that it never leads to an overvaluation of Switzerland's currency.

Every normal person in Switzerland knows that huge waves of speculation on the currency market have led to completely absurd, dangerously high prices for the Swiss franc. And the Swiss central bank has played the short position for years, because no one trusted the market to find the right price. Here, too, if you let the market run its course, it causes damage to the real economy that is often impossible to repair, for example by causing Swiss exporters to lose market share and go out of business.

This kind of thing has happened on the commodity markets too, including many foodstuff markets, and it has put millions of poor people in great distress. It is always the same kind of "investment" dynamic that gets a herd of speculators running with a momentum that cannot be stopped until the herd ultimately runs over a cliff into the abyss.

IV

Money as a Domain of the State

In our search for the market economy that liberals dream of, we have collided with hard and unpleasant realities. We explained in the previous part that the "labour market" is a fiction. The price of labour cannot be a market result because the assumption that independent supply and demand functions exist in the arena of labour relations has nothing to do with reality.

It has also been shown that the so-called financial markets, in particular foreign exchange markets, are generally not in a position to find prices that can be regarded as efficient. Are these mere market imperfections, or have we come across indications of problems that might require us to generally call into question a market-centred organisation of the monetary and financial system? In other words, can we trust the market to do a reasonable job of allocating financial capital? Can the market interest rate ensure that capital is managed in the public interest? Does it make sense for the allocation of "capital" to be oriented towards achieving the highest possible financial profit, and for capital investors to compete with each other for solvent creditors?

Finally, we must also answer the question of whether the so-called independence of central banks, which has become a matter of iron doctrine in many countries, can be justified.

Money, Banks, and Corporate Liability

Almost nobody really expected the major financial crisis of 2008/09, and its consequences shocked even convinced market apologists in their belief in the efficiency of capital markets. For example, Alan Greenspan admitted in a hearing before the US Congress that the financial crisis was evidence for him that the conceptual framework within which his economic thinking had moved over the past 40 years had proved to be wrong (cf. Irwin *et al.*, 2008). Governments hurriedly formed commissions of so-called experts, most of whom had not foreseen or warned of such a crisis, but of whom it was nevertheless assumed that they would be able to make proposals for a reform of the financial system that would make it impossible for such an event to happen again.

As a rule, however, the experts did not ask themselves whether it was precisely the institutional structure of the monetary and financial system, oriented towards the ideals of the market economy, that was responsible for the system's near-meltdown. Rather, they contented themselves with making a few suggestions for correcting the existing system. For example, they proposed obliging banks to hold more equity capital and more liquidity, or raising the hurdles for engaging in all too absurd betting transactions on the capital markets somewhat.

The fact that politicians have taken up even these mild proposals only hesitantly and to a very limited extent shows that financial market lobbyists are doing an excellent job. However, this remains a side note, given the fact that there is still a widespread refusal to recognise that a market-oriented monetary and financial system makes it impossible to handle payments securely or to provide the real economy with a reliable supply of capital.

Cash and bank deposits

"Money" is the term we have used to describe means of payment that allow their holders to settle debts owed to the state as well as to companies and households. Cash can be used — even if only pursuant to making a prior written application — to pay taxes, and cash allows — even if not without exception — the payment of monetary debts resulting from commercial contracts such as a purchase contract. Cash should therefore be regarded as money.

However, nowadays the payment of debts is usually made by bank transfer. If you want to pay your debts by bank transfer, you need a corresponding credit balance on your current account, and the bank transfer will result in this credit balance being reduced by the amount transferred. A number in a bank account ("current account") thus seems to document a claim allowing the person in whose name the account is held to settle monetary debts in the amount of this number. It therefore seems that sight deposits are money.

Many believe that this appearance is deceptive. It is claimed that sight deposits are not money, but rather are claims for money (cf. Thielemann, 2016). In the opinion of those taking this view, "real money" only takes two forms: cash, or the balances in the accounts that commercial banks hold at the central bank (central bank money). Let us give a name to a representative theorist taking this view. We will call him "Ulrich."

To support this thesis, it is often assumed by someone arguing Ulrich's case that the seller and buyer of an asset maintain their current accounts with two different commercial banks. And indeed, if the bank receiving a transfer requires the other bank to make payment, it is correct that the credit balance of the transferring bank recorded in its account at the central bank is reduced by exactly the amount by which the equivalent account of the bank receiving the transfer increases (i.e. the transfer goes into the account the receiving commercial bank holds at the central bank).

However, if it is assumed that the seller and the buyer both keep their current accounts with the same commercial bank, it is indisputable that no central bank money is required for this transfer. Now, Ulrich can attempt to argue that a buyer's transfer is only a transfer of "money" to the seller if, in the course of the transaction, a credit is also credited to the central bank account of the relevant commercial bank. The fact is, however, that with the transfer from A to B, where both A and B have accounts at the same commercial bank, the money debt of A to B has been settled, and this process does not involve any change in the balance recorded in their bank's account at the central bank. According to our concept of "money," which is based on Knapp, in this case sight deposits are clearly to be regarded as money.

Giro account balances are also money in cases where a transfer leads to a simultaneous reduction in sight deposits and in the relevant banks' account balances at the central bank. Let us consider a tax payment from business entity A to the tax office. This entity A has an account at bank X. A tax payment of EUR 100 from A will reduce the balance-sheet item "demand deposits" on the liabilities side of bank X, and it will also reduce the balance-sheet item "central bank balances" on bank X's assets side by EUR 100. Those who do not have a corresponding sight deposit cannot pay their taxes. Current account balances obviously allow payment obligations to the tax authorities to be settled.

In a last-ditch attempt to defend the claim that sight deposits are technically not "money," Ulrich may reply that in order for A to pay taxes due, it is not only necessary for there to be sufficient funds in A's current account at bank X, it is also necessary for bank X to have a corresponding amount in its account at the central bank, available to transfer to the government revenue department's account. And that is correct. But the question is whether it is possible that a taxpayer, in this case A, who has a balance in his current account large enough to pay his taxes nevertheless cannot pay his taxes because his bank, in this case bank X, does not have a sufficient balance in its account at the central bank.

We now make the following claim: For the entire banking system, and assuming that banks only handle payment transactions and grant loans, this is only possible if the bank goes bankrupt due to credit default and/or the total tax payments are higher than government expenditure (cf. Steinhardt, 9 September 2016).

To explain this thesis, we will assume, for simplicity, that there is only one commercial bank in the relevant currency area. The commercial bank then always has easy access to the required central bank balances. It does not even need to get into debt with the central bank. This is because when the state makes a transfer in the amount T to pay for an asset to a customer C of the commercial bank (let us say the government buys a computer or a car from C), not only the current account balance of C but also the commercial bank's balance in its own account at the central bank automatically increases by T. In other words, if the state spends at least the amount that it later intends to recoup through levying taxes, then the commercial bank always has sufficient central bank money available in its account to process a tax payment from one of its customers.

Defects in the two-stage banking system

The two-stage nature of the banking system is illustrated in this example by the fact that government spending automatically increases both the central bank balance of a commercial bank and the current account balance of a customer of the commercial banking system; whereas tax payments reduce both the taxpayer's current account balance at a commercial bank and his bank's balance in its account at the central bank. If this consideration is correct, how can one explain that in real two-tier banking systems, "commercial banks have had to be saved from the threat of collapse with taxpayers' money'" (Jenner, quoted after Thielemann, 2016).

The reason is easy to see: If a commercial bank has granted a loan of 100 euros to bank customer A, then A can use this to pay for assets she buys from bank customer B. A no longer has the money created by the commercial bank through lending, but of course she still has to service the loan with her commercial bank. If A is now unable to obtain money from third parties — for whatever reason — then she will no longer be able to service this loan. In this case, however, the bank must adjust the value of the loan downwards. If the amount of the downward value adjustments to its loan book exceeds the "equity capital" of a bank, then the bank is bankrupt. Note that a commercial bank does not go bankrupt because it is illiquid but rather because the valuation of its portfolio of asset items has decreased so much due to very specific valuation regulations that the valuation of the residual figure "equity capital" becomes negative.

It should also be clear that in the example case the commercial bank must be rescued, because otherwise the entire payment system will be at risk of collapse. This also applies if we abandon the assumption that there is only one commercial bank. If a bank becomes insolvent, a chain reaction can occur because the bankruptcy of one bank can easily lead to the bankruptcy of other banks to which it has liabilities.

Rescuing a commercial bank is very simple. The central bank simply credits the commercial bank with an amount that restores its equity capital to the legally required level (or higher), in exchange for some securities. However one wants to label this "business transaction," "taxpayers' money" is obviously not needed.

The fact that a commercial bank can in principle go bankrupt, but is generally not allowed to go bankrupt due to the consequences this would entail, shows that our monetary system is defective and needs repair. This defect can be easily identified. If the bankruptcy of commercial banks is in fact not really possible (because if it were allowed to occur, the payment system would collapse), then one must ask what is the point of our system of commercial lending. The core function usually attributed to banks, namely to act like entrepreneurs in the credit market, does not actually exist, because the risk case — business failure and bankruptcy — must never be allowed to occur. This raises the fundamental question of whether the market-economy organisation of commercial banking — and thus the application of the so-called liability principle — makes sense at all.

Are banks normal companies?

The great financial crash of 2008 caused confusion, irritation, and astonishing insights even among the banking elite, as the following quote from Josef Ackermann, then CEO of Deutsche Bank, from 2011 shows: "I am convinced that we must once again thoroughly assess the entirety of our activities in all areas, to see whether we are doing justice to our genuine tasks and responsibilities as servants of the real economy." (Ackermann, 2011)

The primary task of banks should be to provide companies with money to enable them to "produce" goods and services, as the "servant" Ackermann agrees. And we must also agree with him that all activities of a bank should be assessed and audited to see whether they contribute effectively to the fulfillment of this task. It should be added that, in concordance with this logic, all activities of a bank that do not serve this objective, or are detrimental to achieving it, should be explicitly prohibited by the state.

It is to the credit of the EU's political representatives that after the financial crisis, they recognised that such an audit should not be left to the banks themselves. The then head of the Finnish central bank, Erkki Liikanen, was therefore asked to set up a group of experts to look into this important issue. The central result of the group's assessment reads as follows: "The Group's conclusion is that it is necessary to require legal separation of certain particularly risky financial activities from deposit-taking banks within a banking group." (Liikanen, 2012, p. i)

Currently, banks are allowed to (i) buy and sell securities — most of which are tradable on the financial market — on their own account, and (ii) grant loans to households and companies. While a bank's category (ii) activities allow it to make a profit if it has correctly assessed the creditworthiness of its customers, it makes a profit with its category (i) activities if it has correctly assessed the market development for the price of a financial market product.

The category (i) activities recorded in a bank's balance sheet are referred to as financial assets. Since their amount is measured on the market, a bank's equity position fluctuates with the market valuations of its assets. These fluctuations are problematic because lending must be backed by sufficient equity capital and because speculative activities endanger customers' deposits. Nevertheless, the recommendations of the Liikanen Commission were not followed. Instead, reforms have been initiated that are meant to make banks better entrepreneurs, so that the market can efficiently manage the allocation of capital.

The hero in the story told by market-believers is the entrepreneur, motivated by a search for profit opportunities. Entrepreneurs may be greedy creatures, but that is not a bad thing, the liberals believe, because his greed is always held in check by his fear of losing money with his activities. This leads to him exercise a degree of prudence in his decision-making. If the state takes away this fear from the entrepreneur by promising to save him if he is at risk of going under, greed will prevail and "moral hazard" will become the rule. The financial crash of 2007/08, which many economists believe was triggered primarily by banks' reckless lending, serves as proof of this thesis.

According to an article in *Handelsblatt*, for example, economists are consequently calling for "thicker capital cushions to be built up, so that risky loans can be granted less easily, and in order to be better secured in the event of a crisis" (Heide, 2016). While from this point of view greed, i.e. the intention to achieve the highest possible profits from their business activities, is quite positive, it is indispensable that entrepreneurs — in this case, bankers — are also afraid to lose their invested money as a result of misjudgments made in the course of their business activities.

So there are two considerations at the core of the proposal to increase the equity capital cushion of banks: First, the amount of equity providers' money put at risk of loss is to be increased, so that they are more motivated to control the business conduct of "their" bank. Second, an increased equity capital buffer is meant to help ensure that no third parties (the state, for example) are asked to pay for damages caused or losses incurred by a bank.

The so-called European Banking Union, which provides regulations for winding up and settling the accounts of "systemically important" banks, among other things, has its aims in the same direction. The declared aim is to prevent the state (often, as already mentioned above, confused with the taxpayer) from being in a position of having to intervene and save the banks every time there is a bank crisis. In English, such an act of rescue is called a "bail-out" of a bank (or banks) by the state. The new regime, on the other hand, provides for a so-called "bail-in": The goal is not a quick resolution of the crisis by the state, it is to hold accountable — financially and legally — those who are regarded as responsible for the bank's crisis.

The Deutsche Bundesbank published the following remarks about the objectives of this new "settlement regime":

> The new settlement regime for banks, introduced in Europe at the beginning of 2015, should make it possible to settle systemically important institutions in an orderly manner without jeopardising financial stability or burdening taxpayers. The central element of the new settlement framework is the so-called bail-in. The introduction of this instrument of creditor participation makes it possible, for the first time, that in addition to owners and subordinated creditors, non-subordinated lenders can also be called upon to assume liability for a bank's losses outside insolvency proceedings. (Deutsche Bundesbank, 2016, p. 65)

First of all, the bail-in does justice to the fact that is often not possible to implement an orderly insolvency procedure, as doing so would jeopardise "financial stability" and serious effects on the "real economy" can be expected (Deutsche Bundesbank, 2016, p. 68).

In the course of a bail-in, then, insolvency proceedings are to be simulated, to ensure that both the "owners" and the "lenders" (creditors or depositors) are asked to pay up in order to restore the bank to solvency in a manner that allows the principle of liability to unfold. The Deutsche Bundesbank explains why this is important and good: "This principle of liability strengthens incentives to take appropriate account of risks in investment decisions and to limit moral hazard behaviour as much as possible." (Deutsche Bundesbank, 2016, p. 67)

Now, it is hard to deny that a bail-in significantly increases the risk associated with investing in banks. It should therefore be expected that investors will tend to be less willing to invest in banks.

But why are banks thought to be more secure when they have less capital at their disposal? The idea is probably that "investors" who know that they can actually lose the money they have invested will exercise better oversight or control of the bank's business conduct. Unfortunately, the Bundesbank does not disclose which control rights can be exercised by lenders and equity capital providers. Or are they silent about this because they know that the vast majority of "creditors" do not really have any such rights?

The "creditor" who only holds "deposits" with a bank has no control or oversight influence whatsoever. Depositors are, as a rule, persons who have a current account with a bank so that it can process their payment transactions. They are in no position to play an oversight role, and they are even less suitable for playing a role in the "cascade" of those who are supposed to be financially liable for the bank's mistakes. After all, deposits of up to 100,000 euros are to be exempted from bail-ins. Why this should be any different for amounts greater than 100,000 euros remains the secret of the supporters of this European Banking Union. In any case, in the real world it is simply impossible for depositors to monitor "their" bank's management.

It promises to be rather difficult to implement the "principle of liability" in practice. First of all, creditors cannot be placed in a worse position than they would have been in ordinary insolvency proceedings. Therefore, a bail-in for secured creditors is not planned. Only those who took loose talk about a bank being "safe" too literally and made money available to a bank on unsecured terms will be asked to pay. But is it fair that someone who was particularly cautious and therefore secured his investment, but still earned money with the bank's business activities, now has no reason to fear any losses?

This does not even begin to fully describe the absurdities of the planned bail-in approach. Since derivatives are particularly risky and generate high profits, it is logical to ask derivative investors to pay first. However, the opposite is the case: they are expressly excluded from participation in the bail-in, because the unequivocal valuation of these financial instruments is difficult or impossible. The valuation of "savings deposits," whether in the form of bank bonds or in the form of an old-fashioned savings book, on the other hand, is very simple, which is probably why it is only "logical" that they should be drawn on to help pay for bail-ins. Anyone who confuses a bank with a piggy-bank must obviously be taught a lesson!

Banks are not intermediaries

The basic idea behind the liability principle is a conception of a bank's business model that has nothing to do with reality. According to this traditional notion, banks need money made available to them by third parties in order to conduct their business — in particular the business of granting loans but also the purchase of securities. Banks are regarded as intermediaries which take up money (the customers' deposits) and merely pass this money on to borrowers, or invest it. It is claimed that lending is only possible because banks have received money in advance from savers. According to this story, banks are money collectors, which merely have the function of mediating the supply of and demand for money.

However, the idea that banks must have money in advance so that they can pass it on to third parties as loans is wrong. The business of banking is much simpler than is usually assumed. For example, if a bank wants to buy shares issued by a company or grant a loan, it does not need money from anyone. It merely credits the issuer or the borrower with the corresponding amount on their current account. Formally, these credit notes are liabilities of the bank to the holders of the current accounts. In substance, they give the holders the right to demand cash, i.e. government-recognised legal tender, from the bank in the amount of their credit balances (cf. Deutsche Bundesbank, 2017b, p. 15 ff.).[1]

Even though this is so simple and easy, banks, as we have described above, can go bankrupt if they have to write down so many loans that the valuation of their residual "equity capital" becomes negative. If the sole objective of banking reforms is to reduce the risk of banks going bankrupt, then the call for an increase in equity capital is basically correct. However, the primary aim is (or should be) to prevent loans being granted with which speculative bubbles are produced. But it is not clear how an increase in equity capital requirements can help to avoid such transactions.

Money as a Commodity, and Monetarism

The understanding of "money" that prevails among the vast majority of people today, including politicians, economists, and even so-called banking

---

[1] This view is now also shared by the Bundesbank.

experts, can be traced back to Carl Menger's attempt in the 19th century to conceptualize money as a special type of commodity. In Menger's opinion, this commodity is special because it is regarded as particularly valuable by all people, but is only available to a limited extent.

It is this idea of scarcity that is still regarded today as the central pillar of a stable monetary system, and it is money scarcity which the latest reforms of the monetary and financial system aim to reinforce. We are highly critical of these reforms. It is worth taking a closer look at Menger's concept of money and the associated conceptual elements of how the monetary order is constructed.

Money as a commodity

Carl Menger explains what money is by taking us on a journey into the past (or a somewhat mythologised caricature of the past). In this notional past, a division of labour was already in place, but people did not use money; they simply exchanged their produce with each other directly. For example, a carpenter might have exchanged a chair he made for a basket of fish caught by a fisherman.

But the carpenter did not want to eat only fish, he also wanted potatoes and vegetables. He knew a farmer who grew these products and produced more than he needed for himself, but unfortunately the farmer did not want any of his chairs. Our carpenter, however, knew that the farmer loved fish, yet the fisherman grew potatoes and vegetables himself, and therefore did not have to purchase these products from the farmer. A bright fellow, the carpenter realised that he could make a deal with the fisherman, by trading a chair for fish, and then he would be able to exchange some of the fish for vegetables and potatoes from the farmer. From the carpenter's point of view, these fish are no longer a consumer good; they are a means of exchange.

Now our carpenter may have many other wishes for products and services that he cannot directly fulfil with his own work, but might be able to engage in barter for. However, for this to be feasible, he must have well-founded opinions about the value assessments of all possible exchange partners with regard to all possible goods. Menger overcomes this epistemic hurdle by claiming that different goods have different "marketability."

According to Menger's definition, the more the demand for a good deviates from (i.e. exceeds) its availability, the more marketable it is. A clever person will therefore concentrate on such high-marketability goods when seeking to acquire things whose primary function is not their direct use by their owner, but rather their value in exchange:

> This recognition certainly will not have emerged in all members of a community at the same time; rather, as with all cultural progress, at first only a limited number of subjects will have recognized the advantage resulting from the above process for their economy. (Menger, 1970[1892], p. 4)

Not all people have the same epistemic abilities, and some people can be expected to be more successful than others in identifying these marketable goods. The dumber ones, of course, are able to see that the smarter ones are doing better than they are and that this has to do with the fact that they are able to identify marketable goods. They will therefore now also try to exchange the goods they produce for marketable means of exchange. Menger continues:

> Certainly practice, imitation and habit, with their mechanising effect on human actions, have also in this case contributed more than a little to the fact that, in the context of local and temporal conditions, those goods which were most marketable were those which were generally accepted in trade, and so these became commodities, because they were accepted from the outset not only by many, but ultimately by all economic individuals in exchange for the (less salable!) goods also brought to market, with the intention of further exchanging them. (*Ibid.*, p. 13)

In this evolutionary process, precious metals, in particular gold and silver, established themselves as the generally used means of exchange. These metals are physically available only to a limited extent. Of course, Menger saw that even in his time, most payments were not made in gold and silver but in banknotes and state notes. But he saw no problem in this for his determination of the essence of money since, in his conception, these notes were merely redeemable demands for gold or silver.

The conclusion to be drawn from these considerations is simple: If it is possible to regulate the issuance of money in such a way as to ensure that the notes can be cashed at any time and without any problems into a commodity that is valued and appreciated by practically everyone, yet available only in limited quantity — gold, for example — this would also ensure that money is merely a representative of tradable goods. If too much fiat money (e.g. banknotes) is obtained in circulation compared to the limited availability of precious metals, this would naturally lead to a decline in the value of the fiat money.

Chicago style monetarism

In today's pure fiat money systems, however, no such obligation to redeem cash for precious metals exists. So how is one supposed to keep the amount of money in short supply? The answer to this question was given by the monetarists around Milton Friedman. Friedman's idea (which was not original to him — its origins go far back in the history of economics) appears to be captivatingly simple. To keep money scarce, it is only necessary to ensure that the total amount of money put into circulation by the central bank is exactly sufficient to allow all transactions in money-valued goods to be settled. According to the monetarists, this quantity can easily be determined using the so-called quantity theory. The quantity theory, which is actually merely an identity, reads as follows:

$$M^*V = P^*Y$$

where M is money, V is the circulation speed of money, P is the price level, and Y is real national income. V is the variable that, by definition, balances the other variables, because there is always a multiple of the money supply that "finances" the right side, the nominal gross domestic product (or some other income variable).

As the next section explains, this "theory" was to become the fate of the German and European economies for more than 30 years. It allegedly showed that the economy can be kept on a stable, inflation-free growth path almost without need for government intervention. The appropriate rate of money supply growth was to be determined historically, i.e. by extrapolating past growth rates and setting a target rate for inflation. The promise was that this would eliminate the risk of inflation once and for all, without the state having to intervene in the economy over and over again. The idea behind monetarism and this equation was that in the long run, "money is neutral," i.e. it does not influence economic development.

This hope was in turn based on a "theory" about the division of labour between central and commercial banks. According to this theory, while commercial banks circulate money by granting loans, they need to refinance this activity by borrowing the necessary money from the central bank. Since the commercial banks have to pay interest on that money, central banks can therefore, by raising or lowering interest rates, steer towards a target money supply, set in accordance with the economy's requirements, which they calculate from the quantity equation.

Today, monetarism as a guiding theory of economic policy is officially dead. No major central bank in the world continues to hew to the idea of setting a target for the money supply and steering toward it. For the ECB, too, in normal times, economic policy is meant to take place via so-called conventional monetary policy, which consists of either lowering or raising the key interest rate, depending on forecasts about the general trend of the economy — not on any particular money quantity target. The effect is described in an ECB brochure as follows:

> In the short term, a change in money market interest rates set by the central bank will set in motion numerous mechanisms and measures by market participants which will ultimately influence the development of economic variables such as production and prices. (Europäische Zentralbank, 2011, p. 59)

By determining the refinancing costs of commercial banks, a central bank exerts influence on the interest charged by banks to its own borrowers. The level of interest rates, it is further assumed, will have a decisive influence on how many loans are taken out, and the loan volume will in turn be reflected in higher or lower production volumes, and thus also in higher or lower prices for goods and services.

Despite the supposed death of monetarism in the style of Milton Friedman, the idea of money neutrality is so central to neoliberalism that its adherents are loathe to give it up completely. The ECB wrote some surprising sentences in the above-mentioned brochure suggesting that the death of monetarism may have been proclaimed somewhat prematurely after all:

The thesis of money neutrality is generally accepted in expert circles, and empirically proven. In the long term — i.e. after all adjustments in the economy have had their effect — a change in the money supply present in the economy (other factors remaining unchanged) is reflected in a change in the general price level, and does not entail a sustained change in real variables such as macroeconomic production or employment. A change in the money supply in circulation ultimately represents a change in the unit of account (and thus in the general price level) that leaves all other variables unaffected. (Europäische Zentralbank, 2011, p. 59)

So the idea of a neutral money supply — at least for so-called normal times — is by no means dead and buried. It has merely been acknowledged that direct control of monetary quantities (such as central bank reserves, which are called M0, or cheque money, M1) is impossible. Control is now meant to take place indirectly via interest rate adjustments and a resulting influence on the amount of money introduced into the economic cycle via lending. Obviously it is still believed that this is possible, and that the barter economy thought to sit underneath the veil of money can, in the end, be helped to emerge.

This is a thought that even left-wing politicians such as Sahra Wagenknecht seem to find very plausible. They too attribute the many malfunctions of our financial system to the proposition that money can be "multiplied at will" (Wagenknecht, 2011, p. 215). Like other variants of liberal economic theories, the theory of Ordoliberalism, which seems to fascinate Wagenknecht, relies on the market mechanism to ensure the efficient allocation of scarce goods. In this view, if there is not a shortage of goods, there can be no competition, and without competition the market mechanism cannot unfold its beneficial effects. Wagenknecht's conclusion that money must likewise be "kept in short supply" (*Ibid.*, p. 215) is therefore all too understandable in the context of such convictions. It is nevertheless wrong.

Objectified money supply

In the 1970s, the birth decade of the new liberalism, monetarist positions were absolutely dominant in the macroeconomic discourse. The German

Council of Economic Experts, for example, whose work was of great importance for the new paradigm, spent years wondering what was the right quantity with which to measure the money supply, and how, consequently, the "new" ideas of monetarism could be translated into practical policy in a country that was now freed from the "constraints" of the international monetary system.

The great aim of all these efforts was "to objectify the supply of money," as the Council of Economic Experts put it. The aim was not only to entrust a politically largely independent institution with the supply of money but also to create rules that made this institution's decision-making scope as small as possible. The idea was that if such rules could actually be found, then one would not only be able to make a persuasive argument that the state should stay almost completely out of the business of trying to manage the economy; one would have set up the possibility of it actually being in a position to refrain from managing it. Given the right rules for a central bank, the most important price — the rate of interest — would be a pure market result, resulting from the "objective money supply" and the markets' demand for money. Only then would the reformers' task of truly freeing the market economy from state intervention be achieved, and the old monetarist dream of "neutral money" realised.

Today we know that this idea was a powerful illusion. Nowadays, central banks "interfere" in economic activity more frequently and aggressively than ever before, without clearly identifiable, predefined, or even merely comprehensible rules. The central banks in some cases even explicitly admit that they pursue employment goals (the US Federal Reserve has made changes toward a tighter monetary policy dependent on dropping below a certain unemployment rate); this would have been regarded as sacrilege in the 1970s. Nevertheless, many economists have still not understood that the concept of the existence of a money supply quantity that is on offer to bidders on the demand side must be completely abandoned in order to reach reasonable conclusions on monetary policy issues.

There is no economic growth quantity that is largely independent of the supply of liquidity and of interest rates, the magnitude of which could be determined empirically, and which would then only have to be financed by monetary policy. The monetarists believed that in order to implement their ideas in practical terms in a country like Germany, they only had to extrapolate the nominal growth of the last 10 years, and with that, one would have a good measure for the growth of the money supply to be aimed for. "Objectification" therefore consisted of a simple extrapolation, and even then it was not yet known whether nominal money supply growth would be used for more rapid price increases than in the past, which in turn would result in more inflation than desired.

The central bank cannot work mechanically on the basis of predetermined quantitative targets in a world economy that is coming out of a deep crisis, as is the case at present (or as was the case after the oil price explosions of the 1970s). In such a world, nothing is quantitatively predetermined, and an upswing never occurs automatically. Whether, when, and how robustly the economy will return to a growth path depends, among other things, on the central banks' own decisions and behaviour. Contrary to the assertion that money is neutral, in reality, monetary policy has a direct effect on the economic process.

Monetarists cannot completely deny the effectiveness of central bank policies on the economy, since this would be tantamount to saying that monetary policy is obsolete. Monetarists admit the importance of monetary policy insofar as they consider a low and constant inflation rate to be an important element in supporting the real economic process and regard maintaining this condition as the core mission of monetary policy. Monetarism tries to free itself from the logical dilemma that arises from this contradiction by distinguishing between the short run and long run: Monetary policy has a short-term effect, its apologists say, but money is neutral in the long run.

This attempt to distinguish between short-term economic development and a long-term growth path that is somehow determined by other general conditions is featured in neoclassical economic doctrine as well. There, too, the focus is on the idea of a long-term "equilibrium" towards which everything is assumed to tend, and in which, above all, there are no "real" profits (i.e. returns in excess of entrepreneurial wages and interest payments).

Neoclassicism defines away profits, which after all are the really exciting element and driving mainspring of a market economy — and therefore it no longer has anything essential to contribute toward explaining economic development. In parallel fashion, monetarism postulates that because of the (assumed) neutrality of money, monetary policy has no long-term impact on an economy's growth path, and concludes that its only role is to provide a money supply in line with this foreordained path and with the desired rate of inflation.

If one does not accept this dogma, but instead sees the long term as a succession of many individual short terms, it becomes clear that monetary policy always has an influence on the long term due to its influence in the short term. Consequently, monetary policymakers must form their own opinion of the economic situation and use the instruments under their direct control — namely the interest rate — to influence the economy's developing trajectory.

But if monetary policy focuses on steering the interest rate, it cannot logically control the money supply at the same time. That is because the central bank always reacts completely flexibly in the provision of money in response to whatever demand for money arises each day in the banking system, in order to maintain the interest rate it is aiming for. (The size of this provision can be called the "money supply" as long as one remains cognizant of the endogeneity of this quantity.) The central goal that all central banks in the world today focus their efforts on striving to achieve is a certain short-term target interest rate, and if they have no foreign trade–related restrictions to take into consideration (such as a certain target exchange rate), they will achieve that goal. But they succeed in doing so in complete disregard of the development of any money supply quantity. When central banks have retrospectively assessed their data and examined money supply developments (which are always the result of interacting supply and demand for money, and never the one-sided result of an offer by the central bank of a particular target quantity of money), this has merely served to obfuscate the fact that monetarism in its practical implementation (i.e. past attempts to practice central banking by supplying a predetermined target quantity of money) has always been a disaster.

It follows directly from this that the most important price in a market economy is always a price entirely controlled by the state, i.e. the price of money, the interest rate set by the central bank. Independent central banks manage this rate primarily on the basis of their discretionary (not rule-bound) assessment of expected trends in the prices of goods, and real growth opportunities.

What private investors in property, plant, and equipment need, in a market economy, is the most stable and growth-friendly interest rate possible.

If the central bank were to try to push through a steadily growing money supply as their central objective, interest rates would fluctuate sharply whenever demand for money fluctuates sharply. Mistakes made by the central bank in determining the money supply would be reflected in the interest rate, and so would random and unexpected fluctuations in money demand that might occur for a variety of reasons. This would make stable investment activity impossible.

All those who, for whatever reasons, want to see a focus on maintaining a stable "money supply" must grapple with this central problem (which they usually fail to do). Among the motivations for a renewed focus on a stable money supply is the rediscovered notion of fully covered money (variously called 100% central bank reserve backed money, full money, or 100% money) that emerged after the 2008 financial crisis. A full-money system would assign the task of producing money directly and exclusively to the central bank (i.e. the state), which would be asked to produce a quantity of money sufficient for all real production. This system is meant to prevent commercial banks from enabling financial speculation through money creation.

Full money: Monetarism in new clothes

Hans Christoph Binswanger, whom we respect and appreciate very much, wrote the following remarkable sentence in his contribution to the volume *Die Vollgeld-Reform* (*The Full-Money Reform*) in 2012:

> The basic idea is to find an intermediate solution between the gold standard of the past, in which money creation was limited by the redeemability of paper money in gold and thus by the quantity of gold available, and the current monetary system, in which it is possible [for commercial banks] to create unlimited amounts of paper money and book money, such that the central banks are able to control this without creating a crisis [by jacking up interest rates to levels that choke the real economy]. (Binswanger, Huber & Mastronardi, 2014, p. 30)

Advocates of a so-called full-money reform start with an entirely correct recognition: Commercial banks do in fact create money by granting loans.

Yet full-money folks also believe that the "boundless creation of paper and book money" by commercial banks must necessarily lead to financial bubbles. They want to end this situation and allow only politically independent central banks to issue money. They see the sole task of such a central bank, protected from political influences, as ensuring a stable currency, and they are convinced that this goal can be achieved with the help of "potential-oriented" money supply management.

This view is remarkable insofar as we have just had a few decades of trying to steer the money supply through the central bank. This undertaking is usually called monetarism. But monetarism and its failure are usually left unmentioned in the writings of the disciples of the full-money project, although most of them refer, among other things, to the Chicago Plan of the 1930s, and Milton Friedman is regularly cited in support.

In texts written by Joseph Huber, one of Germany's leading advocates of full-money, one can read a lot of sentences that sound exactly like monetarism, though he does not use that term. Money supply has been rising too rapidly for years, the growing money supply is leading to inflation and excessive public debt growth, and an independent central bank should be called upon to manage the money supply "in line with potential." Welcome to the past!

The global financial crisis of 2008–2009 has given new impetus to the full-money idea. Its advocates have made fully justified criticisms of casino-like financial markets in which banks, empowered with the ability to create their own money, engaged in wild sprees of high-risk gambling for years before being rescued by states when it all went sideways.

In order to put an end to the game of "privatisation of profits, socialisation of losses," which we have seen time and again after financial crises, a full-money reform would be a step in the right direction. It is also true that if a bank goes bankrupt, the money balances of its depositors are currently at risk, and a full-money reform would eliminate this exposure. However, there are other ways of getting that problem under control: For example, the state could simply guarantee the entire stock of book money.

Although many sensible points have been raised within the framework of the full-money discourse, the core idea essentially fails because it preaches a supermonetarism that is long out-of-date. We simply do not know what amount of money (liquidity) is "needed" in a developing economy. And we cannot know, because the Central Bank's own decisions must create the conditions for dynamic development in the first place.

That is why monetarism, with its mistaken assumption of the existence of a purportedly somehow predetermined production potential which the central bank is supposed to "objectively" finance, went under. Not only do we not know what amount of real production is to be financed (beyond the amount already inherent in a purely circular economy); we also do not know how the demand for money or liquidity will develop over time, even in the absence of huge speculative bubbles.

There is much to be said for the view that the money market interest rate, and derived from it, interest rates on the capital markets themselves, are key determinants of the level of dynamism of economic development. If that is the case, then the notion of exogenous control over the money supply, in a world where the level of demand for money is unknown, is mistaken from the outset. Full-money representatives and monetarists alike fail to talk about the fact that the interest rate only creates favourable conditions for investment if the rate is low and stable enough to give investors in real capital (property, plant, and equipment) sufficient incentive to make their investments, and the greatest possible certainty with respect to their future funding costs. The central monetary policy insight of the past three decades is that a stable interest rate is only possible if the central bank meets every demand for money at the interest rate it has set. But this is incompatible with the idea of controlling the money supply or setting a certain quantity of circulating money as the target toward which a central bank attempts to steer toward.

Joseph Huber has raised the following objection to such a criticism:

> The quantity theory of money is one of the oldest and most proven economic doctrines of all. It is as fundamental today as it has always been. It implies that the key to safe money and stable finances, or at least its basic prerequisite, lies in the quantity of money and therefore also in monetary policy control over the quantity of money. Apart from the legal authority to issue directives, money — and not only its allocation and distribution, but also its creation and first use — is the most important means of exercising social power and domination. (Huber, no date)

It is astonishing that the so-called quantity theory is still being made use of with such naiveté at the beginning of the 21st century. The quantity theory equation ("Equation of Exchange") $M^*V = P^*Y$ is a mere tautology, as we have already explained above; the values of all its variables are unknown *ex ante* (i.e. in relation to the future). Nobody knows what the right amount of money M should be for a certain level of GDP growth (which level of growth? No one knows that either). Nobody knows the future circulation velocity of money V (how many times a 20 euro banknote changes hands in a given year on average), and nobody knows how real income Y or the price level P will develop.

Even *ex post*, one cannot say whether the level of growth achieved was optimal, or how much the measured money supply and the measured velocity of circulation each separately contributed to it. Price (the inflation rate) is the only variable whose developmental success can be measured on an external criterion — here, on the basis of comparison with a target set beforehand by policymakers. Yet whether this target price level was the level at which growth was optimised cannot be known. All four variables are endogenous, i.e. determined by the overall development of the system.

Monetary policy is not suitable for regulating the banking sector, because it is needed to stimulate investment activity in the real economy. Monetary policy in itself cannot be used as a tool to discriminate between the quality of investments. Central banks cannot make their policy decisions dependent on a review of whether casino-like speculation or real productive investment activity is being financed and promoted in each individual lending case. Only the commercial banking system, which is decentralised and assesses investors locally with regard to their specific projects, can do this. As we have said, a nationalised banking system could do the same thing; but regardless of whether commercial banks are private enterprises or agencies of the state, the task of monetary policy would still have to be separated from the task of distributing money and providing credit.

So the idea of "full money" remains a beautiful dream. If they want to continue defending the idea, its supporters must deal much more concretely with the failure of monetarism and with the central question of how exactly they would effectively manage interest rates for consistency with healthy economic development in a world marked by uncertainty about the future.

Uncle Scrooge and bags of money

The idea that there exists a given quantity of money, akin to a pile of gold coins, is also the basis for the neoclassical economists' explanation of the euro crisis that we previously mentioned in the context of our discussion of Keynesianism. From a neoclassical point of view, large amounts of savings flowed from Germany to Spain, and this caused economic problems that were subsequently reflected in Spain's high current account deficits. This thesis, prominently presented by economist Hans-Werner Sinn, has also been put forward by some Marxian economists such as Frédéric Heine and Thomas Sablowski, who wrote: "The inflow of capital is decisive for the import suction [high volume of imports of goods by southern Europeans from Germany] and the associated current account deficits in the crisis countries" (Heine & Sablowski, 2015).

The leftist theorists' version of Sinn's thesis is based on the "Uncle Scrooge" image of a capitalist: He sits atop bags stuffed full of cash and coins, wearing a top hat, and worries about how he can invest this money profitably. To explain the euro crisis, Uncle Scrooge is transferred to Germany in the early 1990s. He no longer sees any investment opportunities for his "capital" there and is therefore close to despair. To his delight, in mid-1997 the introduction of the euro is announced. Uncle Scrooge can now consider investments in other European countries without having to fear exchange rate volatility.

He looks to Spain and thinks he can distinguish more worthwhile investment opportunities there than in Germany. He therefore takes his bags full of money and transports them to the Iberian Peninsula to invest them in real estate. Uncle Scrooge's money is then used to import construction machinery from Germany and to pay wages to construction workers in Spain, who subsequently buy a Mercedes produced in the Daimler-Benz factory in Untertürkheim, for example.

According to this thesis, Spain's current account deficits were in fact "financed" by foreign capital, and Spain's net foreign debt piled up, over the course of some years, until it amounted to a staggering 1,000 billion euros. For Sinn, these "external debts" are a serious problem for the Eurozone, "because Spain is a large country and its debt is correspondingly huge" (Sinn, 2015).

This picture of banking and the associated interpretation of balance sheets explain why many German commentators were flabbergasted by Trump advisor Peter Navarro's criticism of Germany's large export surpluses. Winand von Petersdorff and Philip Plickert of the *FAZ*, for example, asked whether "a positive balance is necessarily favourable and a negative balance necessarily bad?" Trade expert Gabriel Felbermayr of the Munich-based ifo Institute gave the two journalists the following answer to this question: "The large current account surplus is associated with an export of capital, an outflow of savings." (Petersdorff & Plickert, 2017)

The two *FAZ* journalists concluded that Germany was "giving the buyer countries the necessary financing" to be able to buy German goods. The only correct thing about this view is that the net claims of German legal entities against foreign legal entities always correspond exactly to the current account deficit. It is not true that it follows that it was "capital exports" that financed the current account deficits of Germany's trade partners.

Why not? The relevant financial "capital," i.e. the means thought to trigger a boom such as that of Spain in the late 1990s and early 2000s, is essentially not cash, but rather book money. Uncle Scrooge does not actually sit atop bags full of money; rather, his current account with a commercial bank shows a large positive balance. Money in this form is also not physically passed on from one person to another; it is transferred by crediting the payee's account with an amount x and debiting the payer of the transfer with the same amount x.

For example, if Scrooge invests one million euros in a Spanish property developer, the credit in his German bank account is reduced by this amount, and the credit of the Spanish property developer increases by one million euros. In this case, it certainly makes sense to talk about Uncle Scrooge's "capital export" to Spain, because now a Spaniard has money he can use to invest in a property, and Uncle Scrooge has a right to participate in the potential profits of this investment.

But is this situation comparable to the "foreign debt" resulting from current account deficits? Let us assume that a current account deficit of one million euros arises solely from the purchase of a construction machine from a German supplier by a Spanish construction company. It is clear that this transaction, viewed in isolation, will result in the German contractor's current account balance increasing by this amount. Is this a capital export from Spain to Germany? No, because the Spaniard did not transfer his money to Germany to earn a return; he did so to pay for a construction machine.

The fact is, however, that there is now more money in Germany and less in Spain. It is also a fact that under the assumption that Spain's current account deficit was caused solely by this transaction, a Spanish organisation must now have a liability to a German organisation. We can easily determine the identity of this Spanish organisation: It is the Spanish bank that debited its customer's current account with one million euros to process the purchase. If, during a given time period, a Spanish bank has transferred one million euros more to a German bank, on a net basis, than vice versa, as is assumed here, then the German bank must book a claim and the Spanish bank a liability of one million euros so that the balance sheets of both banks are balanced again. If such an entry were not made, the Spanish bank would "lack" one million euros in liabilities and the German bank one million euros in assets.

However, the assets and liabilities of banks measured in euros relate to central bank reserves. If we call central bank reserves "money," it is clear that no money has flowed yet. Money in the form of central bank reserves will not flow until the Spanish bank pays its liability to the German bank. If the Spanish bank has sufficient central bank reserves to make that payment, then when the payment occurs, it will be reflected in the Spanish balance sheet by a corresponding reduction in its credit balance with the Spanish central bank, and the credit balance of the German bank in its reserve account at the German central bank (Bundesbank) will increase by the same amount.

So far, in this transaction, no inflow of money has been identified at the Spanish bank. However, an inflow of money may be necessary if the Spanish bank does not have sufficient central bank reserves. In this case, it may obtain the necessary reserves by borrowing them from another bank or from the Spanish central bank. In accounting terms, this inflow is reflected by a credit entry in the account of the Spanish bank at the Spanish central bank, and a corresponding loan liability, either to another bank or to the Spanish central bank, depending on from whom the reserves were borrowed. But it should be clear that for our example, the inflow of money is offset by an equally high outflow. There is no net inflow of money to Spain that could cause an investment boom and "import suction."

But what if the Spanish bank borrows more money from a foreign bank than it needs to settle payments? Could it not be that this money will trigger an investment boom and a subsequent "import suction"? Would it not be possible — to stay with Spain as our example — for Spanish banks to have borrowed money (in the form of central bank reserves) from German banks, and then on-lent this money to a real estate developer who wanted to fund the construction of a building? The answer is simply no, because the reality is that banks do not pass on central bank reserves when granting loans.

The misunderstanding arises when both (a) sight deposits of depositors in commercial banks, and (b) claims by banks on each other or on the central bank, are considered or assumed to be "money," and when it is further assumed that the two positions on the assets and liabilities side (those of (a) and those of (b)) can be viewed in isolation. However, this is not possible, because the sight deposit with which a customer pays his monetary liabilities by bank transfer cannot exist without a corresponding balance-sheet item on the assets side of the bank. What appears in the national capital account as "capital exports" is therefore merely an indication of how much more money has been transferred from abroad to Germany than vice versa.

Allocation of capital through interest?

In the opinion of most neoclassical economists, including Hans-Werner Sinn, the level of interest rates is determined exclusively by risk assessments of banks and the capital market. In their view, interest rates have fallen since the start of the European Monetary Union mainly because investors no longer have to take exchange rate risks into account when weighing up their risks. After monetary union, capital flowed into countries that offered higher interest rates. Since, according to neoclassical opinion, an increasing supply must lead to a fall in price, the price of money — the interest rate — naturally also had to fall over time. And since the existence of markets means that arbitrage transactions are impossible over an extended period of time, interest rates in EMU countries had to converge sooner or later.

The following chart shows that long-term interest rates in the EMU countries did indeed converge (Figure 21). But the question arises as to why a market-based allocation of capital with the help of interest rate differentials would trigger a real estate boom in Spain, which ultimately resulted in a crash. Sinn asked himself this question, too. Since he assumed that the market is efficient, i.e. does not make any mistakes, another explanation had to be found: "When it comes to investment decisions, once people have perceived a trend, people tend to extend it arbitrarily far into the future, and in so doing, regularly overshoot the mark." (Sinn, 2015)

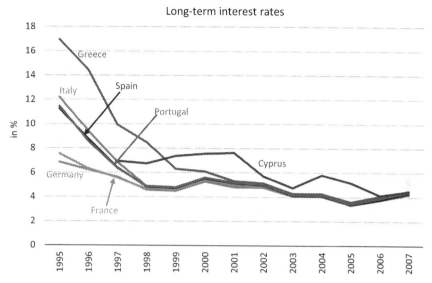

Figure 21:   Long-term interest rates

Source: AMECO, Financial Times, OECD.

But Sinn nevertheless refuses to perceive a market failure. For him, neo-classical theory must always be interpreted normatively, which means that people can make mistakes, but the market cannot. He writes:

> Some economists confuse these expectation errors with market errors. In fact, the problem lies more in the fact that there are no sufficiently far-reaching futures markets in which the future supply of goods and loans is already agreed and coordinated today. So the problem is that markets are missing, not that markets that exist are flawed. That's a subtle but funda-mental difference! (Sinn, 2015)

Such contorted logic is not necessary to explain the phenomenon of converging euro area interest rates after the introduction of the euro. It is enough to deal with reality. In reality, central banks set the short-term inter-est rate and play a significant role in determining the long-term interest rate.

In a reasonably constructed monetary system, this is because (1) com-mercial banks can in fact always refinance themselves with their central bank and (2) central banks always act as lenders of last resort for their state. Based on point (1), interbank interest rates (the basis for short-term interest rates) will generally more or less correspond to the key interest rate set by the central bank.

We further note that because of point (2), government bonds represent a risk-free investment for banks. But given (1), the purchase of government bonds can be refinanced by short-term borrowing from the central bank. The result is that long-term interest rates, which reference long-dated government bonds as a key benchmark, will approach the level of short-term interest rates.

The fact that yields on government bonds fluctuate is due solely to the fact that they are tradable, and central banks set the short-term interest rate. If traders expect the central bank to lower the key interest rate, government bond yields rise; conversely, their yield falls if an increase in the key rate is expected. If yields on government bonds fall or rise above what the central bank considers acceptable, it will intervene by buying or selling government bonds in the secondary market.

Consequently, it is the central banks that determine the level of both short-term and long-term interest rates. These interest rates in turn serve as benchmarks for commercial banks in setting prices for their commercial loans. The interest rate of a commercial loan is made up of the interest rate determined by the central bank, plus a margin, the amount of which depends on the banks' judgements on the creditworthiness of a borrower, and on competition among banks for borrowers. In a currency area constructed in this way, the interest rate that a borrower has to pay is independent of where the borrower is domiciled. That is why interest rates converged in the Eurozone after monetary union.

The State and the Central Bank

In order to shed more light on the connection between politics and the central bank of a country, we will begin with a simplified model of the banking system that assumes all money is paper money, and that the central bank acts as part of the political executive, rather than being "independent." The fact is that in capitalist economies, central banks — i.e. the state — and selected commercial banks are both allowed to "print" money. Let us call the money

Figure 22:   Accounting for lending

the state prints "statenotes" and the money that commercial banks print "banknotes."

How do statenotes and banknotes come into circulation? If we assume that the business of commercial banks is limited to lending and payment transactions, then banknotes come into circulation solely through the granting of loans. Statenotes, on the other hand, always come into circulation when the state uses them to pay for its purchases.

Let us first consider the mechanism for the circulation of banknotes. Let us assume that a company wants a loan to fund an ice cream production facility, and the bank approves this loan after a thorough credit check. The loan is then represented for accounting purposes as follows (Figure 22).

On its liabilities side, the bank has "noted" that it issued banknotes totalling 100 currency units in value to the ice cream producer, and the producer "noted" that he received banknotes worth 100 from the bank. It is already obvious at this point that an expansion of business activities and consequent increase in GDP necessarily involve increasing the "debt mountain." The reason for this is simple: Money is brought into circulation through the granting of credits (loans). In fact, money is a form of transferable debt instrument.

The mechanism for getting government notes ("statenotes") into circulation is somewhat different. Let us assume the state wants to buy a combat aircraft at the price of 100 from an aircraft manufacturer. The process is very simple: The aircraft manufacturer receives statenotes in the amount of 100, and in exchange, the state receives an aircraft. From an accounting point of view, this process can be represented as follows (Figure 23).

But why should the CFO of the armaments manufacturer be so stupid as to take almost worthless pieces of paper with numbers written on them for a real aircraft? Well, he is willing to do that because the state requires companies to pay taxes, which they can only settle with statenotes, and because the state can credibly threaten to throw corporate managers into prison if they fail to deliver the required amounts of statenotes to the state Treasury at

Government			Arms producer		
Airplane	100	State notes 100	State notes	100	Airplane 100

Figure 23:   Booking of aircraft purchase

Treasury Department			Central Bank		
Airplane	100	Credit 100	Credit	100	State notes 100

Figure 24:   Accounting for the refinancing of a government by the central bank

the appointed time. It should be clear now that it is not the state that has a refinancing problem; it is taxpayers who face the problem of obtaining the statenotes they need in order to pay their tax debts.

One may object that the state does not put money directly into circulation in this way anywhere in reality. That is correct. Even in Canada, where so-called monetary finance of public budgets is expressly permitted under the law, the state must take out a loan from its central bank through its Ministry of Finance in order to buy its aircraft this way. From an accounting point of view, this refinancing is recorded as follows (Figure 24).

This form of payment for the aircraft via the central bank has now caused the debt mountain to grow by a further 100 monetary units. However, one should not worry about this very much, because such "loans" are not associated with any costs, and of course do not have to be repaid. As long as the central bank, like the Ministry of Finance, is a "department" of the state, it remains possible to consolidate both balance sheets and simply cancel the credit and debit side. In either case — whether the state Treasury first gets a "loan" from the central bank, or simply records a credit to the aircraft-maker directly — the state always buys its aircraft in a way that amounts to turning on the money-printing press.

It is important at this point to recognise that statenotes come into circulation when the state uses them to make expenditures (pay suppliers of goods and services), and that some of these statenotes are later taken out of circulation again when taxes are paid to the state. What has already been said about bank debt thus applies to public debt too: The bigger these debts are (bank debts and state debts), the bigger the GDP. A growing economy is therefore normally accompanied by rising public debt. There is absolutely nothing problematic about this *per se*.

However, monetary public financing is banned in most countries, and even in Canada it is not really practised. Doesn't the above description therefore ignore the institutional realities of most modern monetary systems? This objection seems correct at first glance, because under the current institutional arrangements, budget deficits must be refinanced by issuing government bonds.

However, it can be shown that the assets and liabilities of the entities involved, and all resulting balances connected with a government bond issue, do not differ from direct financing by the central bank (Fullwiler, 2011). One can only suggest as a counterargument that the issuance of government bonds could in principle fail, since no one can force commercial banks to buy them. Commercial banks thus decide whether and, above all, to what extent the state may borrow to cover government expenditure.

But even in the event that a central bank would never, under any circumstances, be willing to take liabilities of its Ministry of Finance directly onto its balance sheet, it cannot be concluded from this that commercial banks will not always subscribe government bonds in any quantity the state requires and desires. That is because as long as it is clear that a central bank is available to commercial banks as their lender of last resort, commercial banks will not forego income in connection with the issuance of a government bond.

In principle, these relationships describe the functioning of most modern monetary systems very well, even if it appears on the surface as though states are dependent on money from private financial markets. The only real problem with the story we have sketched out here is the assumption that central banks are always executive agents of their governments.

In the crisis surrounding Greece in the first half of the 2010s, it became clear that central banks could, under special circumstances, force politicians to carry out pro-market "reforms" by threatening to cut off a country's money supply. An action of this nature by a central bank against its government is a clear violation of the Central Bank's mandate to support state economic policy. Since the ECB was the central bank responsible for Greece (one of the member states of the euro monetary union), this undoubtedly also applies to the ECB's actions during the Greek crisis in June 2015. There are some indications that the ECB has since recognised that it had thoroughly misunderstood its mandate in this case.

Money is therefore, very much as Georg Friedrich Knapp wrote in his 1923 book *State Theory of Money*, a means of state control, whose acceptance as a means of payment is based on the ability of a state to enforce tax payments in its currency. Once this is recognised, it becomes obvious that the central element of a new monetary order must be to enable the state to generate money under clearly defined conditions.

Central bank financing and inflation

Bundesbank President Jens Weidmann does not deny that a state is in principle free to "refinance" its expenditure via the central bank, and is therefore not dependent on tax revenues or refinancing via the financial market. However, he claims that inflation (or even hyperinflation) would result, and thus severe economic damage, perhaps even an economic collapse. To justify this claim, he quotes Goethe's Faust as follows: "Such a paper, in gold and pearls' stead, is so convenient; you know what you have. You do not have to go to market first, nor to trade; you can get drunk as you please on love and wine." (Weidmann, 2012)

Goethe, as quoted by Weidmann, thus considers the creation of money by the state to be problematic, because the state, unlike private individuals, does not first have to have provided a service in order to be able to get money in its hands. Unlike everyone else, once it has made a pact with the devil, the state can consume without having produced beforehand.

This is a monetarist argument. Public-choice theorists such as economics Nobel Laureate James Buchanan would add that precisely because the financial conduct of democratically elected governments is not subject to market discipline, inflation is to be expected. Politicians who want to be elected must align their policies with the interests of the median voter. Their policies will therefore always aim to increase the income of this category of voter, and they will react to the associated inflationary effects with further measures to increase income. This is how James Buchanan and Richard Wagner sum up the consequences of such a policy:

> Inflation destroys expectations and creates uncertainty; it increases the sense of felt injustice and causes alienation. It prompts behavioral responses that reflect a generalised shortening of time horizons. "Enjoy, enjoy" — the

imperative of our time — becomes a rational response in a setting where tomorrow remains insecure and where the plans made yesterday seem to have been made in folly. (Buchanan & Wagner, 1977)

Now it must be admitted that an abuse of state money creation certainly cannot be ruled out. However, there is no reason to adopt the extremely pessimistic worldview of public-choice theorists, according to which all people and thus all politicians and administrative staff are ruthless and selfish. Moreover, the fact that a state is allowed to create money for democratically legitimate expenditures does not mean that no institutional precautions need to be taken to prevent abuse. For example, one could demand that the state's money creation prerogative may only be used for productive or investment purposes and that the expenditure of the state must be monitored by specified oversight organisations (in Germany, for example, the Federal Audit Office).

The real question is whether central bank financing of public expenditures is more likely or less likely to be abused, and inflation is thereby more likely or less likely to be generated, than by having profit-oriented commercial banks make money available to the state through loans.

This question is answered in the affirmative by the majority of economists: In order not to get into a dangerous situation, they say, a lender must carefully examine the creditworthiness of potential borrowers and secure itself against default risk by putting a lien on an appropriate value of a borrower's assets. While banks have an interest in granting as many loans as possible in order to achieve the highest possible profits, fear of losing their hard-earned earnings is incentive enough to grant only those loans whose service can be assessed as appropriately secured.

However, this risk assessment does not apply to governments, as we have shown above, because there is no default risk — at least not if the government has a functioning central bank. The European Treaties (more precisely: Section 123 of the Lisbon Treaty) therefore prohibit member states of the euro area from "refinancing" government expenditure via the central bank. Corresponding regulations can be found in other currency areas as well.

And yet government bonds are nevertheless routinely encountered as assets in the balance sheets of their respective central banks. This shows that there are quite obviously ways and means that do allow countries to ensure the "refinancing" of their state budgets through central bank balance sheets. Whether and to what extent a particular state can finance itself through its central bank is primarily determined by the extent to which legal regulations allow a central bank to take government bonds onto its balance sheet, and whether and to what extent governments can influence the corresponding decisions of "their" central bank.

There is an additional connection that is easily overlooked. The central bank always controls the interest rate at which commercial banks can borrow reserves, and every day, it supplies whatever amount of money its borrowers demand at that rate. But even if it is completely independent of the rest of government, the central bank cannot prevent the state Treasury from raising as much money on the capital market at that interest rate as the Treasury deems appropriate. If the central bank has had to cut interest rates to zero because there is too little demand on the capital market, as is currently the case, then the state can finance itself on terms that are very nearly as favourable as would be the case with direct central bank financing.

The separation of central bank and fiscal policy is then only of a formal nature; the two policy areas substantially merge. This is obvious to everyone in light of the recently common practice of "quantitative easing," or QE, a jargon term that denotes a programme of central bank purchases of large quantities of government bonds and other long-term securities. In carrying out QE, the central bank buys these bonds and securities from secondary financial markets, not directly from their issuers, i.e. it does not buy government bonds directly from the government Treasury. But that makes little real difference, in net effect, compared to a scenario in which the central bank would buy bonds directly from the Treasury.

Some of these government bonds are purchased by the central bank from commercial banks. And commercial banks, as we have seen, can buy government bonds from the Treasury without first needing to collect any money from depositors or investors to do so; these purchases are a simple balance-sheet operation, a swap in which newly created commercial bank money is traded for newly created government bonds.

It follows from this that in an environment when central banks are running large-scale QE programmes, banks have no real selection task in financing government operations, since they know their government bond-holdings can be sold to the central bank, whose liquidity is unbounded. (Unlike commercial banks, a central bank cannot formally go bankrupt; its balance sheet is indefinitely flexible.) At high interest rates, however, commercial banks receive a subsidy through this process that has no functional purpose: Simply for carrying out a risk-free balance-sheet operation, they gain massive profits. This unheard-of privilege can only be justified, if at all, by observing that by playing their part in this charade, they are carrying out tasks that are essentially part of the machinery of sovereign governance.

Constellations thus arise in interest rate management by the central bank where, due to unorthodox measures like QE, *de facto* direct public finance of government operations occurs even though fiscal and monetary policy are formally separated. Such constellations can, as Japan's decades-long QE programme shows, last for decades without generating consumer price inflation. Japan's example demonstrates that the whole discourse about the alleged hyperinflationary dangers of central bank financing of government operations is extremely dogmatic and disconnected from empirical reality, and misses the point.

In fact, due to the deep structural connections between the balance sheets of the central bank and the Treasury, the state always has the financial resources available that would enable it to set up a state job-creation programme to combat recession and unemployment, even to the extent of providing an iron-clad job guarantee as "employer of last resort." There is no reason to expect that such a programme would lead to inflation, nor that other principles would be thrown overboard that have not already been thrown overboard long ago anyway.

Disciplining the state through the markets?

Economic liberalism claims that the efficient allocation of money requires that all those who need money should only receive it via the market, and thus submit to "market discipline." States, in this view, should be no exception; an "anonymous financial market" should gauge the creditworthiness of a national government and decide whether, and on what terms (at what interest rate), a loan to the government can be justified. Words to this effect were written by the German Council of Economic Experts in its special report of 2015 entitled "Consequences of the Greek crisis for a more stable euro area" (Bofinger *et al.*, 2015, p. 14).

German Chancellor Angela Merkel had the dubious honour of already having expressed, in remarks at a CDU party conference in Stuttgart in 2009, the theory that state debt creation had been the root cause of the recent capers of the financial markets:

> Suddenly one reads everywhere [explanations of] why the financial markets were on the brink of collapse, even [explanations written by] those who had previously recommended investments they themselves did not understand. But it is actually quite simple. Here in Stuttgart, in Baden-Württemberg, one could simply have asked a Swabian housewife. She would have told us a wisdom that is as short as it is true, which is that you cannot live beyond your means in the long run. This is the heart of the crisis. (Quoted from Polster, 2014, p. 32)

In 2009, the German government followed up this analysis of the reasons for the financial crisis of 2008 with a law prohibiting Germany from taking out new loans to finance its expenditures, effective from 2016. A large majority — 68.3 percent — of all members of the Bundestag voted for this measure, which was not formulated as an ordinary law, but rather as an amendment to the Basic Law (the German Constitution). Only the Left Party faction had fundamental reservations. Otherwise, all parties considered a constitutional amendment to limit state debts to be good policy.

Figure 21 has already shown that the long-term yields on government bonds of Germany, France, Greece, Spain, and Portugal were close together even at the height of the financial crisis in 2008. So what explains why they diverged so noticeably starting in late 2009, and then moved towards each other again since 2012 — with the exception of Greece? The answer to this question seems very simple to the German Council of Economic Experts: "The financial markets' doubts about the solvency of the crisis countries were expressed in sharply rising risk premiums for government bonds. This was followed by a self-reinforcing process of rising debt, waning confidence, and increasing risk premiums." (*Ibid.*, p. 16)

This is the story told by German market fundamentalists. However, it has nothing to do with reality, although the course of interest rates over the first few years since 2009 does seem to suggest such an interpretation (Figure 25).

In reality, the sharp rise in interest rates in some countries of the monetary union is solely due to the fact that the ECB chose not to behave as would

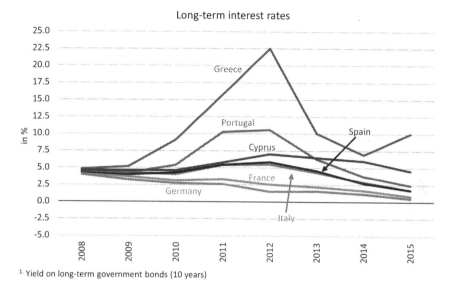

Figure 25:   Long-term interest rates

Source: AMECO, Financial Times, OECD.

normally be expected of the central bank of a sovereign state. A European Central Bank whose leaders had understood its core mission as serving as the guardian of the integrity of the monetary area would not have hesitated for a second and, by intervening directly in the bond markets, would have ensured that the interest rates on government bonds did not diverge, regardless of which member state issued them.

But even within the governing councils of the ECB, voices were heard at the time expressing concern that Greece might withdraw from the monetary union, and at the EU summit of 11 December 2009, it was proclaimed that the ECB would not use the ECB's balance sheet to "help" Greece by buying up Greek government bonds on secondary markets in amounts sufficient to reassure financial markets. This policy was a blatant failure on the part of politicians and those responsible for the ECB under its then President Jean-Claude Trichet. A currency crisis was thus turned into a sovereign debt crisis.

But how exactly does the "discipline of the market" come into play on government bond markets? If this discipline actually exists, it should be

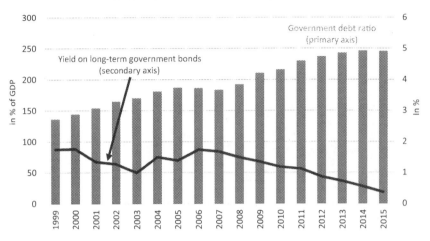

Figure 26:   Government debt and interest rates in Japan

Source: AMECO.

possible to show that rising government debt ratios are systematically accompanied by higher yields on government bonds. Well, do they? To answer this question, let us look at the evolution of Japan's government debt ratio. Japan is the country with the highest government debt ratio in the world. Figure 26 shows the yields on Japanese government bonds between 1999 and 2015.

From a neoclassical monetary theory perspective, Japan is a country that cannot exist. Contrary to what would have been expected on the basis of this theory, yields on government bonds have not risen with the sharp rise in Japan's public debt ratio — they have fallen throughout! Yields on Spanish government bonds also appear to have little to do with the Spanish government's debt ratio, as shown in Figure 27. We see that a sharp rise in Spain's public debt ratio was accompanied by a sharp decline in yields from 2013 onward.

The explanation for these phenomena is very simple. In 2012, Mario Draghi, who had taken over the presidency of the ECB after Trichet retired in 2011, made it clear to the public that from now on the ECB would act like a normal central bank and protect its member states from insolvency: "Within our mandate, the ECB is ready to do whatever it takes to preserve the euro. And believe me, it will be enough." (Draghi, 2012)

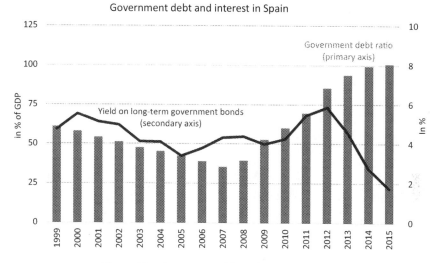

Figure 27:   Government debt and interest in Spain

Source: AMECO.

And lo and behold, the interest rates charged by bond markets on the bonds of most of the euro currency areas' member states converged again shortly thereafter. What had been called a sovereign debt crisis was actually, on closer inspection, a crisis of the euro currency order. The lesson is clear: Anyone concerned about financial market stability in the Eurozone must demand a reform of the rules of EMU that gives the financial markets certainty that the central bank will always ensure that government bonds of "its" countries are always serviced.

Insolvency regime for states?

However, market fundamentalists — and such are the majority of the members of Germany's Council of Economic Experts — cannot tolerate such a monetary order. They want to degrade states to mere market players, and therefore reject the "privileged treatment of government bonds in banking regulation." Instead, they have called for an "insolvency regime for states" (Bofinger *et al.*, 2015, p. 31) to ensure that states, no differently than any private household or corporation, are forced into a "sound" budget policy by means of "appropriate risk premia" (Bofinger *et al.*, 2015, p. 15).

In order to make it unmistakably clear to the financial markets that the euro is a monetary order in which the "guiding principle of liability and control" is relevant for the states involved (Bofinger *et al.*, 2015, p. 2), the markets have been taught a lesson through the cases of Greece and Cyprus that continues to be regarded as exemplary by our economic experts: "In the event of excessive debt or gross violation of fiscal rules, an ESM adjustment programme should only be approved after a haircut [partial write-down of the relevant government bond assets] for private creditors." (Bofinger *et al.*, 2015, p. 2)

In other words, for the financial markets to be motivated to actually exercise their "disciplining function" (Bofinger *et al.*, 2015, p. 8), they have to lose money on dodgy assets from time to time. In the case of Greece, therefore, when its government was faced with an inability to refinance its debt obligations in 2011, private creditors were forced to write off a portion of the value of the Greek government bond portfolio they owned. In the case of Cyprus, in addition to shareholders and bondholders, even savers with large deposits in two bankruptcy-threatened Cypriot commercial banks were indirectly forced to take a "haircut" in the form of a "bail-in," in which part of the deposits of depositors with holdings of more than €100,000 in those two banks were forced to trade deposits for equity in a recapitalised merged bank. Eurogroup leader Jeroen Dijsselbloem even spoke of the rescue of the Cyprus banks as a blueprint for the European rescue mechanism.

In addition, the "rescue" of states and their banks will not be left to the ECB, but instead has been entrusted to special purpose vehicles such as the so-called European Stability Mechanism (ESM), which are dependent on guarantees from EU states for their refinancing on the financial market. The establishment of this "crisis mechanism" has ensured that national governments, and not the central bank, will decide whether and under what conditions a Eurozone member state can benefit from a financial "aid package."

Against this background, it comes as no surprise that the financial markets are concerned about the solvency of some members of the European Monetary Union. As Council of Experts member Peter Bofinger rightly says in his minority report, the members of a monetary order committed to the "guiding principle of unity of liability and control" find themselves in a situation that is otherwise only known to emerging countries "unable to borrow in their own currency." (Bofinger *et al.*, 2015, p. 43)

If the economic wise men's proposals to include "appropriate risk premiums" in government bonds were to be adopted, the yields on long-term government bonds of the euro countries would certainly differ. But since this yield is the basis on which banks set interest rate for long-term corporate financing, companies would have to pay different financing costs depending on which Member State they are domiciled in. This contradicts the basic idea of a single internal market. After all, in an internal market, the success of companies should only depend on their ability to sell their products and services profitably in competition with others, based on quality and finance; they should not face differential financing costs based simply on the criterion of which side of an internal European national territorial demarcation they find themselves on. The political framework conditions should be largely comparable for all companies within the Eurozone.

If the political framework conditions — such as taxation and the wage regime, but also the refinancing conditions — substantially differ, even as the movements of goods, services, persons, and capital are largely free of restrictions, then one should speak of a free trade zone, not an internal market. Under such conditions, competition between companies is substituted by a location competition, which will be won by the jurisdiction that offers the easiest conditions for companies to make a profit. Such competitions necessarily lead to a race to the bottom, not to prosperity for all. Consequently, such a free trade area would require national currencies and flexible exchange rates.

The ECB's policy of recent years must be interpreted as an important contribution against the "competition of nations" desired by market fundamentalists and deserves the support of all those who have an interest in the development of a Europe based on solidarity and the common good. To see this requires more than merely good will; it requires a recognition that we have to say goodbye to neoliberal regulatory dogmas and ideological assumptions that obscure our view of reality.

The European Crisis is not a "Sovereign Debt Crisis"

There is one thing the liberals must be credited with: They have great reflexes. Immediately after the onset of the grand crisis of private financial capital in 2008 and the euro crisis that resulted, the neoliberal mainstream and its cheerleading media succeeded in reinterpreting the private crisis as a crisis of public debt. The states had rescued the private debtors by taking huge amounts of private debt onto the public balance sheets by rescuing banks. How was this fact interpreted? A sovereign debt crisis was diagnosed, and the banks' reckless gambling was exculpated. The neoliberals succeeded in changing the channel.

Even the European crisis, which is undoubtedly a crisis of competitiveness for which Germany clearly bears a large share of the blame, was immediately characterised by interested parties, including such institutions as the Deutsche Bundesbank, as an expression of a sovereign debt crisis. Greece was a waterfall on the millwheels of the neoliberals because it "proved" that it was a misconduct of the state, and only the state, that had led to the crisis in the Eurozone.

This misdiagnosis, which the neoliberals came up with in order to impose their agenda on Europe, has serious consequences for European economies. An unbearably long recession, high levels of unemployment, and high cumulative income losses have resulted from the successful efforts of those who quickly and resolutely spread the false narrative that Europe's core economic problem was a public debt crisis. Austerity policy became a hallmark of the bitter medicine administered by the Eurogroup (the group of European finance ministers) under German leadership, and this medicine was poison from the very beginning.

Some critics of neoliberalism conclude from the European crisis that it was not so much the misconduct of one or more countries that was to blame for the crisis but rather the European Monetary Union as such was not suitable for uniting the Eurozone's very different countries and economies. If the countries had only had greater autonomy, they could have taken countermeasures in terms of economic policy.

However, with open borders for goods and capital, there can be no Isle of the Blessed, and there is no monetary policy method available that can serve to completely isolate a country from events in the rest of the world. It is probably one of this century's greatest errors of economics to have, for a long time, given politicians the idea that national sovereignty in economic policy could be achieved, if only a currency system were installed that would "flexibly" absorb all external shocks. But this cannot be the case, because real currency systems cannot even properly compensate for mere monetary disturbances in a relatively friction-free manner, to say nothing of real-economy shocks, as we will show later.

The loss of national or regional economic sovereignty is not primarily the result of an unsuitable currency system. It is essentially the result of the fact that almost every country in the world has opted for open markets and borders for goods and financial capital. Given this context, well-wrought economic policy can merely shape the way in which crises can be addressed and effectively combated, or in the best case, avoided. Since changes in real exchange rates upwards and downwards — or resulting unsustainable interest rate constellations — regularly play a central role in crisis-like escalations, let us begin our examination of policy options here.

One type of intervention consists in establishing "revaluation bands" for exchange rates. These exclusively serve the single central objective of keeping the real exchange rate (i.e. the competitive positions between countries) more or less constant over longer time periods. Nominal devaluations and revaluations of constituent currencies can be made at certain intervals, either on a discretionary basis or in accordance with agreed rules; but these revaluations must reflect accumulated differences in inflation and unit labour costs.

Any country that decides in favour of absolutely fixed exchange rates, or in the extreme case for joining a monetary union, binds its own hands in many respects ("to tie your own hands" was a slogan that was very popular in Austria in the 1970s), and hopes in so doing to largely avoid the caprices of international capital markets by connecting to a large partner with whom an economic policy approach is broadly shared. This may be an absolutely rational strategy, as long as everyone involved keeps the implicit promises on which such a system is based. What went wrong in EMU was exactly this: Those implicit promises were not kept.

Fixed exchange rates and firm promises

Even 10 years after the crisis began, the connections between Germany's current account surpluses and the problems in European monetary union are still barely understood, or are simply ignored. Let us now look at the situation in EMU again, in a slightly different way.

Not even liberals deny that the idea of "competition" normally refers to competition between companies. And they want to do everything in their

194 Failed Globalisation: Inequality, Money, and the Renaissance of the State

power to ensure that competition between companies is fair. Companies should prove themselves in competition, and the best company should be able to assert itself and be successful under otherwise equal conditions (including, first and foremost, equal pay for equal work) through efforts to improve productivity in production processes or quality of goods and services produced.

At the same time, however, liberals are generally in favour of competition between nations. This is strange and contradictory, because competition between companies is naturally distorted when, for reasons that have nothing to do with the individual company, a country gives all its companies an advantage.

The specific type of advantage does not play a major role here — what matters is that this creates a systemic distortion: the playing field is no longer level. This can result when one country imposes import duties, or cuts taxes on its companies particularly sharply, or pays its companies high subsidies. It can result when a country's currency is undervalued.

It can also result when a country which is a member in a multi-country system of fixed exchange rates (or in a monetary union) implements a years-long national wage-restraint policy, leading wages in all its domestic enterprises to rise less (in relation to productivity) than in the countries with which it has agreed on a fixed exchange rate. This leads to a systemic competitive advantage for all of the country's enterprises, which systematically harms the competitors in the partner countries, regardless of whether they are good or bad enterprises in any company-specific dimension.

It was undisputed for many decades that other countries were of course allowed to defend themselves against these artificial advantages, and protect their companies from the associated disadvantages. It is therefore permitted (according to the rules of the World Trade Organisation) for a country to impose tariffs, devalue its own currency, or initiate dumping proceedings against countries that take measures such as those listed above, i.e. countries that have sought to obtain an unfair advantage for their domestic companies by tilting the competitive playing-field. Getting into a race to the bottom by applying downward national policy pressure on the wages of one's own workers, to compensate for the foreign wage advantage in systems of fixed exchange rates, is among the defensive options.

In the past, the simplest method was often currency devaluation. If a country got into a balance of payments crisis, i.e. was in danger of no longer being able to pay its own imports without having to accept large interest premiums on the capital market, the solution was usually sought in a devaluation. This occurred in the contexts both of flexible exchange rates and adaptable exchange rates (as in the Bretton Woods system or the European Monetary System, EMS for short). A devaluation reduced imports and strengthened exports, and thus reduced the devaluing currency area's dependence on the capital market.

Fixed exchange rates are, in essence, an implicit promise of the participating national trading partners among themselves to refrain from undercutting the others, through whatever tactic, in any way that would make an exchange rate adjustment necessary. Obviously, the stronger the link between exchange rates, the stronger the trading partners' promise of non-undercutting must be for the system to be able to hold together.

Germany has chosen to underbid its partners in the European Monetary Union by mercantilist measures, in the form of its belt-tightening and national wage-restraint policies (cf. Flassbeck, 2013b). In doing so, it broke the promise inherent in the agreement to enter into monetary union. If the EMU Treaty contracts had been reasonably constructed, the trading partners would no longer have to abide by the treaty's free trade requirements and would be allowed to impose import duties on German products and services to compensate for German wage dumping.

But the European treaties were not reasonably constructed. The European Commission's competition bureau takes vigorous measures, including legal actions before the European Court of Justice, in cases where it deems states have distorted competition by favouring a single company. For example, if Volkswagen receives a subsidy from the state, whether in the form of a discount on a plot of state-owned land or an implicit state guarantee of survival in the form of a state taking an equity stake in the company through share ownership, the Commission suspects a distortion of competition to the detriment of other car-manufacturing companies in the EU and demands compensation or an end to the subsidy.

But if a country benefits all its companies through tax cuts or wage pressure, this falls under the rubric of "competition between nations" or "national tax policy sovereignty," and the Commission does nothing. Yet such a lump-sum subsidy in Germany can distort a French company's situation *vis-à-vis* its German competitors in exactly the same way as an individual subsidy. Overall, however, the damage is much greater than with a single subsidy, because all French companies now suffer from system-level German dumping. Absent the European treaties, France could bring dumping proceedings against Germany before the World Trade Organisation with a great prospect of success. Alternatively, if France were joined with Germany in a managed system of currencies that would allow the French currency to depreciate somewhat without major distortions, the problem could also be easily solved.

This argument shows that the issue is not whether a nation is hard-working or productive. Each nation can be as productive as it wants or is able to be. However, no nation may deliberately live below its means (i.e. at a living-standard below the possibilities created by its productivity), because otherwise it deprives other nations of the opportunity to adapt to their own conditions and to enjoy the full fruits of their own productivity. Since it would be extremely foolish for all nations to try to engage in a race-to-the-bottom competition in which all of them live below their means just because one nation does so, we collectively need compensatory mechanisms of the kind described above (i.e. customs duties, currency devaluations, or criminal proceedings) so that trading-partners can defend themselves against troublemakers.

Some will object and say that competition between nations must not simply be ruled out. But yes — it must. It must, because competition between nations is actually anti-competitive at the microeconomic level, i.e. between firms, and it systematically causes nations to live below their means. As we have already shown above, the idea of a "competition of nations" is certainly one of the stupidest ideas of all time, because nations should rigorously avoid doing exactly what we likewise expect companies that compete with each other to refrain from doing.

We believe that competition between companies makes sense because we assume that companies, or the people behind them, are inventive and innovative precisely when they are *not* given the opportunity to outdo their competitors with illegal tricks, tax evasion, bribery, or the primitive blackmail of their employees. If you do not do any of this and still succeed because you make a new discovery or develop a new product, we pay homage to you as a great entrepreneur.

It is not innovative for one state to lower taxes and force all other states to do the same. This is exactly analogous to one of those cheap tricks that we rightly scourge as abuse in business competition. When the state puts pressure on unions to accept wage settlements below the rate of productivity improvement, with the intent of underbidding neighbouring countries, this is just as little an innovation at the state level as it is at the business level. Nations invent nothing. They have no ideas; they are not capable of developing new products or implementing new production processes. Precisely because we want to leave these activities largely to companies in a market economy, a state which is a member of a multi-state free trade agreement must not be allowed to favour a certain group of companies through blanket cost reductions. If it does so, other states must be able to defend themselves against this unfair, competition-distorting behaviour with measures that must be left entirely in the defending states' hands.

These simple principles have been thrown overboard in the EU as a result of the neoliberal revolution. Perhaps we could live with it as long as it was only small states such as the Netherlands, Finland, or Ireland that violated these principles. But now that the biggest state in the Union is doing so too, the fact that the European institutions long ignored the smaller states' competitive policy malfeasance is generating a bitter harvest. Now the problem can no longer be ignored, because the economic effects in the states neighbouring neomercantilist Germany are enormous.

But instead of at least diagnosing the problem openly and calling out these dysfunctional developments, the EU Commission is hiding behind the mercantilist state and calling on everyone else to emulate Germany's policies. This cannot go well, and it is not going well. Deflation and recession in the Eurozone are clear evidence of this. The fact that several states, including the Eurozone's largest, have broken their promise to refrain from undercutting competition through various forms of dumping, requires the reintroduction of flexible exchange rates or the end of free trade. Holding on to fixed exchange rates, defending free trade, and ignoring the broken promise, as at present, essentially will amount to stubbornly holding a match to the fuse of a European powder keg until it explodes.

Currency relations must not be left to the market

Acute currency crises have occurred repeatedly in recent economic history. The clearest proof that neoliberal globalisation has failed can be found here. Nevertheless, these crises were and are ignored by the prevailing doctrine in economics. Politicians, for their part, ignore them because some people make a great deal of money from currency speculation, and lobbyists representing banks and hedge funds have successfully defended the speculators' lucrative perks.

The basic pattern of these crises is always the same, and easy to understand: If countries with different inflation and unit labour cost trends completely open their borders to goods and capital, crisis-like consequences for the money and currency system can hardly be avoided, regardless of the details of the monetary system involved. This can be illustrated as follows: Country A, which has an annual increase in unit labour costs and an inflation rate of 10 percent, opens its borders to Country B, which has unit labour cost increases and an inflation rate of 2 percent. Let us assume that in order to enable domestic investments and a strong expansion of domestic demand, Country A imposes a nominal interest rate of 12 percent (i.e. a real interest rate of 2 percent). Assume further that Country B keeps the nominal interest rate at 4 percent in order to achieve the same real interest rate. Country A therefore offers a nominal interest rate of 12 percent, and Country B a nominal interest rate of only 4 percent.

For managers of financial capital seeking short-term returns on purely financial instruments in another country (e.g. bonds), it is not the real interest rate but the nominal interest rate that is relevant, because there is no intention of buying any goods or production facilities. At 12 percent, Country A offers a much more attractive interest rate than Country B with 4 percent. This attracts investment money to A and tendentially leads to an increase in currency A's exchange rate valuation.

Now that the borders between Countries A and B are open to trade and financial flows, in order to maintain its competitiveness, i.e. to compensate for the difference in unit labour costs and inflation and to avoid real appreciation, Country A's currency would have to depreciate by 8 percent in each time period in order to offset the interest rate difference. That is because given its higher rate of inflation, Country A's goods and services will increase in price in terms of foreign currencies unless A's currency devalues at precisely the same rate that the prices (in domestic currency) of its goods and services increase.

But if, instead, the foreign financial capital inflow stimulated by Country A's high nominal interest rates leads to a nominal appreciation in

A's currency in the short term, or even if currency A merely remains nominally constant, Country A quickly loses international competitiveness, because the prices of its goods and services (as measured in foreign currencies) increase in real terms. As a result, sooner or later, a currency crisis is inevitable.

The "solution" offered in the neoclassical economic literature to this problem, i.e. the problem of differential inflation rates between countries with free trade and flexible exchange rates, is unfortunately — as so often — irrelevant. The theorists simply assume "purchasing power parity" in any given period (i.e. the expectation that exchange rate movements always and immediately exactly compensate for inflation rate differences). This theory is built into the minds of most forex traders, who tend to be adherents of the so-called "rational expectations" dogma. If the purchasing power parity hypothesis is true, then the problem described above does not exist, because then the expected exchange rate movement (w^*), which in our case is an expected devaluation, always corresponds to the interest rate difference ($i\text{A}-i\text{B}$) and the inflation rate difference ($p\text{A}-p\text{B}$), so that internal and external equilibrium is always guaranteed in both countries:

$$(w^*) = (i\text{A}-i\text{B}) = (p\text{A}-p\text{B})$$

Unfortunately, ugly reality once again intrudes to kill a beautifully simple theory. If one recognises that the interest rate differential, i.e. the wide-open gap in interest rates available in Countries A and B, tends to be of greater importance to currency traders' short-term decisions than the purely fictitious purchasing power parity concept, there is no solution to the dilemma, because exchange rate movements will not, in fact, precisely offset and compensate for inflation rate differentials between A and B.

Politically, the way into a resulting currency crisis is paved primarily by the fact that the governments and central banks of countries in the position of Country A tend to be inordinately proud of the "stability" of their currency in the short term, and fail to take into account the negative consequences of this stability, which are inevitable in the longer term.

Durable solutions to this conundrum can only be found by intervening in the free movement of capital in the broadest sense (i.e. by imposing controls on the movement of financial capital across national borders), or by fully aligning inflation and unit labour cost trends between the countries involved. There are no hands-off shortcuts available that would solve the problem automatically.

The exchange rate and real shocks

Europe's monetary crisis provokes the question of whether the exchange rate can be used at all as an instrument of economic policy, and if so, in what way. Even after more than 50 years of intensive discussions, no satisfactory answer has emerged. Economists on the monetarist side of the debate tend to regard the exchange rate as a crucial anchor price, whose determination by free-market trading is necessary in principle for the successful functioning of a money economy, which of course makes state manipulation of, or even just state influence on, this "price of two monies" problematic *a priori*.

Such considerations can be easily accentuated and illustrated by the question of how to assess the formation of European monetary union, which *ex definitionem* excludes the exchange rate as an instrument.

Right from the start, many economists were very sceptical about the European Monetary Union because, in their view, the politicians, who had been given poor economic and political advice, had only launched the euro-money supertanker for "political" reasons. The economies (especially the labour markets) of most participating countries are far too inflexible to get along without the exchange rate acting as a "shock absorber," they said. Only a flexible, or at least adaptable, exchange-rate course could allow the consequences of so-called asymmetric shocks to be absorbed without undue economic dislocation. (Examples of asymmetric shocks might be, for example, an earthquake in just one member state, or a political quake like the unification of East and West Germany after the fall of the Berlin Wall.)

However, as soon as one thinks about this thesis in more concrete terms, doubts arise. Is the exchange rate — that is, a depreciation or appreciation of a country's currency — really an efficient tool of economic policy, as a large number of economists from all theoretical schools continue to believe?

Let us consider a simple case: An earthquake devastates large parts of a country's real capital stock (factories, etc.). Absent outside help, the real income of this country must fall in consequence. A largely frictionless adjustment to this shock appears possible if all sections of the population easily accept the inevitable loss of real income the earthquake entails. This would be the case, for example, if workers accepted the one-off price increase following the shock without reacting to it with higher nominal wage claims against the state and companies. Inflexible, rigid nominal wages lead in this case to a high flexibility of real wages (wages in relation to prices).

A problem undoubtedly arises for the country concerned when nominal wages are flexible and real wages are rigid, which means that workers can demand and enforce compensation for the price increase caused by the earthquake. In this case, either profits will fall, which has an additional negative impact on investment activity and the number of jobs, or companies will be able to pass through excessive wage demands by raising prices, in the context of an accommodative monetary policy. Under the latter circumstance, the one-off price increase will become a real, probably permanent inflation.

Those who talk about inflexible, encrusted labour markets in Europe apparently have the latter case in mind. They postulate a resulting need for an exchange rate buffer. But would a devaluation of the currency in the wake of the earthquake have the desired effect? We are assuming that workers in our hypothetical earthquake-ravaged country are not prepared to accept the inevitable loss of real income for society as a whole. However, according to exchange rate theorists, the same workers will readily accept a currency devaluation which — due to declining terms of trade — itself represents nothing other than an additional loss of real income.

If this thesis is false, i.e. if the earthquake zone's economic subjects do not distinguish between earthquake-caused and devaluation-related price increases and refuse to accept a loss of their purchasing power in either case, then given an accommodative monetary policy, after the devaluation, the rate of inflation will actually rise more strongly (because workers will demand and get further wage rises, without having increased their productivity to justify this). With inflation rising faster, the eventual need for a restrictive monetary policy will become all the greater.

At the end of the day, the currency of the earthquake-devastated country will sooner or later depreciate if real wages are inflexible after the quake. Yet the devaluation does not serve as a "buffer" for the real shock (the consequences of the earthquake); at best, it compensates for the negative secondary effects of the shock (i.e. a further increase in inflation and a deterioration in the country's international competitive position).

With its thesis that the exchange rate serves as a buffer for real shocks, economics has incorporated a strange inconsistency into its system of statements. On the one hand, it has rightly stated that economic policy cannot operate in an environment of continual significant downward changes in the value of money over time, i.e. with inflation, without economic agents losing the "money illusion" and adjusting their nominal claims to the rising inflation rate. On the other hand, many economists regard changes in monetary value over geographic space, i.e. changes in exchange rates, as a tool of economic policy that can be used at any time, without acknowledging that economic subjects will of course eventually see through this specific form of money illusion as well, and thus completely deprive it of its effect.

A reduction in the external value of money (i.e. devaluation) is no more a suitable tool of economic policy than a reduction in the internal value of money (i.e. inflation), in the long term. Changes in exchange rates cannot be a "buffer" for real shocks any more than can changes in the inflation rate. Earlier generations of economists were aware of this, but somehow, late in the 20th century, it seems to have been forgotten. Knut Wicksell, one of the great innovators, wrote at the beginning of the 20th century that "a stable value of money in time as well as in space" was the central prerequisite for a functioning market economy (see Wicksell, 1958). Most conservative economists today are firmly convinced that stable money is a crucial prerequisite for efficient economic activity, but are only concerned with safeguarding price stability. They explicitly reject a stabilisation of money's external value (i.e. its value in relation to other currencies).

According to Wicksell's logic, the only function that exchange rate shifts can have is to compensate for general price inflation rate differences, or differences in the rate of change in unit labour costs, between countries. Currency devaluation applies especially to countries that are not (yet) in a position to limit the internal devaluation of money as well as Europe or the USA manages to do. Exchange rate adjustments can be used to prevent fundamental imbalances in trade arising, because through adjustments of the nominal exchange rate, the real exchange rate remains constant, and all countries involved maintain their competitiveness. In the past, flexible exchange rates guaranteed this outcome very poorly in the short term, but tolerably well in the longer term.

It also follows from Wicksell's logic that the "Asian and Latin American model of the early 1990s," which sought to import price stability by fixing the exchange rate with the US dollar, bore the seeds of the currency crisis in those regions, because a real appreciation of local currencies was inevitable in the countries concerned. The many and diverse experiences with such models in the run-up to European monetary union has shown that controlled flexibility of the nominal exchange rate can ultimately be a successful tool if the potential currency-devaluing countries eventually succeed in stabilising their currencies' internal monetary value on their own.

V

Modern Economic Policy and the Role of the State

On the previous pages, we have fundamentally questioned the dominant neoliberal economic and social theory and the zeitgeist associated with it. It is now time to draw economic policy conclusions from our analysis of the current economic, political, and social malaise. After all, anyone who claims to have a valid economic theory, as we do, must be able to propose effective therapies for the many social and economic problems diagnosed.

So what should we do if we think that a desirable state of affairs is a society that is as open as possible inside and as borderless as possible to the outside? It should have become clear in the course of this text that the realisation of this progressive project cannot rely on spontaneous self-organisation. The state has a central role to play in organising and activating the abilities of social actors in the service of optimising the common good.

However, we are a very long distance apart from those who favour a state-planned economy. Rather, we seek to combine the indisputable advantages of a decentralised and profit-oriented production of economic goods with intelligent state steering of the market. At the end of the day, the market and its players are not in a position to take macroeconomic requirements into account. That is necessarily the role of the state.

A clear-eyed and unbiased analysis, as we have tried to provide in this book, gives nation-states the task of managing economic activity in such a way as to enable the market economy to optimise the prosperity of all nations. For the state to take on this task with prospects of success, however, it is essential to say goodbye to a belief in the existence of self-regulated, self-guiding markets. Neither a labour market nor financial markets really exist in the true sense of the word "market." Nor can social welfare services essential for the cohesion of society be guaranteed via self-determining markets.

What are the Challenges of Globalisation in Economic Policy?

As we explained in Part I, there is no such thing as "globalisation" in the sense of a phenomenon that we can abstract from the great flow of economic development and analyse in isolation. It is of course possible to construct models in which certain parameters can be introduced, which in turn can be said to be characteristic of globalisation. However, there are no existing models in neoclassical economics that capture what we call economic dynamics. All static equilibrium models, or even dynamised static models, as conventionally used in so-called growth theory, are unsuitable from the outset to depict what is at stake.

Economic development always consists of an interplay of forces, such as those of globalisation and automation on the one hand and counter-reactions consisting of human action, including economic policies, on the other. Monetary, financial, wage, regional, and social policies, as well as the different mechanisms used by nationally organised economies to protect themselves against excessive externally generated economic shocks, are not foreign to the market economy system. They are an integral part of society's efforts to use the system for its own purposes. Anyone who talks about globalisation and automation without talking about economic policy is working from a fundamentally wrong premise.

In order to arrive at reasonable conclusions, one must radically detach oneself from the idea that there is a divine or natural order of some kind which independently controls or guides the coexistence of people, and whose smooth functioning and effectiveness is only disturbed, not enhanced, by actions aimed at shaping and controlling a historically evolved economic order. This ideology, reinvented by German Ordoliberalism after the Second World War and spread throughout the world by neoliberalism, claims a connection between market and state that has nothing to do with the reality of our money-based market economies.

The reality is that there is no such thing as a market whose development could be described and analysed without considering the state as a major player. This applies to the legal framework set by the state, to taxation and social systems, to the demand side of the economy, and especially to the monetary system. The conceptual separation of regulatory and procedural policy, another idea launched into the world by the German ordoliberals, is also to a large extent pure fiction.

Likewise, the cooperation of national economies in the globalised economy is governed by states and nobody else. Whether fixed or flexible exchange rates determine relations between the currencies of different economies, whether there are tariffs or other trade barriers, it is always the states, and not markets, that decide how and with what effects goods, capital, and people move across borders.

Financial markets, especially international ones, cannot regulate themselves, as naive neoclassical theory claims. More importantly, industrial relations do not follow the "laws" of neoclassical economics anywhere in the world. There can exist no functioning labour markets in the neoclassical sense because, as we have shown, there exist no independent supply and demand functions of "labour." In order for industrial relations to function properly, the state must continually play an active role in shaping these relations in a variety of ways.

International shocks and economic policy shocks

It can generally be assumed that most of what are often referred to as "international shocks" are price shocks — i.e. changes in important prices, which for a time develop in an unsustainable direction (mostly driven by speculation) and then collapse. As we have already said, the most frequent of these are exchange rate shocks. But there have also been commodity price shocks and property price shocks, most recently during the great crisis of 2008/09.

The second and quantitatively most important type of shock is directly caused by economic policy and is usually national (or limited to a currency area): Shocks arising from a restrictive monetary and fiscal policy. Restrictive monetary policy (or shock-like changes in policy) has usually occurred historically when policymakers significantly increased interest rates at a certain point in the economic cycle in order to reduce the risk of inflation. During the euro crisis, massively restrictive fiscal policy (austerity policy) was pursued on a grand scale. Also during the euro crisis, another type of shock was used to improve national competitiveness: Wage restraint shock, which led to an immediate drop in domestic demand, and thus to an increase in unemployment (Flassbeck & Bibow, 2018).

All these shocks overtax the adaptability of economic agents and in (almost) all cases lead to a reduction in aggregate demand, which cannot be offset by any other (endogenous) effects. The typical reaction of companies is to lay off workers, which further exacerbates the crisis, which continues until economic policy changes direction.

Globalisation and automation could in principle trigger such economic policy responses, but this does not often happen. The most striking example of a shock exacerbated by globalisation (through its impact on global markets and global economic policy) was the oil price explosion of the 1970s, which led to an excessive economic policy response and consequently to unemployment. In this case, however, as in almost every case, it was the rapid and sharp rise in unemployment that exogenously threw the system off its rails.

Flexible labour markets?

What is crucial when shocks occur is an appropriate economic policy response. Unfortunately, the most frequently discussed question in the currently dominant theory of economics in connection with globalisation and automation is whether existing mechanisms promoting "flexibility of the labour market" are sufficient to cushion the shocks emanating from these two processes, or whether there is a need for new policies specifically aimed at ensuring appropriate wage flexibility. So should wages in a certain industry, at a certain level of worker qualification, or in a severely affected region be induced to fall, if pressure comes to bear on domestic producers because foreign suppliers become cheaper?

The blanket answer is: No! In general, it is not appropriate to slow down such processes by countering them by reducing wages relative to the offshore competitors. Rationalisation and globalisation are usually irreversible, because new circumstances have permanently changed international and national price and cost structures, which means that anyone who opposes the trend is playing the role of King Canute, attempting to order the incoming tide to retreat. Once self-driving trucks have been successfully introduced, continuing to employ (i.e. pay salaries to) unneeded truck drivers makes little sense. Moreover, by embracing rather than resisting the incoming changes, it is almost always possible to find opportunities to be successful in some newly emerging economic niche, and thus increase overall economic income.

What is always required is the flexibility on the part of the workforce to give up their old jobs, retrain, and qualify for new ones. There is no need for wage flexibility. The famous wage flexibility that for some reason is usually expected only from lower-income workers does not help. If manufacturing production has migrated to a corporate subsidiary in a low-wage country where wages are only 20 percent of those in the high-wage country, it cannot be brought back "home" by reducing workers' wages in the company concerned by 10 percent in the home country. Indeed, attempting to impose such wage reductions would immediately lead workers to seek employment elsewhere in an otherwise fully employed economy.

The best form of support the state can provide in order to help with globalisation-related adjustments is to pursue a full employment policy, i.e. to ensure that there are certainly new jobs available for workers made redundant by offshoring. In the early 1970s, people in trade union circles seriously discussed pushing for full employment in the form of a state guarantee of every worker's job. But that would have been a mistake — such a policy is a direct path to a centrally planned economy. It makes no sense to want to guarantee the permanence of a specific job. What the state can easily guarantee in a market economy, however, is that everyone will be provided a new job if they lose a previous one due to structural changes.

Of course, there is also the possibility of facilitating the adjustment process for companies and workers negatively affected by rapid structural change by placing the workers in transitional measures or temporary employment companies, as was done in East Germany in the wake of the huge shock of German unification. However, in the absence of such unusually severe shocks, to run a successful full employment policy, it should suffice to offer retraining to workers. Given a full employment policy and a sufficiently strong social safety net to support people well during phases of unemployment, the amount of time an employee must spend unemployed is usually very short.

However, there are some economic sectors (or subsectors) that have special features that make it necessary for the state to intervene directly in economic processes. In agriculture, for example, there are areas such as milk and pork production where the elasticity of demand for their relatively homogeneous products is very high. This means that even very small supply surpluses can result in large price declines, which presents producers with insoluble financial problems without them having done anything wrong.

In such cases (cf. Flassbeck, 2016b), it makes sense for the state to intervene by acting as a "market maker," i.e. by establishing a regulated market to prevent extreme price fluctuations. This can happen far below the threshold where the state — as in the European agricultural market of the past — assumes full responsibility for farmers' incomes. Instead, the state can establish minimum price guarantees to secure farmers' basic solvency, and with it, the security that helps encourage and enable private investment even on the part of small farmers.

Creative destruction and full employment

In a society in which the state sees its everyday task as steering the macroeconomy towards full employment, problems arising from structural adjustment requirements (caused by new products, processes, or offshore competitors) are manageable. That said, even if shock-like changes can be largely excluded (or if the state is able to compensate for them quickly), adjustments at the level of individual employees and entrepreneurs are still unavoidable. They will not affect entire groups of employees, such as low-paid workers; they will generally affect individual companies or particular technical skills categories within the workforce.

Today, it is very difficult to imagine a world operating at close to full employment. In such a world, fears of job loss fade into the background, because losing a job is not a devastating blow; it can be readily accepted and even experienced as an opportunity to find a better one. Over the past 40 years, however, most people have been so programmed by neoliberalism to fear for their jobs that they can hardly imagine such a world. This is the only reason why many people are afraid of processes such as globalisation and automation. Yet it is not these processes that are responsible for the high unemployment that industrialised countries have been suffering from since the 1970s. Rather, it is a systematically wrong economic policy caused by the domination of neoliberalism.

Absurd liberal economic policies based on the ideas of neoclassical economic theory have robbed the market economy of the most important capacity that it once had: The ability to evolve based on price signals, and to start something new immediately following on the passing of the old. This is the famous paradigm of "creative destruction" first described and analysed by Schumpeter. Contrary to what is usually claimed, however, this is not a microeconomic phenomenon. The market economy can only be understood at the macroeconomic level, and it only works if the state plays its part — that is, if it ensures dynamic economic development at all times. Macroeconomic dynamism is not the result of entrepreneurial dynamism — it is the prerequisite for it.

It may be worth revisiting the old idea is that there are two levels of policy response: The macroeconomic level, and the underlying structural level (where changes in economic structures happen that do not necessarily have an impact on the macroeconomic level). If the processes of globalisation and automation becoming amplified into veritable shocks for the economy can be prevented, then, for the rest, it is in principle sufficient to use known macroeconomic instruments (financial, monetary, and wage policy) to work consistently towards dynamic economic development. That means an economic environment in which employment can increase in line with the volume of work desired by the workforce; at the same time, inflation is also kept within limits by a reasonable wage policy.

Avoiding internationally induced shocks requires the international monetary system to be designed to prevent abrupt exchange rate shifts. In both the Bretton Woods system and the European successor system EMS (European Monetary System, 1979–1999), adjustments to losses or gains in international competitiveness usually happened through sudden, shock-like dislocations. Large trade imbalances had to build up before the system's internal mechanisms could compensate for them. Systems of more flexible (i.e. market-driven) exchange rates are even worse; in many cases, floating exchange rates have themselves been responsible for imbalances since exchange rates were driven in the wrong direction by speculators (primarily by means of the carry trades described earlier) before the inevitable correction in the form of sudden devaluations of these currencies took place during major financial crises.

Mercantilism as a solution?

Whether and to what extent globalisation has negative effects for industrial-ised countries can generally best be determined by assessing the development of current account balances. Only if it were the case that developing coun-tries achieved high and rising trade surpluses over a longer period could it be inferred that their foreign trade was having negative consequences for their trading partners. It is only through the current account balances that the various positive and negative effects on particular industries or companies can be appropriately summarised and weighted.

The current account balance is the most comprehensive expression of the effects of trade and globalisation. Anyone who claims that globalisation and the integration of developing countries into world trade is damaging to industrialised countries would need to show that developing countries are economically displacing industrialised countries through increasing interna-tional market shares and a long-term trend of rising current account surpluses.[1]

But this is not the case. A global comparison of current account bal-ances shows that judging by the size of their current account surpluses in relation to their GDP, it is not developing countries that seem to view inter-national trade as a one-way street and thus harm their trading partners, but primarily some mercantilist-oriented countries in northern Europe (Figures 28 and 29) along with a couple of developed industrial economies in south-east Asia.

In 2015, Switzerland was the country with the world's highest surplus (after we removed a few mini-states from the data, e.g. Singapore), followed by Ireland (a case where there are many foreign companies with subsidiaries in the country, as is the case in China), and then Norway (an oil exporting country). Then come the two big mercantilists of the Eurogroup: Germany and the Netherlands.

Most developing countries have deficits. China, Thailand, and South Korea are the Asian countries with the highest surpluses (when city-states like

---

[1] In recent years, however, there have been industrialised countries in Europe with increasing surpluses, even though they cannot be counted as members of the mercantilist class. These are countries such as Italy, Spain and Portugal. Their exports are not rising — rather, their imports are falling as they experience prolonged, deep recessions.

Current account balance in % of GDP in 2015

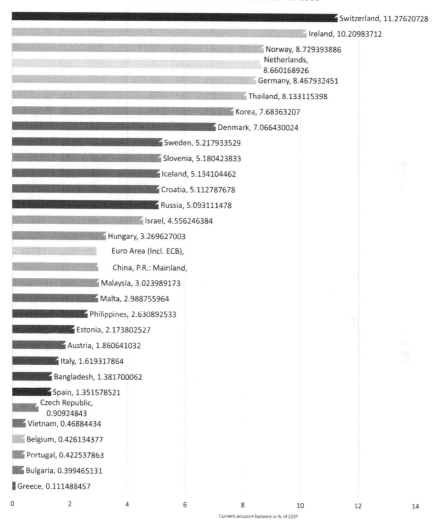

Switzerland, 11.27620728
Ireland, 10.20983712
Norway, 8.729393886
Netherlands, 8.660168926
Germany, 8.467932451
Thailand, 8.133115398
Korea, 7.68363207
Denmark, 7.066430024
Sweden, 5.217933529
Slovenia, 5.180423833
Iceland, 5.134104462
Croatia, 5.112787678
Russia, 5.093111478
Israel, 4.556246384
Hungary, 3.269627003
Euro Area (Incl. ECB),
China, P.R.: Mainland,
Malaysia, 3.023989173
Malta, 2.988755964
Philippines, 2.630892533
Estonia, 2.173802527
Austria, 1.860641032
Italy, 1.619317864
Bangladesh, 1.381700062
Spain, 1.351578521
Czech Republic, 0.90924843
Vietnam, 0.46884434
Belgium, 0.426134377
Portugal, 0.422537863
Bulgaria, 0.399465131
Greece, 0.111488457

Current account balance in % of GDP

Figure 28:   Current account balance as a percentage of GDP in 2015
Source: IMF.

Singapore are excluded). Thailand and South Korea experienced how dangerous it can be to be a deficit country during the Asian financial crisis of 1997.
South Korea has mercantilist reflexes similar to Germany's. Russia is an oil-
exporting country; its currency depreciated sharply in 2014–2015 and

Current account balance in % of GDP in 2015

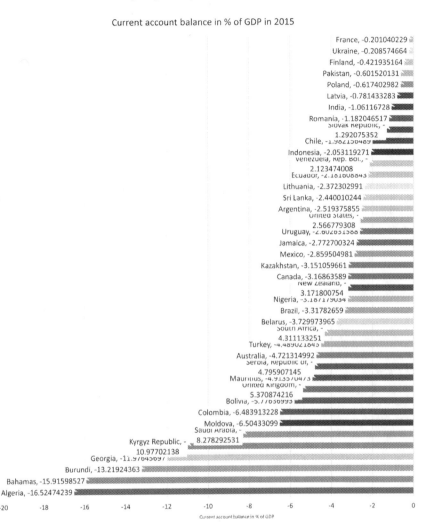

Figure 29:   Current account balance as a percentage of GDP in 2015

Source: IMF.

therefore, due to a deep recession, it had a fairly high surplus. Saudi Arabia also normally has had extremely high surpluses, but like Russia, in 2015 it was suffering from an extreme fall in oil prices.

In view of these facts, it is clear that low-wage developing countries have not triggered any processes in recent years that caused great damage to the labour markets of industrialised countries. In this respect, complaints about globalisation heard in the industrialised countries are as void as the fear of automation.

In industrialised countries plagued by large chronic trade deficits, such as the USA, the situation may be viewed differently. China is, however, a special case, because Western companies themselves have assumed the role of wage-dumping champions by offshoring their production to China. Moreover, China's surpluses have dramatically declined in recent years. If China is excluded from American current account data, then what emerges is that it has primarily been industrialised countries that caused damage to American production by running chronic trade surpluses against the USA (which the new American president apparently understands, see Müller & Flassbeck, 2017).

Most of the countries that have caused damage to their trading partners by running large chronic trade surpluses are found in Europe. Germany is by far the largest mercantilist among the major industrial countries. Germany is also the only G20 country that has continued to increase its surpluses in recent years despite many calls from this very group urging it to reduce them. In 2017, Germany's current account surplus amounted to almost eight percent of gross domestic product.

China's integration into the world economy

Quantitatively, China's integration into the world economy was and is certainly of the greatest importance for globalisation. This has to do with the sheer size of China's economy, but also a special kind of integration. Much more than other Asian countries before it, China followed a development model that was largely supported by direct investment from industrialised countries.

As a result of the strict pursuit of this model, the relocation impacts were at times very large; the combination of high Western productivity with low Chinese wages promised production-offshoring companies enormous monopoly profits, as explained above. At the same time, however, positive effects resulting from the size of the Chinese domestic market were considerable. Western companies were able to supply the entire world market from China, and at the same time expand into the Chinese market, which quickly became an Eldorado for them in view of the rising incomes of the mass of the population.

It is an open question whether the positive effects on industrialised-world economies resulting from the expansion of the Chinese economy have in themselves offset (or perhaps even more than offset) the negative effects of the relocation of production capacities. In any case, it is certain that the enormous productivity progress China has made has given the global economy considerable impetus over many years. In China, there was a timely recognition by the leadership that only an increase in real incomes of the mass of the population, in line with the increase in national productivity, would make it possible to integrate the country into the world economy and end the extreme dependence on exports that still existed at the beginning of the 21st century.

China's case exemplifies how even enormous restructuring can be easily managed if major shock-like changes are avoided. This requires the consistent use of appropriate adjustment mechanisms available for such integration. First and foremost, the real effective exchange rate, which determines the relative competitiveness of all national economies, must be managed properly. In addition, differential growth rates naturally also play a major role; these favour economies that are in a catching-up phase in terms of capital stock and productivity, in relation to industrialised economies.

China has taken advantage of both factors. It has appreciated strongly in real terms in recent years, i.e. increased nominal wages far more than the increase in productivity (the nominal appreciation of the Chinese currency played only a minor role). Because real wages also rose sharply, the volume effects of Chinese growth were very large, and quantitatively significant for Western economies as well. In this way, the surplus in China's current account, which had at times been very big, shrank considerably, which is why it should no longer be a seen as a major stumbling block in the international debate today.

Recall the Importance of Work to Economic Development

As we have already described earlier (Figure 1), the most important factor to understanding the importance of work and wages for macroeconomic development can be found in a simple empirical relationship: The strong correlation between the development of unit labour costs and prices of goods and services, over many decades and in almost all countries of the world. This key fact could be the starting point of a comprehensive, general economic theory, if economists had not thrown it away long ago for ideological reasons.

The crucial fact that inflation rates and unit labour cost increases have risen at almost the same rate on average for many years brings with it implications that acolytes of the ruling neoliberal doctrine fear it like the devil fears holy water, because they threaten to blow away their entire theoretical model like a straw hut in a hurricane. Even many left-wing economists are afraid of dealing with the implications of this correlation, although it is hard to understand why they duck the issue, given that in so doing, they're forfeiting the opportunity to advocate, on the basis of compelling arguments, a new and rational division of roles between market and state.

The most important economic policy implication of this empirical finding is also the simplest: If wages are correlated with prices in the long term, then wages cannot also be responsible for the level of employment.

If a few years after a wage shock (a period when wages suddenly rise or fall sharply), prices adjust to once again reflect unit labour costs, what does this imply for the neoclassical idea that labour gets cheaper in relation to capital in the long term (i.e. that factor price relations can change permanently)?

It implies that this claim is meaningless from the outset. Companies will not restructure production in the neoclassical sense if they have to expect that the real wage, which has fallen in the short term, will be brought back almost to its old level through price reductions forced by competition among companies. And they do have to expect this in view of the close empirical correlation between wages and prices.

One must say "almost to its old level," because the trend line in the above graph does not run exactly along the 45-degree line. Instead, prices always rise somewhat more strongly than unit labour costs. Perhaps prices would fall more sharply in absolute terms if wages were to fall, but there is — as yet — insufficient empirical evidence to support this. The data show, in any case, that the system has a certain tendency towards redistribution of macroeconomic income at the expense of workers. This may be due to a lack of competition. Another reason could be that in the past, there have been more inflationary exogenous shocks (such as oil price hikes) than deflationary shocks, which has led central banks to halt economic upswings prematurely, i.e. before full employment was reached.

Of course, quite apart from these long-term considerations, the neoclassical employment and labour market theory must also be fundamentally rejected because it ignores the short-term negative demand effects of falling real wages as well as the positive effects of rising real wages. Neoclassical theorists can easily dismiss this as "the usual short-term demand considerations of the Keynesians," but this is an untenable posture given the empirical finding that prices correlate closely with wages in the long term too.

All in all, it is clear that reasonable people should wholly reject one of the core theoretical assumptions of neoclassical theory — namely the proposition that there exists a "labour market" that functions no differently than a potato market or an iron-ore market. This in no way precludes sensible people from also recognising that in an open trading economy, wage cuts can result in a positive effect on global market share and hence on employment levels in the wage-dumping country, if there are no exchange rate reactions and no countermeasures from other countries (Flassbeck & Spiecker, 2016). It would be absurd to suggest that one tends towards agreeing with neoclassical economic theory merely because one recognises that there are many ways to manipulate foreign trade results (see also Ehnts, 2016).

Left-wing economists do not like working with this empirical finding of a long-term link between real prices and wages either, and the reasons are easy enough to understand. The finding also implies that attempts at redistribution on the part of employees and trade unions through collective bargaining can succeed only to a very limited extent in the long term. That is because companies always have the opportunity to turn high nominal wage increases into lower real wage increases through upward price adjustments. As a result, any attempt to directly change primary distribution by means of across-the-board wage hikes faces great difficulties.

Here one could argue that in the past few decades significant redistribution at the expense of employees has occurred (see above), and that amount, at least, must be redressable by imposing generous annual wage hikes for a few years in a row. Unfortunately, however, it is not that simple. As already mentioned above, there is a strong asymmetry here, which systematically makes life difficult for trade unions: If nominal wages are reduced, or increased by less than the sum of productivity growth plus target inflation rate, then only the pressure of competition can force companies to adjust prices downwards (thereby generating a *de facto* real wage increase). If the trade unions try to reverse the outcome of past wage-restraint policies by demanding substantial wage hikes, they face resistance not only from employers but also from the central bank — because those wage hikes will provoke nominal price increases.

Virtually all central banks in the western world stand ready to use their interest-rate-setting power to squelch nominal price hikes (i.e. inflation), irrespective of the current level of the wage ratio, i.e. irrespective of past redistribution results. This makes any attempt at redistribution in favour of the workers' side practically impossible. If employees, through their union representatives, make high wage settlement demands during collective bargaining, central banks tend to immediately react with threats to hike interest rates to counteract what they see as "too high" wage settlements. Wage settlements in excess of productivity increases plus the target inflation rate are the only way to achieve redistribution — yet faced with such a prospect, central banks are always prepared to apply a strangulating interest rate to the economy, causing increased unemployment, and thus weakening the trade unions' negotiating position.

Through establishing the principle of independence of central banks and giving them a strict mandate to guarantee low inflation at all times, a system has been created that undoubtedly promotes redistribution in favour of businesses. (This effect is more serious in Europe than in the USA, where it is at least formally the task of the central bank to promote employment as a co-equal goal with low and stable inflation.)

In part, the lopsidedness of the central banks' actions is due to the inability of central banks to combat deflation as effectively as inflation, as long as the only tool in their toolkit is setting interest rates. But to an even greater extent, it is due to the fact that a decades-long, almost constant decline in the wage share of national income, as in Germany, has not even been acknowledged by the central bank. This decline in the wage share was not accompanied by open deflation (as measured in the consumer price index), and consequently is simply not taken into account by the central bank in assessing the "inflation risk" that could emanate from high wage demands (which would have to be central to any trade union–driven national income redistribution strategy in favour of workers).

Fighting inequality

Almost everyone complains about inequality — but hardly anyone dares to demand really far-reaching and effective changes. The critics' list of policy proposals is usually limited to demands for a slightly higher tax on elite incomes, or a modest tax on wealth or inheritance, and a call for more educational opportunities for the poor. But what is it that really stands in the way of a rapid and thorough solution to the problem of inequality in a capitalist or market economy order?

Above all, two interlinked prejudices prevent the majority of inequality critics from demanding serious systemic changes: First, a firm belief in the validity of the so-called marginal productivity theory; and second, the idea that the labour market functions like any other ordinary market — like markets for shoes or wheat, for example.

The first prejudice is incredibly deep among most economists, because it forms the core of the so-called marginal utility revolution that took hold in economics in the 19th century. As we have shown in this book, this theory is fundamentally wrong, since there is no measurable and thus verifiable marginal productivity in societies organised around division of labour. If this neoclassical idea is not correct, then there is no obstacle for a nation to establish (by law) financial participation in society's progressive productivity increases that encompasses everyone, i.e. the entire population (e.g. in the form of equal percentage salary raises calculated on current gross monthly income). On the contrary, this is a prerequisite for successful economic development.

In light of these considerations, what would a benevolent ruler do who, on the one hand, wants to vigorously wage war on inequality but, on the other hand, does not want to shake the foundations of the existing market economy? He would acknowledge that there is no such thing as individual marginal utility or individual productivity, but also that the differences in people's wages cannot be eliminated overnight.

It is precisely at this last point that the benevolent ruler would begin. Even if wealth and income differences cannot be eliminated overnight, the primary goal of a long-term policy against inequality must be to significantly improve the opportunities for individuals to change their wealth positions over the course of their lives, i.e. to rise from the status of the proverbial dishwasher to that of a millionaire. This so-called social mobility is, as many studies show, much less a reality than one might expect, even in the USA.

The social and material circumstances of one's family of origin play a much larger role than generally assumed. This applies to Germany as well, as Michael Hartmann, among others, has shown (Hartmann, 2002; cf. also Heinemann, 2002).

In order to increase social mobility, a benevolent ruler would start on both sides of the income pyramid. First, he would make income tax very progressive in order to siphon off extremely high and mostly non-functional profits from those who have the power to pay themselves princely dividends and incomes. For this purpose, the highest marginal tax rate could be applied on far higher incomes than is currently the case in Germany, but that rate could be set well above 50 percent.

The state would largely dispense with taxation on low incomes, and at the same time massively improve the opportunity to take advantage of educational opportunities. To be clear, nothing can justify the fact that the children of rich parents can systematically afford the best (and often the most expensive) educational institutions, while children of equal or greater talent who happen to be from poorer families are excluded from them. Such being the case, the fees for studying at Harvard, for example, should be part of the normal scope of state educational support for poor but talented kids.

It is scarcely necessary to mention that robust wealth and inheritance taxes are high priorities on the agenda of any fight against inequality. High wealth ownership and large inheritances are central elements of the permanent privilege of the ownership class. Neither inherited wealth nor extreme levels of self-concentrating wealth from property ownership can reasonably be said to bear any positive relationship to the principle of rewarding superior performance or contributive merit.

We should not forget that taxation of companies must be normalised again. In the course of the supply-side revolution, enormous privileges were created for corporations through the radical step of halving corporate taxes in Germany at the beginning of the 2000s (see our analysis in Chapter III). This turned out to have no economic benefits whatsoever, because no boost in entrepreneurial investment activity resulted. Corporate profits should be taxed at the maximum marginal rate of income tax, as had been the case earlier. Businesses should be encouraged to invest in real productive capital through generous depreciation rules, which means privileging those who invest rather than privileging all businesses, as is currently the case.

In addition to minimum wages, which is currently around half the average or median wage, it will be unavoidable in view of the current imbalance of power in companies to set maximum limits for management income. For this purpose, it is appropriate to use salary schedules applied in wide areas of the public service as a reference point. A ratio of 1 to 5 is often the maximum of what is allowed between the lowest and the highest salary group in public service. A 1 to 10 multiple would therefore already be a very generous rule for setting top incomes in the private sector, even if this is far below the absurd ratios of 1 to 100 and more often seen today.

Finally, the incomes of the mass of the population must be systematically involved in the macroeconomic progress (productivity improvements) achieved in a country. Since trade unions can no longer enforce this, in view of their political weakness (and in many cases, an all-too-cozy closeness to management), the state must intervene here as well. An indexing rule would be suitable. Indexation rules have rightly fallen into disrepute in the past, because they usually provided for the indexation of wages to a backward-looking quantity such as the past rate of inflation (as famously practised, for example, in the Italian *scala mobile*). In an improved version of indexation, the productivity component of the calculation must be based on the past, but the inflation rate component must be based on the inflation target, not the past rate of inflation. Wages, salaries, and pensions should increase every year as much as the average productivity increase of the past five or ten years plus the inflation target (see Flassbeck, 2016a).

With this rule, wage policy would provide a buffer for supply shocks such as sudden changes in oil prices, and at the same time, everything would be done on the demand side to prevent mass unemployment. Taken together, the mass of people would be able to buy all the products produced by the economy. In addition, the international competitiveness of the economy would be maintained, at least as long as currency relations develop reasonably.

With these simple measures, none of which are revolutionary or system-changing, it would be possible to combat inequality effectively without causing economic damage — on the contrary, such measures would make it much easier and more efficient to control a modern economy than has been the case with the antiquated methods of the neoclassical school.

Equal price for equal work

There was a time in Germany when people understood how important it was that equal pay was given for equally qualified work at every location and in every company in the country. This rule is not, as is often assumed, a product of trade unionists' fantasies about overcoming the capitalist system; rather, it is the heart and soul of a market economy (Flassbeck & Spiecker, 2016; the following section is largely based on this work). The implementation of this simple rule was guaranteed in Germany by blanket collective agreements covering a given sector, valid for the whole nation.

However, the blanket collective agreement became a repeated focus of criticism on the part of employers. They argued that uniform wages, even for comparable work, were a violation of market economy principles, which include a promise of flexibility. Under employer-association pressure, trade union resistance eventually crumbled. While "flexibility" was the magic word of market ideologues, trade unions promoted a relaxation of the "rigid" agreements out of a concern for showing "consideration for the employees in the companies," i.e. to avoid causing job losses in companies that could not afford to pay national-standard wages. This concession thrust the extremely important institution of the blanket collective agreement into a political dilemma through which it was largely destroyed.

The question of whether the transfer of collective bargaining to the company level (rather than keeping it at the sectoral level) tends to promote employment and efficiency for the economy as a whole should be at the centre of any debate on the future of the blanket collective agreement. Naturally, in a market economy, agreements to secure employment at the company level are possible and usually effective. However, it does not necessarily follow from this that such agreements are also macroeconomically efficient and reasonable. The simple assumption that wage agreements that take account of the different earnings and competitive situations of individual companies are better from the outset than wage agreements geared to the economy as a whole is a fallacy of composition. It is not possible to draw conclusions about the impacts on employment in the economy as a whole from the impacts on job security in a single company.

The hallmarks and driving force of a market economy system are the different earning situations of the individual companies. These result from differences in the individual productivity development of companies, in a context of uniform prices for all production factors, and competition for market share on this basis. These production factors include all precursor products that the company obtains from supply chains in Germany and abroad, external financial capital, and — of course — work.

Under pure competitive conditions, all companies would pay exactly the same price for all comparable inputs, i.e. all functionally identical and equally scarce inputs. This means that all companies would pay lenders the same price for financial capital of the same maturity (taking into account individual default risk, because interest and repayment are only a price promised for the future, not a price paid immediately today). They would also pay the same price for imported raw materials, such as oil or steel. From the point of view of the individual company, inflexibility of prices is virtually a prerequisite for the functioning of the market economy, i.e. for competition on a level playing field.

This must logically also apply to labour as a production factor. This is undisputed in countries where the workforce is as mobile as it is in the USA, for example. If a company does not pay the uniform market price for a worker, the worker leaves and seeks an employer who will pay him the going rate. In countries with lower labour mobility, alternative solutions (functional equivalents) have emerged in the course of industrialisation, which also create market economy conditions for companies on the labour market. The most important of these alternative solutions is the blanket collective agreement.

If, by means of process innovations, a company increases its productivity more than its competitors under pure competitive conditions or when a blanket collective agreement applies, then its profit increases because it has to pay no more than its weaker competitors for its inputs, including labour. This is the decisive incentive for the pioneering entrepreneur to strive to develop innovations and implement them in products brought to market. Conversely, companies fall behind the competition if they can no longer keep up with the pace of productivity improvements achieved by their competitors. They will then slip into the red, due to higher costs or inferior products, and will have to withdraw from the competition sooner or later.

If the accountability mechanism for a company's decisions — normally through temporary losses, in extreme cases through bankruptcy — is mitigated or eliminated, the desired market economy logic is weakened or even abolished. Instruments for eliminating these market economy mechanisms are price differentiation in inputs, including for equally qualified labour, or government subsidies for an enterprise or sector.

Flexible wages or flexible profits?

Generally speaking, systems characterised by supply chain input prices that are rigid at the level of the individual company are controlled by flexible profits. Systems of flexible input prices, on the other hand, tend toward inflexible profit targets and thus require different control mechanisms. The more inflexible the prices for inputs — including labour — for an individual company trading on the market, the more flexible and efficient the company's profit is in controlling the system. Conversely, the more flexible prices for inputs are — including labour — the more rigid and thus inefficient profit is as a control instrument.

It is surprising that employers tend to prefer a system of inflexible profits over a system of flexible profits. From an employer's point of view, does it make sense to demand a system in which every productivity advantage that a company acquires is offset to a considerable extent by price increases for its specific inputs, including labour? What variable in this system decides whether a company can remain on the market, if it can survive despite permanently weak productivity development, because it has to pay far less than its competitors for its inputs, including labour?

From the trade unions' point of view, does it make sense to demand a system in which a company's productivity advantage benefits only or predominantly its own workers? Who then decides which employees are allowed to work in good and which in bad companies, and thus earn high or low wages? The labour force's alacrity of response to lower wages or worse working conditions in a relatively "bad" company (in a system in which wages paid differ according to a company's individual profitability) is limited by the costs and stresses associated with moving to a new job elsewhere; but at some point, the costs of staying with a low-paying company outweigh the costs of moving.

The "labour market flexibility" (in the sense of different prices for the same services) demanded in politicians' Sunday speeches on the "challenges of globalisation" has nothing to do with price flexibility in a functioning market economy. The latter does not mean that every supplier or customer in a well-defined market (or market segment) can agree on his individual price at the same time; rather, it means that at a given point in time, a uniform price is paid by all participants in a market for a given input. This price can then change over time, i.e. "flexibly" adapt to a wide variety of influences. But then it changes in the same way for all market participants, and not in one way for a few players, a different way for a few others, and not at all for still others.

It sounds paradoxical, but price flexibility is greatest when the observable differences in prices of similar products and services are close to zero. For example: If a bagel of the same size and quality costs 40 cents in all the bakeries in a city during a certain month, nobody would talk about overly rigid structures or a supplier cartel. If the price of bagels rises to 44 cents in the following month due to devastating wheat crop damage and a corresponding increase in the price of flour in all bakeries, the necessary market economy flexibility, i.e. the ability to react quickly to changing conditions, would demonstrably exist.

In the labour market, the microeconomic principle of flexible prices basically works the same way. The main difference to the above example is the lower mobility of the workforce compared to that of bagel customers. While consumers of a mass product can easily react to price differences by migrating to the competition (switching suppliers does not involve high costs for the consumer), changing jobs in response to different wage prospects is more difficult and usually associated with high transaction costs for an employee, as she may have to move house, or at least accept longer commuting distances. In the worst case, she may have to move a whole family, disrupting the lives of her children, and her partner may have to give up his job.

Despite these factors which tend to cause immobility of the workforce, the law of equal price for equal scarcity can be made to apply. This is best guaranteed by a blanket collective agreement for each sector, with as few exceptions as possible. Only in such a system does the control of economic development work through profits, instead of through substitute mechanisms such as company-specific labour agreements. Just as is the case with state subsidies for ailing industries, a deviation from the principle of the same price for the same input must be the exception, not the rule, for all factors of production, including labour. Many past examples have shown that making the exception the rule not only destroys the structures of social dialogue that have evolved and grown in Germany for many good reasons, they also damage the efficiency of a dynamically developing market-economy system.

Now, to return to the above example of a local bagel market, critics of the blanket collective agreement could argue that the flexible reaction of the bagel price to a significant increase in the flour price, due to damage caused to cereal crops, cannot exist for wages, since these are fixed for considerably longer periods than mere months — wages tend to be fixed for a year or even several years. This argument is correct insofar as it is true that the duration of price agreements on the labour market, i.e. the duration of collective agreements — for good reasons, such as increased planning security for both employers and employees — is significantly longer than the validity period of prices on goods markets. What is wrong with the argument, however, is the proposition that this reduced flexibility of wages over time is problematic for economic development.

If individual sectors, e.g. bakeries, are affected by exogenous shocks such as poor harvests, passing on the resulting cost increases in a higher price for the sector's goods (bread) is unproblematic for companies, since all suppliers in the sector are affected by the same shock, i.e. no company can avoid the price increase and thereby break ranks to gain market share for itself. For workers in the sector concerned (in this case, bakeries), the short-term consequences of the absolute and relative price increase of the goods they produce are the same as for all other workers: Their real income decreases (or rises more slowly) in accordance with the unexpected price increase that the goods in question trigger in their individual shopping baskets.

If however the employees of the sector affected by the shock react to it by accepting a cutback in their wages, in the spirit of a "flexible collective agreement," so that the producing companies (here, bakeries) can avoid passing on the input factor cost increase (a higher cost of flour) in the retail price of their product (bread), then the employees of the sector would be alone in bearing the loss of macroeconomic real income caused by the shock. The sector's customer, in this case buyers of bread, would not help bear the increased cost burden. This cannot be justified from the point of view of distributional fairness. Nor can it be justified in terms of the efficient functioning of a market economy: The industry's commodity market price would lose its control function in terms of signalling scarcity. The commodity (bread) would be offered too cheaply, and thus consumed in too large quantities, in view of the input scarcity shock.

In the medium to long term, depending on their degree of mobility, employees in the sector affected by the shock will withdraw and move to sectors where their qualifications are needed and their work performance is remunerated at unabated wages. In the long term, the original, pre-shock wage levels in the bakery sector would have to be restored, in order to prevent or at least curb outmigration of labour to other sectors; this ultimately would lead to roughly the same price increase that would have occurred from the outset, had collective sectoral wage agreements and inflexible sectoral wages been in effect.

Even the introduction of profit-sharing for employees, which is proposed time and again, does not change these conclusions. If employees receive more or less wages (or receive equity shares instead of wages) depending on the company's current profitability, the risk of unemployment is indeed reduced. The employees are more involved in the company's entrepreneurial risk. The liability for management errors is then passed along to the employees not only in terms of the risk of dismissals but also income adjustments. This reduces fluctuations in the company's profits, but in so doing, it also reduced the control function of profits in the sense described above. In choosing between profit-sharing vs. fixed wage packets, employees are choosing between income risk and dismissal risk.

However, nothing is gained from such flexibility in macroeconomic terms. Indeed, there is another aspect to the macroeconomy that makes flexible-wage systems even more unstable. For the macroeconomy as a whole (unlike for individual companies), a "flexible" response of employees' incomes in the event of an exogenous shock does not automatically help to cushion the shock. For example, if an economy's export demand falls, as in the Asian crisis, neither a reduction in wages, nor a disemployment of part of the labour force, nor any combination of these two measures is an appropriate response, because this generally further destabilises overall demand. Only fiscal policy and/or monetary policy can (and must) take countermeasures in such a case. A system in which workers share a limited liability for corporate profits is therefore not a substitute for a macroeconomic policy, in contrast to what is often believed today.

Is there a "services gap"?

The blanket collective agreement came to be seen in Germany not only as an obstacle to change in corporate structures; it was also blamed for "too rigid" sectoral wage structures. The best-known example is the claim that there is a "services gap" in Germany, i.e. "too few" employees in the tertiary sector. According to this claim, the blanket collective agreement burdens less productive services in the same way it burdens highly productive industries.

According to this view, the best way to create employment is to promote labour-intensive activities. Apart from expressing "regulatory" concerns, economics has so far failed to bring much in the way of conceptual content to the table in opposition to this agenda, because the majority of economists are trapped in their neoclassical world-view — which assumes that if unemployment is high, the reason must be that wages are too high. Moreover, many economists have endorsed the claim that there is a lack of "structural" flexibility in wages — and that this is a bad thing — without considering the serious implications of this claim for other areas of economic analysis.

The solution to the "services gap" problem is simple: If productivity gains in services tend to be lower than in industry, and if the same price is to be paid for equally scarce work in all domains, then the price side does indeed generate a built-in brake on the expansion of service sectors within the framework of sectoral changes in the structure of the economy. However, if there is a "natural" tendency for consumer preferences to change in favour of services as prosperity increases, the situation is quite different. In that case, the negative price effect will always be offset by a positive income effect driving the expansion of services. Which of these directionally opposite effects is quantitatively greater is completely open.

An agenda of "filling the services gap" has been proposed that cannot actually ever achieve the core objective of creating more jobs. That is because the underlying hypothesis the advocates of wage differentiation have adopted is wrong: Promoting a sector with low labour productivity does not increase overall employment. All considerations aimed at slowing down or accelerating sectoral structural change — depending on which side one is looking at — by discriminating against capital-intensive sectors, are wrong from the outset because they have no rational economic basis.

All such proposals are premised on the simple idea that a given production volume can be produced with either more or less manpower, depending on the sectoral structure. But the reality is that in a dynamically developing economy, there is no predetermined production volume. A high increase in productivity leads to a high increase in production, and a lower growth in productivity to a lower expansion of production. This rather obvious fact must be completely ignored in order for someone to imagine that it is possible to achieve positive effects on employment as a whole by controlling and guiding sectoral and entrepreneurial structural change toward lower-productivity services sectors. But in a sound macroeconomic analysis, this must not be ignored, since otherwise no coherent statements about overall macroeconomic or employment effects can be made.

To sum up, wage differentiation for equally scarce work, with wage rates dependent on which individual companies or sectors people work for, violates the basic principles of a market economy. In a rapidly developing economy, calling for "flexible" wages in this sense is an abuse of the concept of flexibility, because flexible wages dampen macroeconomic dynamism by reducing incentives for productivity-improving pioneers and subsidising less successful companies. But the key thing is this: In a temporally open-ended, dynamically developing economic system, it cannot be demonstrated that generating wage differentiation through dampening the progress of productivity increases can trigger positive employment effects. On the contrary, the negative income effects of such actions are clear.

A New Distribution of Economic Policy Roles

The tasks of monetary, financial, and wage policy

We have noted above that monetary theory has made great progress over the past 20 years and that the time is more than overdue for policymakers to respond with institutional adjustments. For example, if one recognises that in all developed economies, unit labour costs are decisive for inflation development, inflation control can no longer be assigned exclusively to monetary policy. In general, monetary policy must then be assigned a completely different role, namely that of promoting private and public investment.

The task of wage policy in such a redistribution of roles is threefold: First, by adjusting real wages, it must ensure that domestic demand is stabilised and sufficient at all times to purchase all products produced. Second, wage policy must stabilise the inflation rate and prevent one-off price shocks from becoming permanent deviations of the inflation rate from the inflation target. Third, through these mechanisms, wage policy can prevent the economy as a whole from losing competitiveness *vis-à-vis* other countries, assuming the international monetary system performs its task of balancing out different inflation rates by means of compensatory currency devaluations and revaluations.

Whether the wage-bargaining partners (employers' associations and trade unions) can do all this on their own or whether they need the help of a mediating or even intervening state must be discussed. To refuse to have this discussion from the outset because people fear the holy cow of independent bargaining might be slaughtered in the process is more than problematic, because it plays exactly into the hands of the market fundamentalists and their trickle-up redistribution agenda. To them, independent bargaining only has value if a power advantage for corporations results from it.

Redistribution of income and wealth must be an urgent priority for the state. And, as we have shown above, there is no question but that the state can do a great deal in this regard without destabilising or overturning the system. In addition, the state — supported by monetary policy — must ensure that the private sector's attempts to hoard money (i.e. the approximately 250 billion euros that German households and companies are currently socking away in unspent net savings year after year) lead neither to a recession nor to a senseless attempt to permanently push foreign countries into the role of debtors as Germany's private sector attempts to "improve its own competitiveness."

This means that the state has enormous leeway to directly positively influence the economy through its own deficit spending and public investments, and at the same time (above all through state financing of excellent public infrastructure, including investments in ecological sustainability and regeneration) to create the conditions for private investments to flourish and be channelled in the right direction.

This is how the market economy works, or how "capitalism" works, depending on what you want to call the system in which we live. Unless one wants to put the system entirely into question, redistribution rhetoric and recitations of clichéd slogans about evil capitalists are unhelpful. Obviously people have (and should have) the right to put the market economy or capitalist system entirely into question. However, to claim that one finds the system to be good in principle, but to completely reject its results in terms of income distribution, is disingenuous at best. It is quite surprising to read of

Left Party ex-leader Sahra Wagenknecht in a paraphrase of Karl Marx: "The capitalist buys the labour and sells the product of the worker, and because [the prices of] these differ, he has made a cut without violating the laws of equal exchange." (Wagenknecht, 2016, p. 131)

Wagenknecht's thesis correctly describes the underlying principle of profit, namely that the employee (with the help of capital) produces more than he gets paid, i.e. that part of the income generated from work (and capital!) goes to the owner of the company. But that is capitalism! That this occurs has nothing to do with a supposed lack of competition that Ms. Wagenknecht has elsewhere complained about and would like to correct with the means proposed by Ordoliberals of the Freiburg school. The capitalist gets a cut even when there is complete competition. No one has yet encountered (or invented) a capitalist system in which the results of production (i.e. productivity) generated by workers in combination with capital are distributed without a cut going to the owner of capital. One must not shrink from the clear empirical finding that there is no capitalism without the laws of capitalism.

Fundamentals of a reform of commercial and central banks

The political system's responses to the financial crisis of 2007/08 that have arisen so far can be interpreted as a revival of a sociological figure who, as Werner Polster has correctly put it, originates in the "way of doing business characteristic of small owner-operated goods producers and traders" who "lived and worked in the period between the late Middle Ages and the early 19th century."

> We are talking about the figure of the "Honourable Merchant." On the map of sociological types, an outside observer would expect this figure to be located more in the periphery regions [not in major urban centres], in the provinces, perhaps in a mechanical engineering based community in southern Germany, where such patriarchal figures from small and medium-sized enterprises are to be found on municipal councils; at any rate, one would not have expected to suddenly meet the Honourable Merchant on the stages of international finance capital. (Polster 2014, p. 28)

The attempt to resuscitate this paradigmatic narrative figure has an important precedent in German academic economics. In the early days of

Ordoliberalism, the figure of the "Honourable Merchant" was celebrated with the less dusty-sounding term "bearer of liability." It is hardly surprising that attempts to get systemic problems of the current financial system under control with regulatory concepts that originated in a time long past, whose economic structures are no longer comparable to those of modern economies, are doomed to failure.

This insight must necessarily lead to a departure from the idea that more liability-based regulation of the operation of commercial banks, as provided for in the recently established European Banking Union, can improve financial stability. On the contrary, all attempts to strengthen the liability principle in the operation of banks can be expected to be ineffective at best. In practice, this approach will most likely further undermine the financial stability of the euro area.

We must also say goodbye to the idea that "independent" central banks, which are not democratically legitimated, might be well suited to ensuring that economic policy is oriented towards the common good. Central banks must once again be regarded as an integral part of the executive branch, whose task is "to ensure price stability, a high level of employment, and a balance of foreign trade while maintaining steady and appropriate economic growth," as required by the "Law on the Promotion of Stability and Growth of the Economy" adopted in 1967.

Commercial banking reform

The 2008/09 financial crisis was triggered by the insolvency of Lehman Brothers. This event should have made it more than clear that banks must always be rescued from collapse, because they are essential for the settlement of payment transactions and the granting of loans to the real economy. However, if, as we have shown, the investment banking business is associated with large uncontrollable risks, then the consequence must be that the state must ensure that these activities — lending to the real economy vs. investment banking — are strictly separated from one another.

This is not a new insight. It is a hard lesson learned in the USA as early as 1932, as expressed in the so-called "Glass–Steagall Act," and it needs to be relearned and implemented. The commercial lending and savings deposit business must be completely separated from investment banking. In such a banking system, commercial banks will no longer be allowed to use their money-creation privilege and their access to central bank reserves to speculate on the financial markets with money they have created themselves.

The primary goal of separating investment banking from commercial banking is to ensure that, whatever happens on the financial markets, the settlement of payment transactions and the supply of credit to the real economy will not be impaired. Whether and to what extent this separation will establish sufficient control over the world of casino finance to prevent egregiously harmful effects on the real economy is a separate issue that will not be discussed here.

A legal separation of the lending and deposit business from investment banking does not yet guarantee that financial market crises will no longer destabilise the banking system. The separation of these two business areas must be complete, not only legally but also functionally. Banks should be prohibited from granting loans for financial market transactions and from collateralising loans with financial market products.

Development of a more stable financial system will also require ensuring that the credit relationship between a bank and its customers will be maintained throughout the term of a loan. Asset-based securitisations, which are created by turning a portfolio of loans into a tradable security that can be bought and sold on capital markets, must be prohibited. Instruments such as these triggered a real estate boom in the USA that had no real economic basis whatsoever. It is not without irony that this "financial innovation" was selected by the EU Commission as a means to improve the refinancing possibilities of small and medium-sized enterprises in Europe.

Implementing a stable financial system will certainly require a state supervisory body that develops criteria for commercial lending and employs personnel that can monitor compliance with them. It is also essential that banks that do not comply with regulatory requirements are effectively sanctioned. These sanctions must range from fines all the way to the withdrawal of a banking licence. Above all, in the event of infringements, the senior management of banks must be denied the right to manage a bank ever again. The current practice of supervisory authorities is to rely on banks' internal risk management systems or even on the assessment of rating agencies such as Standard & Poor's; this practice must be ended immediately. Every bank must be obliged to assess the creditworthiness of a potential borrower on the basis of an independent credit analysis.

Even a bank with an exemplary business concept, overseen by financial supervisory authorities that have an appropriate mandate and are equipped to fulfil their duty to supervise the business conduct of banks, will inevitably get into difficulties in a recessionary environment, as is currently the case in Italy, for example. It is therefore essential for a country's central bank to act as a financial backstop, a lender of last resort, for all banks in its national territory. This means the central bank must use its balance sheet to ensure with ultimate consequence that these banks can never become illiquid. The safety of retail clients' current account balances, the uninterrupted flow of payment transactions, and the granting of credit are, as our previous remarks should have demonstrated, public goods.

The granting of credit by a bank to a non-financial business is to be regarded as a service which consists of checking whether a company can use resources profitably. If this assessment is positive, the bank simply enters the appropriate figures in the company's current account, which the company can then use as a means of payment for the acquisition of production factors. From this point of view, it would make more sense to pay banks a fee for their credit assessment service, instead of an interest rate.

Because banks can suffer losses due to a borrower's default on loan repayments, they normally grant loans only against provision of collateral. No matter how good a business idea someone may have, if they do not own the appropriate collateral, they will not receive a loan. The inherent tendency of the current credit system to primarily focus on extending secured loans is reinforced by the fact that the capital requirements that banks must meet vary depending on the collateral provided.

It is therefore not really surprising that by far the biggest chunk of private sector debt is composed of mortgage loans. These in turn are used primarily to finance the purchase of existing properties and — in cases where homeowners borrow money secured against homes they already own — to provide cash flow for consumer purposes. Loans used to finance transfers of existing properties contribute very little to GDP. Credits granted for building up real capital stock (e.g. factories, production facilities, equipment) or to finance consumption, on the other hand, do contribute to increasing GDP.

The consequence to be drawn from this is that loans should primarily be made for investments that are expected to generate a cash flow that allows the loans to be serviced on time. Assessments of the creditworthiness of potential borrowers will be best carried out by banks that are geographically close to their customers, and therefore aware of the specific conditions under which a company operates. Against this background, Germany's savings banks and cooperative banking system seem particularly suitable for providing small and medium-sized enterprises with capital for promising investments.

A potentially infinite supply of money always faces a limited supply of potential borrowers. Any commercial bank that enters into a lending transaction that has been rejected by another bank due to risk considerations will initially be able to report higher profits than its competitor. However, since the success of any business is primarily measured in terms of return on equity, and the salaries of commercial banks' senior executives are heavily dependent on this criterion, it is realistic to assume that over time, commercial banks will take on increasingly risky credit exposures in order to generate higher short-term apparent profits. These "profits" tend to disappear as soon as a recession arrives, because riskier loan portfolios are more likely to see high levels of borrower defaults. This can lead to bank insolvencies.

If competition in the banking sector is potentially damaging in this sense, and if, moreover, each bank's business practices require extensive monitoring by appropriate state supervisory bodies, there is much to be said in favour of operating such institutions as publicly owned organisations staffed with civil servants. Civil servants have not only completed training that enables them to carry out their work competently, but are also explicitly committed to the common good. Since they are obliged to base their actions on explicit and verifiable rules that can be enforced with sanctions, they can be effectively controlled by monitoring bodies set up for this purpose.

Lending by banks under the current system is based solely on whether a borrower is in a position to achieve monetary surpluses that allow him to service his loan. However, since the total resources available at any given time are always scarce in relation to the sum of objectives of all the individual members of a nation's population, it is an open question whether the achievement of a surplus can, in a democracy, be the sole criterion for granting credit.

A possible means of subjecting the use of resources in an economy to a certain degree of democratic control is the provision of credit guidance to commercial banks by supervisory authorities. This was practised, albeit only very rudimentarily, by the Deutsche Bundesbank at the beginning of the 1970s under the name "Kreditplafondierung" (credit ceilings). Banks' credit-granting can be managed both quantitatively and qualitatively by the central bank's setting lending-volume targets for banks as well as specifying how the total volume of loans granted is to be distributed regionally and sectorally. For example, if the responsible authority is concerned that a real estate bubble is inflating in Munich, it might limit the granting of mortgage loans in the region.

Central bank reform

When monetarism lost its lustre, it should have been obvious that the function of a central bank cannot consist in providing an "objective supply of money" to the economy. The financial crisis has also revealed that a central bank cannot fulfil even the more limited task of ensuring a uniform interest rate in its currency area if it is not fully available to its state (or member states) as lender of last resort.

When Mario Draghi reassured the nervous "markets" in July 2012 in response to rising interest rates for Spanish and Italian government bonds that the ECB would assume the lender of last resort function, he in no way, as Jürgen Habermas mistakenly claimed, "simulated a fiscal sovereignty he did not even possess." Rather, he made the capital markets understand that would not allow the ECB's fiscal sovereignty, namely its ability to supply the countries of the European Monetary Union (EMU) with "printed" money, to be limited by the public finance ban in Section 123 of the Lisbon Treaty.

But why should a state not make use of this ability of its central bank more routinely? Why should states not use the instrument of monetary (central bank) financing of a portion of public expenditures, if the smooth functioning of state bonds issuance via the capital market is in any case only assured if their repayment is effectively guaranteed by the state's central bank?

Horror stories about impending state or central bank bankruptcies and the spectre of galloping inflation associated with monetary finance of public expenditures are, as we have shown in this book's previous parts, neoliberal myths that only show what their narrators really think of democracy. Certainly, however, it is necessary to discuss which resources the state should activate for which purposes with its ability to "print" money for itself. For if a state with its ability to create money "from nothing" enables the production of certain goods, then the real resources required for this are no longer available for the production of other goods. It is therefore a question of determining which resources are left to the private sector to produce goods that are in demand from private individuals and which goods a state demands and possibly also produces (or pays the private sector to produce) on its own initiative.

But is the post-war German economic miracle not striking proof that an institutional containment of democracy by an independent central bank makes sense? And is it not misleading to criticise the lack of democratic legitimacy of independent central banks, even though the Bundesbank, for example, is an institution that enjoys the trust of the vast majority of the population?

First of all, it should be noted that for almost 25 years after the Second World War, until the end of the Bretton Woods system, the function of the Bundesbank was limited to being the mouthpiece of neoliberal ideological convictions. After that, the Bundesbank zealously adopted the half-baked doctrines of monetarism for 30 years and, with its dogmatism, hindered a successful economic policy wherever it could. Even conservative Finance Minister Franz Josef Strauß complained during his term of office (1966–1969) that the Bundesbank did not sufficiently support the Federal Government's economic policy.

However, it is by no means necessary to go that far back in history to identify other cases of the "beneficial effects" of independent central banks. In Greece, with the help of an independent central bank called the ECB, the citizens' democratic "no" to "structural reforms" (radical austerity policies), expressed in a national referendum, was firmly put in its designated place (in the trash can). There is no doubt that it was the ECB's threat to bring down the entire Greek banking system which finally "convinced" the Greek parliament to adopt the "structural reforms" agenda dictated by the troika (European Commission, ECB, and IMF).

On the basis of the overview provided in this text, it should now be clear that a central bank must be part of the state and that its actions must be coordinated with those of other state actors in such a way as to optimally serve the public interest. In times when companies as well as households are net savers, it is obvious that monetary policy is no longer sufficient to successfully manage an economy in order to ensure full employment and the associated growth of GDP. In addition to the promotion or restriction of economic activities through interest rate policy, a policy designed to meet the requirements of the abovementioned Stability Law of 1967 requires increased use of fiscal and tax policy.

Abba P. Lerner, an economist who was trained in England and taught in the USA, had already convincingly demonstrated in the 1940s that attempts by the private sector to save must necessarily lead to a decline in GDP. In such a situation it is therefore, in Lerner's opinion, the task of the state to compensate for the resulting loss of demand either indirectly, through tax reductions, or directly by increases in expenditure. In the case of an overheating economy, which is reflected in inappropriately high inflation rates, taxes must be increased and/or government spending reduced (Lerner, 1943).

However, the economic effects of tax policy are often difficult to assess. It cannot be ruled out, for example, that higher disposable incomes of households will predominantly lead to an increase in savings rates instead of more consumer spending. Expenditure policy is much more suitable for demand management purposes. If, for example, a state makes additional investments in an environment of weak private-sector demand, there is no doubt that economic activity will pick up speed immediately.

But if it is easy for a state to "print" money in any desired quantity, and to use this ability to control the aggregate demand level of an economy in such a way that full employment results, why are the majority of economists so reluctant to endorse the use of fiscal policy to achieve these ends? Lerner asked himself this very question as early on as the 1940s, and answered with a reference to a bit of dogma that goes by the name "sound fiscal policy," which was recently expressed by the German Federal Ministry of Finance as follows: "The view of the Federal Ministry of Finance, which is also shared by many in the academic world, is [...] that sound public finances strengthen the confidence of the private sector and thus promote investment and growth." (Bundesministerium für Finanzen, 2015, p. 4)

The success of the "sound fiscal policy" dogma is due to the fact that the devotees of the neoliberal narrative believe that a state's debt is comparable to that of private sector actors. However, as we have explained in previous sections, this equation is a very dangerous mistake. The reality is that the state can create "money from nothing" in any quantity. And since it can do that, there is no way it will ever get into financial difficulties in its own currency. A state will therefore always and easily be able to afford to pay for budget deficits to stimulate the economy with appropriate levels of aggregate demand, without any difficulty, if the real capacities of its domestic economy are not fully utilised. The state should only want to achieve budget surpluses if it wants to put inflationary tendencies in check.

But then why do so many believe that the "escalating national debt" will necessarily end in national bankruptcy? There are certainly those who actually do believe that. However, there are others who know perfectly well that states with a sovereign currency can never become insolvent, but still claim the opposite. These people are propagating a big lie in pursuit of certain political purposes. For example, Nobel Prize for Economics awardee Paul Samuelson belongs to the latter group. Samuelson admitted in a moment of incautious frankness that the belief that a balanced state budget was necessary to avoid a "debt trap" is a myth... A myth which, he said, must be maintained under all circumstances in order to prevent state intervention in the "efficient market mechanism" (Samuelson, quoted in Wray, 2012, p. 200).

As soon as we have lost our collective fear of dispensing with this myth, nothing more will stand in the way of an economic policy which, with its coordinated monetary, fiscal, and tax policy elements, "ensures that total expenditure in the economy is no more and no less than the expenditure sufficient to achieve the full employment level of production at current prices" (Lerner, 1951, p. 7).

Public services provision

We have shown in many places in this book that all important institutions that have to do with an economy's provision for the future (i.e. with investment and its prerequisites) should be located at the level of the nation state. This applies in particular, of course, to public services and social security systems, with state-guaranteed pensions in pole position. The pensions system has arguably been the most important state achievement of the last hundred years; probably more than any other achievement, pensions have given people the feeling of being part of a political community with a shared destiny. Pension insurance has enabled the economically active generation to help their parents and grandparents age with dignity. Today, this mechanism no longer has the same form and function, as the ongoing discussion about poverty among the elderly shows.

In a modern society in which the division of labour into specialisms is constantly increasing, citizens are becoming increasingly dependent on the state. They are no longer in a position to meet their needs by themselves, or together with acquaintances or kin. All those who integrate themselves into the division of labour are dependent on abstract production and distribution processes that are no longer transparent to them and whose functioning must be guaranteed by the state. Contrary to what neoliberals claim, more and more processes of social organisation require activation by the state. Consequently, the economy must become increasingly subject to the primacy of public policy.

Economic liberals believe, as we have explained in detail in this book, that the state must merely provide a legal framework that enables profit-oriented companies to produce goods and services in competition with others, without state intervention. In such a legal framework, the price mechanism alone should ensure that all citizens are supplied efficiently with all conceivable economic goods. What liberals completely ignore is that the results of the process of producing goods and services create power constellations that systematically put employees caught up in the specialist division of labour in a bad negotiating position.

To counteract this tendency, public services and social welfare systems must be set up to ensure that the threat of (even if only temporary) exclusion of a worker from an active role in production loses much of its coercive force. A social welfare system, a safety net, is the only way for workers to defend themselves against powerful negotiating partners, because its existence means they can look for alternative employment without being under extreme existential pressure.

The most important means of correcting the balance of power is without question a consistent full employment policy. However, this alone is not enough to cover the life risks imposed by the market in such a way that ordinary citizens can participate in society on an equal footing with companies and their lobby groups.

It is this fact that explains why the share of government spending as a percentage of GDP in developed economies is rarely below 40 percent and in some cases as high as 60 percent. Social security, transport and finance, defence, research, kindergartens, schools, universities, police, justice, health care, culture, housing, tax administration, water and energy supply, waste disposal, sewerage, kindergartens, and many other goods require a state guarantee to ensure their comprehensive provision.

In principle, publicly funded services and infrastructure can be delivered either by public or private companies. However, the delivery of services by private providers faces two problems. One is that many typical public services are produced by so-called natural monopolies; the other is that their provision in sufficient quality or quantity by profit-oriented companies is not always assured.

Nevertheless, in political practice over the past decades, the prevailing opinion has been that the provision of services by private companies is more efficient even in such areas. This conviction was expressed in Section 7 of the Federal Budget Code (BHO) at the end of 1993. The following sentence was added immediately after a passage directing public authorities to comply with the principle of "efficiency and economy" in their expenditure: "These principles require an examination of the extent to which governmental tasks or economic activities serving public purposes can be carried out through subcontracting, denationalisation or privatisation."

Although the privatisation of public services had already begun in the 1960s, the first major wave of privatisation came with the election of Helmut Kohl as German Chancellor and the intellectual and moral change he proclaimed in the early 1980s. In his government declaration of 4 May 1983, the centre-right Christian Democratic Union Chancellor made it unequivocally clear that he wanted to curtail the role of the state and pave the way for an enhanced role for the market: "An economic order is all the more successful the more the state holds back and allows the individual his freedom. We don't want more state, we want less; we want more personal freedom, not less."

One must give Kohl some credit for being serious about his agenda — he put his words into action. According to the OECD, during Kohl's reign, the number of companies with federal government ownership participation fell from 808 to 132 (Mattert *et al.*, 2017, p. 41). The air transport and energy sectors, rail, postal services, and telecommunications were particularly affected. It was consistently claimed that the same or at least a comparable result would be achieved, but at significantly lower cost, as private companies simply operate more efficiently than state-owned ones.

The second major privatisation wave began at the beginning of the new millennium under a red–green government. In those "times of tight budgets," social security systems were privatised. This particularly affected the health and nursing care sector, but also statutory pension insurance (see the following section for more details about that).

How problematic the privatisation of public services can turn out to be can be seen in the example of the privatisation of energy supply, which is partly material and partly "only" formal. In this domain, local authorities were legally forced to facilitate competition between different providers. As a result, a resource- and environmentally friendly energy supply could no longer be ensured in some municipalities. For example, the use of waste heat generated during electricity production for heating purposes requires that energy production takes place on a sufficiently large scale. If a municipality offering its citizens district heating loses the services of a large electricity supplier to a competitor, it may no longer be possible to supply district heating.

The problem is thus not only substantive privatisation but also so-called formal privatisation, which consists in the transformation of publicly organised companies into companies organised under private law. However, the production of public goods requires, according to the administrative and parliamentary lawyer Albert Janssen, "a certain organisation and a certain procedure [...] for the completion of tasks" (Janssen, 2014, p. 414).

In fact, it requires an organisation that impartially weighs up the interests of all those affected by the actions of a producer of public goods. Such organisations are called public administrations; their tasks are carried out by civil servants, whose decisions are based on explicit rules, which means they can be held publicly accountable for their decisions.

What might prevent the state from taking companies which are essential for provision of core public services back into public ownership, and from financially structuring the relevant administrative units in such a way that they can provide these services reliably? The short answer is: Rampant market fundamentalism and an endemic fading of the state from active memory. What we need first and foremost is a departure from the belief that the market and thus profit-oriented companies can do everything better, and that the state only gets in the way of people's welfare. The narratives of "necessary reform" with which privatisations were and are justified have in most cases simply been lies.

As we have described in detail in this book, a state with its own currency has no problem refinancing public infrastructure projects to the required extent and in the desired quality. The debt brakes established at EU, federal, state, and local levels are the best proof of this: It is precisely because a state is in a position to refinance any amount of expenditure at any time that these institutional hurdles, some of which even enjoy constitutional status, have been built up.

The current hurdles to efficient public services provision thus primarily take the form of government regulations that could, in principle, be changed. However, this does not make it easier to overcome these hurdles. After all, the new model of private delivery of public services did not fall from the sky. Those who directly or indirectly benefit financially from privatisation have spent a lot of time and money implanting the idea of its preferability into people's brains. The mechanisms have included so-called "endowed professorships" and, relatedly, the increasingly necessary acquisition of third-party funding by universities; teacher training courses supported with the provision of free teaching materials by lobby organisations; as well as a permanent drumbeat of neoliberal dogma broadcast by leading media. In this way, the privatisation lobby has ensured that market solutions to services provision are widely considered to lack serious alternatives and that people have increasingly attuned their thoughts and actions to conform with neoliberal ideology.

The intensity of resistance we can expect if we want to pave the way for public services to once again be provided by public agencies becomes clear when we consider, for example, how the privatisation of pensions was achieved. So-called "experts" who prepared the relevant laws were and are employed in various "functions connected with the insurance industry [...], for which an extremely profitable market was opened up with the development and expansion of private old-age provision" (Engartner, 2016, p. 141).

But it was not only "experts" who were bought. Every tenth member of the Bundestag and an even larger proportion of the members of the relevant parliamentary committees were associated with the finance and insurance sector between 1998 and 2002. A particularly blatant example of this was the then Federal Minister of Labour and Social Affairs, Walter Riester, who reported 69 paid part-time jobs during his time in the Bundestag, most of them with financial service providers, i.e. the group that directly benefited from the private pension savings reform ("Riester-Rente") named after him.

No less remarkable, Carsten Maschmeyer, the head of the largest door-to-door sales organisation in Germany, paid his personal friend, Chancellor

Gerhard Schröder, two million euros for the rights to his memoirs while Schröder was still in office. Maschmeyer profited enormously from the establishment of the Riester-Rente by pushing sales of these private pension investment plans. Six months after the end of his chancellorship, Schröder was cashing generous paycheques as an "advisor" to an investment bank (*Ibid.*, p. 142 f.). Not surprisingly, given this context, other people from the Schröder government's sphere of influence later earned outsized pay packets at outfits like Lehman Brothers, Deutsche Bank, Allianz, Maschmeyer's financial consulting firm AWD, etc.

The new model of private delivery of what had previously been public services has been reflected in corresponding laws, which have created facts on the ground that have permanently damaged the ability of state administrations to act. Criticising the ideological background of these laws is not enough; the laws need to be changed.

In regards to the widespread and mistaken belief that a "sound budget policy" requires state budgets to be more-or-less balanced: Anyone who thinks this popular misunderstanding need not or cannot be corrected, and therefore believes that politicians must present plans to finance any public infrastructure or services delivery investment from tax revenues (i.e. to avoid new public debt), has already lost the battle. The challenge before policymakers and influencers is to communicate effectively to the general public that money is not a scarce resource for a state but is rather a means of economic management which the state can and should use to activate resources located in its territory for public-interest projects and purposes.

It is certainly worth intensively investigating how this means of economic management can be institutionalised in such a way that its misuse can be largely ruled out. In this context, it goes without saying that effective control mechanisms must be developed and greater involvement of citizens in investment decisions considered. However, such proposals regularly neglect the importance of the material and social status of career civil servants. The current negative image of civil servants among the general public, and the consistently poorer pay of civil servants compared to similar professional roles in the private sector, urgently need to be corrected. To put it bluntly, we need talented and effective mandarins to implement the democratic will. Pay and prestige should motivate the "best brains" of a country to want to become "servants" of society, and appropriate training should enable them to perform their work with competence and moral integrity.

First of all, however, it is essential that all public debt brakes, whether at EU, federal, state, or municipal level, be immediately removed, without replacement. The "golden rule" laid down in Article 115 of the Basic Law (Germany's Constitution) formulated a reasonable limit on the extent to which the state should be able to exercise disposition over the country's resources using debt financing: "Revenue from loans may not exceed the sum of the expenditures for investments budgeted for in the budget; exceptions are only permissible to avert a disturbance of the macroeconomic balance."

Once the nonsensical debt brakes have been removed, the main priority will be to provide the municipalities in particular with the financial resources they need to deal with accumulated infrastructure investment arrears of around 120 billion euros as quickly as possible. (The federal government's dogged determination over the past several years to balance its budget, regardless of the real-economy context, is the cause of the scandalous decay of Germany's infrastructure.) To manage the relevant projects, it will be essential to equip municipal administrative offices with qualified personnel as quickly as possible. This alone will be a Herculean task, as becomes apparent when one considers that the number of full-time jobs in Germany's municipal administrations was halved between 1990 and 2010 (cf. Mattert *et al.*, 2017, p. 34).

In order for public services to be provided properly, it will also be necessary to end the current dependence of local authorities on their own income, in particular the trade tax (income tax on locally registered businesses). In future, the level and quality of public services must no longer be based on the income of the relevant administrative units, but solely on actual needs.

The notion that private companies are able to provide public services more efficiently and that the state's only task should consist of tendering service contract competitions and establishing financial incentive systems has been impressively refuted in practice. It is precisely the private provision of services ultimately paid for with public funds that opens the door to nepotism and political corruption. Public infrastructure and services must in future be provided predominantly and directly by public-law organisations, which *expressis verbis* must not be managed according to the profit principle.

Pensions

It was just over 125 years ago that Germany, in a genuine social innovation, gave the majority of people the security of not having to starve or beg in old age. Fatefully, however, most citizens and "experts" have still not really understood this innovation. Even 125 years after the introduction of general pension insurance, they still wonder how this system actually works. It thus behooves us to recall some simple macroeconomic relationships that convey very clear ideas about how a society can make provision for the future.

This lack of understanding of the pension system became very obvious in a programme broadcast by ZDF, a major public broadcaster, in 2014 on the occasion of the 125th anniversary of the introduction of general pension insurance. According to the moderator, Bismarck's principle was that the young pay the pensions of the old — but, he said, that is no longer how it works today. At that point, a chart showing the declining level of pensions relative to average income was displayed on the TV screen, making it appear that the publicly funded PAYGo (pay-as-you-go) pension was no longer viable. This message was underpinned by brief interview clips of young people in front of the Reichstag building in Berlin saying that they did not expect to be able to live from the statutory pension insurance in their old age.

However, the declining curve in pension levels over the years is solely due to the fact that the statutory pension system was torpedoed by ignorant politicians who imposed nonsensical dogmas such as limiting social security contributions to a maximum of 22 percent of income. Demographics (a story about the aging population) was pushed forward as an excuse to justify limiting the flow of money to the statutory pension system, and thereby divert money to private pension schemes instead — as a gift to German insurance companies.

Further proof of this fundamental lack of comprehension of the workings of the state pension system was provided by Chancellor Angela Merkel, who said at its 125th anniversary celebration that the pay-as-you-go system was used in the 1950s because there was no financial capital stock (accumulated savings) from which to pay pensions; a country with demographic problems, in contrast, needs to cover these expenses with a savings pool.

This argument is almost ingeniously wrong. Let us assume that in the 1950s there had been claims by retirees on a pension savings scheme that had been accumulated during the decades before. What would the younger, working generation and the politicians have done then? Given that capital had been destroyed on a gigantic scale in the war, they would have been put in a position of deciding whether to say "sorry, there's no money in the kitty" and let the pensioners beg and starve, or instead, to acknowledge and honour the retirees' pension claims despite the fact that there were no savings available from which to pay them out.

If the decision had been made to pay pensioners according to their accumulated entitlements (even if there was no physical capital left to meet those entitlements), the result would have been the same as with the pay-as-you-go system: The currently working generation would have paid the retirees' pensions.

Similarly, after the fall of the GDR (the postwar East German regime), had retiring GDR citizens possessed papers promising them payouts from a financial savings fund composed of claims on the productivity of an accumulated East German capital stock (which was uncompetitive compared to Western industrial capital and became largely worthless after the Wall came down), West German society would have had to decide whether or not to pay a reasonable pension to pensioners whose capital stock had largely disappeared — just as it would have had to do anyway in the absence of any such papers.

We now have demographic developments in the form of an aging society, and because of this — usefully and sensibly, according to Ms. Merkel — savings-funded pension schemes like the Riester-Rente have become necessary. But if you think about it, 30 years from now, in the context of an ageing society, it will be of no particular use to people who are just entering retirement age to hold such papers in their hands. Such pieces of paper in the hands of retirees will not change the volume of real production prevalent at that time. Once again, the then-working generation will have to decide whether they really will pay the financial benefits promised on the pensioners' papers, or whether they will instead make the pensioners beg and starve. If 30 years from now, the system will have evolved such that there is once again only a pay-as-you-go system, the outcome would be no different: the working generation will have to pay pension benefits to retirees. And if they do not pay it, nobody pays it.

In this context, "to pay" pensions simply means "to produce goods, and then partially cede claims to their use and ownership to others." The details according to which the claims of the elderly are "securitised," i.e. whether these take the form of a legislated pay-as-you-go system in which the young promise that they will honour the pension claims of the elderly, or instead take the form of a funded system based on accumulated financial savings, in which the young promise they will repurchase financial securities held by the elderly, does not play a major role in establishing the validity of the retirees' claims.

The only real relevance of the different forms of pension claims relates to distributional issues. The actors looking to influence the details of how social production is redistributed to various subgroups of the elderly can be found in different camps: Politicians like to intervene in the details of the pay-as-you-go system, whereas managing the details of a funded system composed of privately accumulated savings involves fees, commissions, and distributional decisions that are of interest principally to speculative financial market players.

On average, however, both systems are affected by demographic shifts in exactly the same way — just as they are equally affected by the destruction of capital stock caused by wars or natural disasters. If a societal collapse has led to a situation in which the existing capital stock is poor in quality or quantity — as Angela Merkel, who grew up in East Germany, should have understood — then the young can only provide a modest flow of goods and services for the old, delivered in a pay-as-you-go arrangement, because they themselves have very little income, and first have to rebuild society's physical production capital to generate a surplus that can be redistributed.

This means that the securities issued today under so-called "funded" private pension savings schemes do not guarantee that there will be a physically large and economically efficient capital stock in 30 years' time. If it does not then exist — for whatever reason — there will not be any interest payments on pensioners' financial securities either. At that point, once again, the working generation will have to decide between making pensioners beg and starve, or paying them a pension, regardless of whether (or how much) they paid into a public pension fund.

However, the almost always overlooked, yet crucial sticking point in the whole debate is this: Attempting to fund pensions by means of financial savings accumulated in private pension funds worsens the prospects of having a large and efficient capital stock in the future. That is because a higher savings ratio today (in the sense of a larger gap between income and expenditure of private households) hinders investment (as we explained in detail in Part II). Savings-funded pension plans lead to lower aggregate real-economy investments and thus to a smaller capital stock in the future — or at least, that is what they do when they succeed in increasing the overall savings ratio (which does not apply to the Riester-Rente pension scheme, because the savings rate of private households did not increase after it was introduced, as it happens; in aggregate, Riester-Rente merely shifted some money from other savings instruments).

This phenomenon was observable in the wake of the global financial crisis. When funded pension schemes were first introduced in Germany and other countries, everyone (especially every bank and insurance salesperson) believed that the interest rate on private investments and government bonds would permanently be far above the (implicit) interest rate of the pay-as-you-go system. As it turns out, however, interest rates on financial securities are now approaching zero, and if — as in Japan — they remain at zero for another 20 years, there will be no return on invested money. Whether the absolute sum (the principal) of the invested money will be recovered is also an open question — because if many people try to sell their papers at the same time, a large part of the original value can quickly be lost.

What Norbert Blüm, who was Germany's federal Minister of Labour and Social Services from 1982 to 1998, said many years ago remains unchanged today: The pay-as-you-go pension is safe. It is as safe and secure as anything can be in an insecure world. As long as our children are willing and able to honour their parents for their work, with pay-as-you-go, their pensions are secure.

Which monetary order is best for developing and emerging countries?

Currency prices are the most important prices for the international exchange of goods, services, and capital. However, as we explained in Part IV, exchange rate adjustments cannot work miracles. In Europe in recent years, it has been common to hear the mantra repeated that monetary union should not have been implemented, because EMU member countries are so "structurally" different. But this is were true, then the reverse would also be the case:

"Structurally" different countries would only be able to trade with each other without running into major difficulties within a flexible exchange rate regime.

This is wrong, because changes in currency relations, i.e. a change in macroeconomically effective monetary parameters, cannot cure an economy's structural deficits, as we show below. This does not contradict the often expressed view that a prolonged undervaluation can help developing and emerging countries to assert themselves in international trade and thereby receive important growth impulses. The catching-up processes of Germany and Japan after the Second World War are usually cited as classic examples of this. However, it would be difficult for today's developing and emerging countries to following the post-war examples of those two countries. At the time, Germany and Japan were members of a global, US-led monetary system (the Bretton Woods system), which tolerated the undervaluation of the currencies of some smaller countries that had been hard-hit by the consequences of the war. No catching-up country today has the opportunity to choose to join a system like Bretton Woods — much less on such favourable terms. Today, there exists no monetary system like the one Germany and Japan, and also France and Italy, had access to after the war.

Interventions by a country's central bank (i.e. the systematic purchase of foreign currency with its own currency) would make undervaluations possible, but this type of intervention to weaken a country's own currency is virtually proscribed internationally. Doing it, as the example of China has shown, leads to considerable international political pressure on a country's leadership to leave the valuation of its currency to the market — even if the central bank only is attempting to prolong, for a while, an undervaluation that resulted from an economic crisis. Moreover, especially for the central banks of "structurally" weak countries with relatively high inflation rates, it is difficult to generate relatively high import prices through currency undervaluation without causing these import-related inflationary impulses to be transferred to the domestic goods and services market.

That is why many countries have chosen the reverse option in the past, namely to exert downward pressure on their own inflation rate by overvaluing their own currency (resulting in low import prices). Very few have dared to go the way of China (and some smaller Asian countries, after the great Asian currency crisis of 1996/97), which fixed its currency in a state of undervaluation unilaterally, i.e. without the help of other countries.

In contrast, most countries that have temporarily benefited from an undervaluation in the last 30 years owe this outcome to a crisis which caused their own currency to be significantly devalued. But since this in turn was usually the result of a previous overvaluation, these countries did not gain much on balance; in general, they suffered a net loss. Only in the case of Argentina, where a terrible crisis raged in 2002 and the devaluation was extremely strong (the Argentine peso depreciated by 65 percent against the weighted average of its trading partners at the time), did the devaluation have such a strong impact on trade flows that lost ground could be made up for in the first five to six years after the devaluation. After that, however, inflation returned and destroyed much of what the devaluation had made possible.

Only if, as in China's case, interventions in the currency market and the fixing of the exchange rate is combined with intelligently managed income policies (i.e. an explicit rejection of the neoliberal/neoclassical hypothesis of flexibilisation), so as to keep domestic inflation in check, can a long-lasting undervaluation really be beneficial on balance.

Most financial crises of recent decades were currency crises, i.e. crises in which the currency of a country or group of countries ended up with a lower valuation. These crises have occurred in all types of monetary systems. However, acknowledging the key importance of currency crises violates one of the most important doctrines of the prevailing economic theory, namely the dogma that financial markets are efficient. Even Paul Krugman, for example, criticised the financial markets after the 2008 crisis (Krugman, 2013b), but failed to underscore a central point: The fact that the currency markets were an important part of this great crisis.

This is a key point that neither the International Monetary Fund nor other international organisations significantly controlled by the industrialised countries want to (or are permitted to) acknowledge. The problem is that anyone who admits that foreign exchange markets regularly and systematically produce absurd results would have no choice but to abandon the even more important dogma of efficient free trade: If exchange rates do not adequately reflect the fundamentals of the economies involved in a free trade agreement, there will be no stopping protectionist measures that countries could take if their currency is unjustifiably driven to overvaluation by the currency markets.

A new international financial architecture

There must be global rules for global trade, just as there are national rules for trade within the borders of existing nation states. These cannot be set by individual states, but only by the international community of states. Just as they have taken a driving and leading role in trade liberalisation, developed countries must now take the lead in developing a system of internationally recognised and enforceable financial and currency rules.

A new world monetary order must regulate monetary relations between the major blocs, and at the same time give smaller countries the opportunity to tie their currency to one of the major blocs with a high prospect of enduring success. Systems of fixed exchange rates or a monetary union can only be sustained in the long run if all participating nations succeed in keeping their internal cost development and inflation rates within agreed limits that all members are prepared to accept. If goods and capital are to move freely worldwide, however, sustainable solutions must also be found for a monetary order encompassing currency relations between regions which, for various reasons, will not be able to achieve rapid convergence in their respective cost and inflation trends.

Strong fluctuations in exchange rates that go beyond offsetting inflation differences cause distortions in the allocation of resources and in investment decisions, in the same way that fluctuations in the internal value of a currency, i.e. its purchasing power, cause such distortions. Under a new international system, exchange rate adjustments should only be implemented in order to compensate for differences in inflation rates. As a guideline for a new world monetary order, it follows that exchange rates must be stable enough to allow rational economic decisions, yet also flexible enough to maintain the international competitiveness of all states.

In order to establish such a system of controlled flexibility, international cooperation in currency relations management must be considerably strengthened. This applies to the relationships between major industrial nations, and also to those between large economies and smaller ones. In view of advancing globalisation and the ever stronger integration of the world economy, smaller nations — irrespective of their monetary system — are increasingly unable to pursue their own independent economic policies. If they want to keep their product and capital markets open, they must be included in a global system of currency relations supervision and cooperation to avoid excessive exchange rate fluctuations.

If a new world monetary system is to be successful, the international community will need effective institutions. In recent decades, the two Bretton Woods institutions — the International Monetary Fund and World Bank — have adapted their roles and distribution of tasks to the changing conditions of the global economy. The tasks of both institutions will need be redefined again as a new global financial architecture emerges.

For the IMF, this will mean a return to its original role in the Bretton Woods system. In particular, it will have to provide short-term monitoring of the functioning of monetary systems and currency relations as well as macroeconomic advice to participating nations. Its monitoring functions must include, for example, the establishment and operation of an early warning system which recognises emerging risks of serious external trade imbalances, warns the countries concerned, and informs the other participants. The IMF would also continue to be responsible for organising and implementing short-term support measures for countries that are facing a critical worsening of their financial situation.

In the new architecture, another institution, plausibly the Bank for International Settlements in Basel, would have to play a far greater role than previously in analysing systemic risks in the entire financial sphere and recommending countermeasures at an early stage when emerging problems are identified. In globalised markets, there is no alternative to setting up rules for assumption of financial risks and introducing information requirements, i.e. to establishing credit supervision in the broadest sense. This requires a multilateral agreement. However, regulations in this area must not be limited to an agreement between states. The private sector, i.e. all those who want to take advantage of the opportunities offered by the global financial market, must be involved in covering risks to a meaningful extent, as we have described earlier.

It is often feared that the emergence of a new world monetary order and a global financial architecture will lead to a loss of national sovereignty. But the panoply of global and regional crises since 2008 shows that there can be no sovereignty in the sense of an effective decoupling from these events. All nations of the world are affected in one way or another. Experience with various monetary systems after the Second World War has made it clear that none of the various monetary systems applied allowed effective decoupling. A partial loss of national sovereignty is a direct result of the opening of product and capital markets, not the result of an inappropriate monetary order. There is no alternative to international cooperation on exchange rate policy if effective and sustainable trade relationships are to be enabled.

Climate Change and Environmental Protection

Climate and environmental protection are the two grand challenges that will remain even if economic problems, as conventionally defined, are largely solved. Here again, many mistaken economic preconceptions stand as obstacles in the way of humanity's progress. Regardless of whether one considers climate change or the overuse of natural resources to be the greater problem, the key question is always how necessary, desirable, and lasting behavioural changes can be achieved within the framework of the global market economy system.

Here again, progress is not possible absent a realistic theory of economic dynamics. This is why attempts to ensure effective protection of environmental systems necessary for human flourishing on planet Earth have so far failed.

Climate change and the dynamics of the market economy

With regard to environmental and climate protection, the conditions prevalent in each nation will determine the concrete path to be taken by politics, given the strong path dependency that emerges from past development patterns. A country such as Switzerland that has relied on hydropower to generate electricity will deal with its share of the climate policy challenge very differently from Germany, where lignite and coal have been the most important inputs for electricity generation. France, with its focus on nuclear energy, has different conditions again.

However, the prevention or mitigation of climate change is indisputably a global challenge. That is why, irrespective of different starting conditions, efficient strategies for reducing the use of fossil fuels can only exist if at least the most important countries agree to coordinate.

Economic principles can be of decisive help in responding to ecological challenges because the focus here is on the increasing scarcity of natural resources. The analysis begins — but does not end — with classical microeconomics. A first step is to ask how much of a given set of goods people are prepared to sacrifice if they have to use more resources to ensure a healthy environment, for example to avoid or remediate damage caused by production of consumer goods or to prevent less pollutants from escaping in future production. This involves weighing up costs associated with refraining from producing consumer goods or services by conventional methods, against the benefits of preventing environmental damage. The second step is to address the question of what this means at the macroeconomic level.

Environmental protection as a preference

The most important problem with the initial problem statement described in the foregoing paragraph — a problem which has been fiercely discussed by economists — is that the ordinary microeconomic subject has no immediate benefit from reducing the emission of harmful gases during production, because she may not live anywhere near the production plant where the damage is done. In addition, she does not know whether economic agents in other regions or countries are also changing their behaviours, which would be necessary for a significant overall environmental benefit to be achieved by her ethical consumer choices. Conversely, if negative environmental effects occur in the production of a particular good, it can be difficult to attribute this negative effect to any particular actor in the supply-and-demand chain, and as a result, the overall effect does not appear in any individual cost–benefit considerations. Economists say that "negative externalities" have been produced that harm society, but for which no one can be held individually liable.

Often, the benefits from using a product are concentrated, but the harms are diffuse — and mostly passed along to others, not sustained by those using the product. To give a simple example, the combustion of fuels in automobiles produces harmful emissions that do not directly harm the driver of the car; instead, they harm the people in the next car behind, or a nearby cyclist, and society as a whole. So no driver has an interest in making his car cleaner unless he can be sure that everyone else is reciprocally doing the same. Consequently, the state must intervene and force everyone to do something about harmful emissions. To prevent the negative external effect, the state can, for example, issue regulations that generally make driving more expensive, or it can enforce technical requirements to reduce pollutant emissions.

However, it can also apply regulations to try to make negative externalities get internalised directly, i.e. to make them perceptible to the individual without the state prescribing any particular technology solution. One example of this would be a simple requirement that all exhaust gases produced by an automobile must first be conducted through the interior of the car that produces them. This sounds radical, but if one takes a long-term view, it would probably have been the best solution. We have no doubt that if this regulation had been enforced by governments a hundred years ago, today we would not be driving any less. However, we would probably be driving battery- or hydrogen-powered cars. In any case we would have left a large part of the oil that has historically been burned in the ground, and produced a much lower volume of greenhouse gases.

This example shows that posing environmental policy questions in microeconomic terms does not get us very far, and in most cases even leads us astray, because the classic consumer-choice decision imputed by the microeconomic conceptual framework cannot be answered in practical reality. This is because the information that would be needed to be able to ask the majority of people a simple decision-making question of the kind "What do you want? More environmental protection or more goods?" is generally not even available. This begins with the fact that there is no uniquely given set of goods to trade off against each other. After all, we are operating in a dynamic system in which people's inventiveness is permanently generating increases in the range, quality, and supply of goods and dramatically changing the structure of society's basket of available goods and services. People cannot really know their preferences in any enduring sense, certainly not on a forward-looking basis, because they will only develop relative preferences for goods that are yet to be invented after these emerge, at some point in the future. The landscape is constantly shifting, and so therefore are people's preferences. Within that temporal context, it is also clear that technical progress is continually changing the available means for implementing environmental protection.

No one can predict many years in advance what (if any) the trade-off between "normal" goods and "environmental" goods will be, or whether it will be relevant at all. Let us take the above example again: Let us imagine that hydrogen technology has been introduced for automobiles, because industry decides it is the most cost-competitive way to meet the aforementioned hypothetical regulation that exhaust gases must be routed through cars' cabins. Once mass production hydrogen powered cars exist, it is completely irrelevant for the subsequent hundred years how expensive the introduction was, and how many "normal" (i.e. environmentally more harmful) goods were not consumed because of that expense, or how much lost benefit humanity temporarily had to "suffer" because it relied on an "expensive" technology early on.

Until now, we have been working with the idea that environmental damage regularly occurs as side effects (externalities) during the processing of people's "normal" preferences by the market system, and must be internalised by the state in one way or another. But this conception becomes incoherent when environmental protection becomes an important part of people's preferences. When people become aware that they have neglected and abused the natural environment, and that there is a great need to restore, regenerate, and protect it, then the desire to repair damage that has already occurred and/or to prevent new damage itself becomes a consumer preference and competes at the micro-level with "normal" preferences.

In this case, entrepreneurs are needed who will take up and implement these preferences. Since these preferences are not necessarily expressed in a concrete demand for better products but rather in an abstract willingness to pay for more environmental protection, it is the state that must be the entrepreneur for environmental protection and serve these preferences. By imposing, in one way or another, a general obligation on companies to take certain precautionary measures (such as fitting catalytic converters, filters, or other exhaust devices in cars), the state meets citizens' preferences for better air quality while implicitly forcing them to pay for it. However, this compulsion results only from the fact that without it, there would be many free riders who would rely on "others" to pay for pollution reduction measures, so that they themselves could escape the relevant payment. Moreover, everyone knows that "free riders" would be extremely numerous absent regulations, so much so that perhaps almost no one would bother taking pollution avoidance measures, since their efforts would not suffice to clean the air — and this might happen even if most people prefer clean air.

Quite differently from what market-fundamentalist apologists would have us believe, state coercion does not mean that people are forced to buy something that they do not really want to have. Rather it means that the state, like any entrepreneur, has to persuade its clients and sell its products — in this case, policies aimed at producing cleaner air, which everyone actually does want. Coercion does not *a priori* mean that the state is imposing something on people that they do not want to have; it does not necessarily mean that the measures imposed by the state are alien to the market, in the broader sense of the word "market."

Let us imagine a further scenario in which the state acts solely on the basis of its better understanding and imposes some costs and regulations on the citizens in order to create "meritorious goods" which the citizens initially may not want to have in the form imposed. Let us assume that in the assessment of a democratically elected state leadership, the measures imposed serve the citizens' well-being. Even in that case, economists cannot simply say that this imposed good is something foreign to the market, and that one must deduct it, so to speak, from a macroeconomic calculation of prosperity.

For example, the state's requirement that children attend school and are not allowed to work may be perceived by some individuals as a compulsion, and when it was first introduced, it may have been unpopular with many families because it deprived them of financial benefits derived from putting their children to work at an early age. But the vast majority of citizens today take the laws prohibiting child labour and requiring them to be sent to school for granted, and understand that it contributes enormously to making society richer both materially and immaterially in the long term.

If, on the basis of these considerations, we classify provision for environmental conservation and climate protection as being among the needs and preferences of citizens and society, a whole class of "problems" goes away which are linked, in the dominant version of economic theory, to environmental protection. This applies in particular to the "problem" which is usually designated by the phrase "the costs of environmental protection."

Costs and jobs

What are the famous costs usually held high by business lobbyists when the talk turns to environmental protection? For example, if Volkswagen, along with all other manufacturers, were obliged to install an exhaust filtering technology in their new cars that is more expensive than the current version, what would be the problem? If the vehicle as a whole were to become more expensive as a result, then the additional costs would be borne by consumers. The additional costs would mean additional income for the manufacturers of the relevant car parts. Consumers would perhaps pay a bit more for the car overall and save on consumption elsewhere, assuming a given income. However, the car manufacturers could also dispense with the installation of some decorative parts to compensate for the now higher environmental component costs, thereby keeping the overall price of the car unchanged.

From a macroeconomic point of view, the result is always the same: Additional income is earned and more jobs are created at the manufacturers of exhaust control system devices, and less money is earned (and jobs are cut) in some other part of the economy where the customers or car manufacturers make the savings, for example in decorative components. This is not a problem; these are entirely normal impulses of structural change, no different than are given millions of times each and every day by consumers' purely private spending decisions. Politicians need not lose any sleep over this at all.

However, if politicians make the mistake of identifying with the interests of an individual automobile manufacturer or even of the car industry, then they find themselves in a predicament. As soon as politicians respond to carmakers' special pleading, they are trapped, because they have to admit that someone loses. The relative income situation of an individual producer (or in some cases, of an industry) may have deteriorated, because state requirements have made production more expensive. It is easy to imagine that, with such an approach, politicians have great difficulty explaining to producers who are spreading panic about prospective job losses that environmental protection is more important than individual jobs. If politicians accept the converse premise, the horse-trading begins, and environmental goals are sacrificed to the financial interests of particular companies or industries. A competent state (i.e. a state whose policymakers think exclusively in macroeconomic categories) should refuse to engage in such horse-trading from the outset.

It is clear from the foregoing that when it is discussed in microeconomic terms, the whole discussion about the conflict between environmental protection on the one hand and jobs or income on the other completely misses the point. In the everyday process of structural change imposed on us by private producers (through advertising, among other things), we never ask whether the results are positive or negative for jobs and income. When a new tablet computer largely replaces older-model desktop machines, many jobs and income opportunities also shift. However, no one would dream of asking whether this development should be stopped or at least weakened so as not to endanger so many individual jobs in the desktop computer–making industry. It is only when the state is involved that every single producer (the big ones in particular) takes it upon himself to ask exactly this question.

Of course, this confusion would not occur if economists really focused on doing economics and not business administration in disguise. In fact, a particularly sad chapter of economic confusion must be noted here. As early on as the 1970s (Flassbeck & Maier-Rigaud, 1982), the dominant economic theory began to form a pentagon out of the "magic square," i.e. the four key macroeconomic objectives (price stability, external trade balance, high employment, adequate growth), in which environmental protection also had its own (fifth) corner.

This was and still is grandiose nonsense, because people's desire for a clean environment (or their understanding of the need for interventions to protect the environment) belongs to the category of microeconomic preferences, but has nothing to do with how the system is controlled macroeconomically or what results are achieved with macro-control.

The classification of environmental protection as among the popular preferences also reveals that the euphoria of many supporters of the green movement, who speak of environmental protection as generating "two dividends", namely the improvement of the environment and more jobs or more incomes, is just as nonsensical as the perception of conflict mentioned above. In our view, environmental protection is a completely normal good, but its production usually has to be initiated by the state. The production of more environmental protection in this sense is neither in conflict with jobs taken in aggregate nor can one expect a particularly large number of jobs from it. An appropriate economic policy takes note of this and carries out its tasks irrespective of how much (and in what way) environmental protection is enforced by other domains of public policy.

The only area where even enlightened economists often believe they have to restrict this logic is in the question of international competitiveness. Indeed, if a state imposes massive environmental requirements and its trading partner does not, then a one-off cost differential arises under otherwise equal conditions; this cost differential can help industries in the state that does nothing in terms of environmental protection to gain market share.

Here, classifying environmental protection as among the normal preferences is no longer effective, because it is quite possible that people's wishes
(or the natural conditions) in the other country are such that their state, with
a certain justification, enforces less environmental protection there. In other
words, in the relationship between these two states, one cannot simply
assume that production for environmental protection is as much in demand
everywhere as production for a normal good, because the preferences of the
majority of citizens for more environmental protection may be different from
country to country. Consequently, all other things being equal, the cost and
price levels of normal goods (and probably of tradable goods) in the country
with stricter environmental regulations are likely going to be higher than in
the country with less strict regulations.

If this cost gap is really quantitatively significant, the state can compensate for it through many different measures. It could permanently impose an
import duty on goods produced in countries with laxer environmental standards, calculated to compensate for their cost advantage. Alternatively, it could
give its own companies a tax advantage or a subsidy that compensates for the
disadvantage. However, one must generally bear in mind that the absolute
cost levels in many countries are in any case massively distorted by government intervention. Tax rates vary widely even within the European Union,
without this resulting in suggestions that this will lead to systematic distortions of competition. Different levels of tax burden are often offset by different levels of infrastructure provided by the state, after all, which benefits
companies in the country with higher taxes. Better training of the workforce
is also part of the infrastructure of higher-tax jurisdictions.

Steer the economy via prices — how else?

When considering the matter of limited natural resources, it is obvious that
the environmental issue is a matter of scarcity and therefore of prices.
Appropriate pricing can encourage people all over the world to be careful
with finite natural resources. Price effects can also directly stimulate people
to use their intelligence and creativity to create processes and technologies
that will help to reduce fossil fuels usage; the potential in this domain goes
far beyond the current state of the art.

If it were possible to impose a global price management system ensuring
that oil and coal prices rise steadily in comparison to clean energy and also

in proportion to consumer incomes, one could expect that much greater efforts would be made to conserve these substances than could ever result from the regulations of one state (or all states). A larger amount of the vast potential of renewable energy is not being exploited precisely because even 40 years after the first oil price crisis, fossil fuels are still as cheap as they were back then.

The first argument put forward against this is the obvious one: "It's going to cost a lot!", many will say. Well, of course, it will cost something! How could there be such huge investments for free? However, this is not a macroeconomic problem, because again, some producers will benefit and others will lose out, but there is no reason to believe that a reduction in money circulation or in GDP will result from a shift to clean energy systems. The resulting structural change is desired and intentional. Like any structural change to supply and demand patterns, the clean energy transition will "cost" something in the sense that customers will no longer buy the same set of things with their money as they did before. Consequently, as shown below, many producers of older-generation fossil-fuel-intensive products will lose market share, but many new-generation suppliers will win. It is clear that existing big fossil fuels companies do not like this, but why should politicians care?

If a country wants to exit from dependence on fossil and nuclear energy, it either has to make fossil and nuclear energy so expensive that renewable energy becomes price-competitive in comparison or it has to subsidise renewable energy directly. It can also use the so-called new market-based instruments and burden those who emit pollutants by forcing them to buy certificates that allow them to emit a certain quantity of pollutants, such that the total quantity of permissible emissions is capped. If the quantity of certificates is then consistently and steadily reduced, so that the price of the certificates continues to rise, the relative prices of fossil vs. clean energy will increasingly shift in favour of renewable energies. Since politicians have not yet dared to implement carbon prices or the new market economy instruments ("cap-and-trade" systems) on a global scale, Germany over the past ten years has chosen to implement subsidies for renewable energy.

The Federal Government has reduced the attractiveness of fossil energy by subsidising the development of renewable energy sources via guaranteed purchase prices. This can be justified in that without such subsidies there would have been no large-scale transition to renewable energy systems, because there is no reason to believe that the market will by itself make oil so expensive soon enough that a timely transition would occur — i.e. a transition that would happen soon enough to prevent catastrophic climate destabilisation.

By the way, subsidies still exist for the nuclear industry too, in the form of future costs for final nuclear waste storage sites (these costs are not fully covered by the electricity price) and the repair of damage to interim storage facilities (keywords in a German context: Asse, Gorleben). The taxpayers will end up paying for the defusing of these time-bombs because the nuclear reactor operating corporations have so far successfully dodged dealing with them.

With its large guaranteed market for renewable electricity sales, established since 2000, Germany has managed a fairly rapid, large-scale build-out of wind and solar power in the country as well as biogas digesters. The pace of conversion from fossil power generation to power generation from renewable sources has been quicker than almost anyone predicted would occur. This example demonstrates one thing very clearly: in order to make progress on the clean energy transition, the flexibility of companies is enormously helpful, even though the financing process has had nothing to do with that of a conventional market economy. Because the state guaranteed a certain purchase price for electricity to all those willing and able to invest in renewable energies (i.e. set a fixed feed-in tariff), investments in renewable energy production were well worthwhile. Consequently, almost everyone who had money to invest (or was able to borrow money cheaply) started looking for a large roof somewhere to cover with solar panels, or a meadow on a hill that a wind turbine could fit on. In almost no time at all, farmers, homeowners, and restaurant operators became electricity producers.

Compensating for distributional effects

This shows how enormously flexible companies can be. Given appropriate financial incentives, they could easily meet global challenges such as climate change. To make it happen, we merely need to more clearly understand how the market economy works. We must stop giving in to the lobbying power of individual major corporate "players" and not let ourselves be misled by ideological barriers (like the notion that "the state must under no circumstances intervene in price formation in the long term").

The German example shows the great effect that is possible with a price that is sufficiently stable for a product to be promoted for a sufficiently long time to gain substantial market share. If in addition to a stable and attractive price, there are also reasonable financing conditions, then even people who have not yet been entrepreneurs or cared a damn about the environment or future generations will invest in protecting the environment and improving the future. But this is not possible without the state — or a community of states. Anyone who waits for unaided markets to fund public goods such as climate stability will wait until the end of time.

The renewable energy subsidy caused increases in the retail price of electricity for ordinary consumers. As it was introduced, some people in Germany moaned and wailed their concern for "the long-suffering electricity customer — and especially the poor!" The people who wailed loudest were people who otherwise had never been noted for their concern about the poor or the income of ordinary people. Yet in fact, there is no denying that such market-based instruments place a much greater burden, calculated as a proportion of income, on those at the lower end of the income scale than those at the upper end. This is true even after taking into account the fact that much more energy is consumed at the upper end.

At this point, we must ask ourselves what we really want. Many examples have shown that subject promotion is more effective than object promotion. In other words, it is usually better to provide direct material support for the less well-off than to refrain from setting the prices that are needed to discourage public or private bads or encourage public goods. If policy does this, the system does not have to refrain from awakening the spirit of entrepreneurial solutions discovery which is only possible with appropriate setting of price incentives.

It is absolutely right to insist that relatively poor citizens should not be burdened more in relation to their income than the relatively well-off. This applies to poorer countries as well as to poorer people. This means that their financial situation must be improved so as to enable to afford rising energy prices. To put it simply: Every welfare recipient should be able to decide for himself whether he wants to spend a higher monthly welfare income on higher heating costs, or whether he prefers to actively participate in energy saving by changing his behaviour in order to use the additional money for other consumer goods.

Consequently, welfare rates must be substantially increased, taxes for low-income earners must be lowered, decent minimum wages introduced across the board and gradually increased as productivity improvements permit, or social security contributions for low-income earners must be systematically reduced, if the necessary change in energy policy is to be achieved. Anyone who rejects this rather obvious solution to the oft-cited "energy poverty" problem abandons credibility.

Even those who believe that social welfare systems should provide regulatory incentives and requirements to take up available work — as does Germany's "Hartz IV" unemployment benefits system, which achieves this in part by setting benefits at a very low monthly rate compared to the incomes of people employed even at the minimum wage — must admit that allowing the costs of the clean energy transition to worsen the living conditions of lower-income groups cannot be justified. Politicians must be prepared from the outset to compensate for the additional burden on the poor in order to avoid social injustice — and in order to take the wind out of the sails of fossil-fuel lobbyists who loudly proffer the "energy poverty" argument simply as a way to derail the clean energy transition.

Global solutions and the market

Both supporters and critics of the German clean energy transition are sceptical as to whether the existing technologies to compensate for strong natural fluctuations in renewable energy sources (wind and sunshine) will soon be available. The German government, too, which must be optimistic on principle, seems to be very cautious in its approach to this issue. Some proponents of the energy transition openly say that if the decision is made to do without nuclear power, then fossil energy will still have to be used for many years or even decades in order to ensure security of electricity generation under all conditions.

This raises a global problem that has not yet been discussed much by the public. It was always clear that for purely economic reasons, an energy revolution in one country cannot by itself solve the global problem of fossil fuel consumption. In a functioning market, underconsumption in one place leads to increased consumption in another, because if one consumer consumes less, the price of fossil fuels will decline, and the market will tend to sell more oil, coal, and gas to other consumers. Many advocates of energy efficiency have not yet understood that there is no "contribution" that a country (much less a smaller unit such as a household or private individual) can make to the global energy transition as long as the market for fossil fuels exists. Given the tremendous utility of cheap energy, this market will be "cleared" at all times by other consumers via reduced prices, as economists put it. Anyone who wants to prevent fossil fuels from being burned must therefore support the creation of nothing less than a global regime to manage and steer this market — with all the consequences that entails. Yet even at the major climate conference in Paris in 2015, this crucial point was not even discussed, much less implemented.

In this respect, the best thing that can be said so far about the German energy transition from a global perspective is that it can be very important that a country shows that such an energy turnaround is technically and financially possible — an important argument that should not be minimised. It can be worthwhile for a rich country to spend a lot of money to demonstrate this. Moreover, Germany's massive build-out of wind and solar power drove the relevant technologies (wind turbines, solar panels, etc.) down the unit cost curve through economies of scale and learning effects — which has greatly helped their market penetration in the rest of the world.

However, if Germany can only secure its energy transition over many years or decades by keeping conventional fossil-fuelled power plants on standby to fill gaps when wind and sun are lacking, then unfortunately this argument will also collapse, since the energy transition will be incredibly expensive. If the whole world were to take Germany as an example and rely on renewable energies, but at the same time (again, if nuclear power were to be phased out) fossil energy-fuelled generating capacity would also be needed as a fallback solution, a functioning market for fossil fuels would continue to be needed.

However, the world cannot drive this fossil-fuel market and the associated global infrastructure to virtually zero for eight months and then simply start it up again during the dark, low-wind winter months. The market for the extraction of oil, coal, and gas, as well as the enormous logistics associated with it, must be operated on a continual basis if it is to be operated at all. But if it exists, then the extracted raw materials will either be used up immediately, or the world urgently will need a global fossil fuels governance system to manage and secure the fossil fuels market on both the supply and demand side, i.e. by taxing demand and rationing supply. Unfortunately, international politics is still not prepared to discuss this point, let alone negotiate seriously towards its implementation.

A global paradox

Here, too, there is a very interesting "fallacy of composition" (i.e. a conclusion that may apply to a part of the system but does not apply to the whole system): When a country makes the transition to renewable energy sources, it can be confident that it will always have enough fossil energy available to compensate for fluctuations in the production of renewable energies, but the world as a whole cannot have that confidence. Given today's energy production and storage technologies, only nuclear power remains available as a non-fossil-fuelled option to compensate for lulls in wind or solar power delivery. One can only hope that long before the natural end of the fossil age (i.e. the depletion of all fossil resources), a completely different secure energy supply system will be available — most likely in the form of cheap and ubiquitous long- and short-term energy storage technologies for storing renewable electricity. Long-term storage, for example, is possible by using electricity to generate hydrogen gas, methane, or even liquid fuels, using "power-to-gas" or "power-to-liquids" technology, which are already available in prototype forms.

But let us not deceive ourselves, until such a system exists, no one in the world (absent a notional "global green dictator") will prevent the large-scale burning of fossil fuels, no matter how many international agreements are concluded in which (some or almost all) countries commit themselves to reducing CO_2 emissions. Measured against the exhortations of climate scientists who urge a rapid absolute reduction in emissions, current global policy is simply not suitable for tackling the issues that matter if we want to prevent further global warming.

These considerations show that the prospects for global climate stabilisation are not good. But if there are no good arguments, it does not help to console oneself with illusions. The International Energy Agency (IEA) has just reported that global CO_2 emissions rose last year after remaining roughly constant over the previous three years (Clark, 2017). Whether this is, on balance, a reason for optimism or pessimism cannot be clearly stated at present, since the IEA assessment took into account that in China, where emissions have fallen by one percent, many new nuclear power plants have been going on line, and that hydropower is also increasingly being used there — technologies which are low-carbon but have other environmental costs.

It must be borne in mind that global economic development (especially industrial development) has been quite weak over the past few years. The estimate of three percent global GDP growth must be treated with great caution, as it does not adequately reflect global industrial dynamics. Even in Europe, where there has been a small reduction in CO_2 emissions in recent years, it is important to note that economic development (here too, especially in industry) has been weak over the last five to six years, which is a trend that should not be continued, for economic and social reasons.

In any case, a drastic absolute reduction in CO_2 emissions from fossil fuels combustion by 2050 (*nota bene*, other anthropogenic CO_2 emissions sources exist as well), as many climate researchers consider necessary (they even talk about achieving zero emissions from combustion), is in our view unrealistic. To achieve this, as we have said, a global clean energy transition would have to be set in motion very quickly, but there are almost no signs of this at present. In addition, a radical global management of fossil energy markets would have to be implemented — and so far, nobody has dared to develop such a thing even conceptually, much less politically or practically.

Prices and quantities

There continues to be great confusion throughout the energy debate as to whether and to what extent "the market" in general can be left to discover the right prices for energy carriers. This applies not only to fossil fuels but also to electricity. Some believe that now that the state has given a boost to increased use of renewable energies, it can largely be left to the market to find the right electricity price.

This idea is not remotely realistic. It is already evident today that a "free" electricity price gives completely confusing and irrational signals. Temporarily negative prices per MWh on wholesale electricity exchanges, as have repeatedly occurred on particularly windy or sunny days since Germany enabled a massive build-out of renewable energy, signal to suppliers of conventionally produced electricity that their product is worth less than nothing, and therefore implicitly call on them to stop production immediately. However, this is not politically desired or intended, because that would deprive the system as a whole of the reliable on-demand generating capacity necessary to offset the inherent volatility of renewable energy sources. But if shutting down non-renewable generating capacity is not the intention, then clearly, we cannot rely on signals from the electricity market; indeed, we must prevent them from driving some crucial business decisions.

This shows a simple and undeniable principle: Those who, for political or other reasons, have set certain quantity of targets must not leave prices to the market. The market only distributes what is currently available, but does not ensure that a given product is produced in a certain quantity in the future. The best example of this is the role of interest rates in macroeconomic developments, as we have already explained above. Because all Western societies are not only looking to distribute existing goods on offer but also to promote economic development, one of the most important prices in the market economy, the interest rate, is almost entirely controlled by the state (or the central bank appointed by it).

Anyone pursuing specific volume targets in energy supply or atmospheric carbon concentrations must not shy away from intervening in the markets, but must actively intervene and steer prices as consistently as possible in line with political priorities. Informed and efficiently functioning states should explain this as clearly as possible to their citizens in order to show that they are serious about the declared objectives.

In light of all this, what US President Donald Trump has recently done, namely pulled out of the Paris Climate Agreement, is likely to prove less dramatic in its consequences than many people fear. Fine declarations of intent by the rest of the world do not amount to a substantive policy to prevent climate change. Moralistic posturing is not a substitute for real policy action.

Many critical thinkers are dissatisfied with the political implementation of what they consider necessary to save the world. Some might even like to replace the cumbersome and unpredictable processes of democracy with a well-intentioned global eco-dictatorship in which a benevolent dictator does what seems appropriate for humanity as a whole. For others, decentralisation, a departure from the centralised state and its inadequate interventions, seems the only way to reconcile humanity with its environment.

Both ideas are very dangerous. In order to solve the macroeconomic control task, which ranges from economic policy to environmental policy objectives, we need an extremely competent state, but there is no reason to believe that a dictatorship could deliver this efficiency — and obviously there are many other grave concerns associated with that governance form. Decentralised economic or political units that function largely without a state are also an illusion. The environmental problem can only be solved globally and at the political level; the contribution that decentral actors can make to it is negligible. The individual may console himself and calm his conscience if he lives in an environmentally conscious way. But to imagine that the example of a few is enough to persuade the masses to change their way of life is, experience has shown, to be grossly out of touch with reality.

Bibliography

Ackermann, Josef (2011). "Verunsicherung der bürgerlichen Mitte", in *Handelsblatt* (8th September). Available online at http://www.handelsblatt.com/unternehmen/banken-versicherungen/rede-von-ackermann-zur-zukunft-europas/4588000-2.html. (Website visited February 2018).

Ameco (2017a). "Domestic demand excluding changes in inventory at constant prices". Available online at http://ec.europa.eu/economy_finance/ameco/user/serie/SelectSerie.cfm. (Website visited February 2018).

Ameco (2017b). "Gross fixed capital formation at current prices: total economy". Available online at http://ec.europa.eu/economy_finance/ameco/user/serie/SelectSerie.cfm. (Website visited February 2018).

Armbruster, Alexander (2017). "Raubt Foxconn Wohlstand und Geld der Amerikaner?", in *Frankfurter Allgemeine Zeitung*. Available online at http://www.faz.net/aktuell/wirtschaft/wirtschaftspolitik/trump-und-china-raubt-foxconn-wohlstand-und-geld-der-amerikaner-14602661.html. (Website visited February 2018).

Austin, John (2001 [1832]). *The Province of Jurisprudence Determined*, Cambridge: Cambridge University Press.

Bicchetti, David & Maystre, Nicolas (2012). "The synchronized and long-lasting structural change on commodity markets: Evidence from high frequency data". Available online at http://unctad.org/en/PublicationsLibrary/osgdp2012d2_en.pdf. (Website visited February 2018).

Binswanger, Hans Christoph, Huber, Joseph & Mastronardi, Philippe (2014). *Die Vollgeld-Reform. Wie Staatsschulden abgebaut und Finanzkrisen verhindert werden können*, Solothurn: Zeitpunkt.

Bofinger, Peter, Schnabel, Isabel, Feld, Lars P., Schmidt, Christoph M. & Wieland, Volker (2015). *Sondergutachten: Konsequenzen aus der Griechenland-Krise für einen stabileren Euro-Raum.* Available online at https://www.sachverstaendigenrat-wirtschaft.de/fileadmin/dateiablage/download/sondergutachten/sg2015.pdf. (Website visited February 2018).

Bofinger, Peter, Schnabel, Isabel, Feld, Lars P., Schmidt, Christoph M. & Wieland, Volker (2016). *Zeit für Reformen. Jahresgutachten 2016/17.* Available online at https://www.sachverstaendigenrat-wirtschaft.de/fileadmin/dateiablage/gutachten/jg201617/ges_jg16_17.pdf. (Website visited February 2018).

Böhm-Bawerk, Eugen von (1914). "Macht oder ökonomisches Gesetz?", in *Zeitschrift für Volkswirtschaft, Sozialpolitik und Verwaltung* 23, pp. 205–271.

Bratu, Christine (2014). *Die Grenzen staatlicher Legitimität*, Münster: Mentis.

Brodbeck, Karl-Heinz (2009), "Scheitern — eine Kritik an der traditionellen Ökonomie". Available online at http://www.khbrodbeck.homepage.t-online.de/scheitern.pdf. (Website visited February 2018).

Buchanan, James & Wagner, Richard E. (1977). "Democracy in deficit: The political legacy of Lord Keynes". Available online at http://www.econlib.org/library/Buchanan/buchCv8c5.html#anchor_n61. (Website visited February 2018).

Bundesministerium für Finanzen (2015). "An morgen denken. Gemeinsam handeln. Die deutsche G7-Präsidentschaft auf der Ebene der Finanzminister und Notenbankgouverneure". Available online at http://www.bundesfinanzministerium.de/Content/DE/Downloads/Broschueren_Bestellservice/2015-05-22-g7-gemeinsam-handeln.pdf?__blob=publicationFile&v=3. (Website visited February 2018).

Bündnis 90/Die Grünen Baden-Württemberg & CDU Baden-Württemberg (2016). *Baden-Württemberg gestalten: Verlässlich. Nachhaltig. Innovativ, Koalitionsvertrag 2016–2021.* Available online at http://www.baden-wuerttemberg.de/fileadmin/redaktion/dateien/PDF/160509_Koalitionsvertrag_B-W_2016-2021_final.PDF. (Website visited February 2018).

Clark, Pilita (2017). "A sharp drop in US-emissions keeps global levels flat", in *Financial Times (17th March).* Available online at https://www.ft.com/content/540ebb0c-0a60-11e7-ac5a-903b21361b43. (Website visited February 2018).

Davidson, Paul (2011 [1994]). *Post Keynesian Macroeconomic Theory: A Foundation for Successful Economic Policies for the Twenty-First Century.* Aldershot: Edward Elgar.

Deutsche Bundesbank (2016). *Monatsbericht: Juli 2016, 68. Jahrgang, Nr. 7.* Available online at https://www.bundesbank.de/Redaktion/DE/Downloads/Veroeffentlichungen/Monatsberichte/2016/2016_07_monatsbericht.pdf?__blob=publicationFile. (Website visited February 2017).

Deutsche Bundesbank (2017a). "Monatsbericht März 2017". Available online at https://www.bundesbank.de/Redaktion/DE/Downloads/Veroeffentlichungen/

Monatsberichte/2017/2017_03_monatsbericht.pdf?__blob=publicationFile. (Website visited February 2018).

Deutsche Bundesbank (2017b). "Monatsbericht April 2017". Available online at https://www.bundesbank.de/Redaktion/DE/Downloads/Veroeffentlichungen/ Monatsberichte/2017/2017_04_monatsbericht.pdf?__blob=publicationFile. (Website visited February 2018).

Deutsche Bundesbank (2017c). "Ergebnisse der gesamtwirtschaftlichen Finanzierungsrechnung für Deutschland — 2011 bis 2016. Statistische Sonderveröffentlichung 4". Available online at https://www.bundesbank.de/ Redaktion/DE/Downloads/Veroeffentlichungen/Statistische_Sondervero- effentlichungen/Statso_4/statso_4_ergebnisse_der_gesamtwirtschaftlichen_ finanzierungsrechnung_2011_2016.pdf?__blob=publicationFile. (Website vis- ited February 2018).

Draghi, Mario (2012). "Speech by Mario Draghi, President of the European Central Bank at the Global Investment Conference in London", 26th July. Available online at https://www.ecb.europa.eu/press/key/date/2012/html/sp120726. en.html. (Website visited February 2018).

Ehnts, Dirk (2016). "Die deutsche Lohnpolitik und die Alleinschuld". Available online at https://makroskop.eu/2016/05/deutsche-lohnpolitik-und-die- alleinschuld-eine-keynesianische-perspektive/. (Website visited February 2018).

Eichengreen, Barry (2017). "Is Germany unbalanced or unhinged?". Available online at https://www.socialeurope.eu/germany-unbalanced-unhinged. (Website vis- ited February 2018).

Engartner, Tim (2016). *Staat im Ausverkauf. Privatisierung in Deutschland*, Frankfurt am Main: Campus.

Europäische Zentralbank (2005). "Monthly bulletin May 2005". Available online at https://www.ecb.europa.eu/pub/pdf/mobu/mb200505en.pdf. (Website visited February 2018).

Europäische Zentralbank (2011). "Die Geldpolitik der EZB 2011". Available online at https://www.ecb.europa.eu/pub/pdf/other/monetarypolicy2011de.pdf?0651- d17c4b69dd55f5d21d93aa600694 abgerufen. (Website visited February 2018).

Feldenkirchen, Markus (2016). "Kretschmann plädiert für Schwarz-Grün im Bund", in *Spiegel online* (26 August). Available online at http://www.spiegel.de/politik/ deutschland/winfried-kretschmann-fuer-schwarz-gruen-geheimtreffen-im- kanzleramt-a-1109581.html. (Website visited February 2018).

Financial Conduct Authority (2014). "Commodity markets update (February)". Available online at https://www.fca.org.uk/publication/newsletters/commodity- market-update-1402.pdf. (Website visited February 2018).

Flassbeck, Heiner (1982). "Was ist Angebotspolitik?", in *Konjunkturpolitik* 28/2–3, pp. 75–138.

Flassbeck, Heiner (1988). *Preise, Zins und Wechselkurs. Zur Theorie der offenen Volkswirtschaft bei flexiblen Wechselkursen*, Tübingen: Mohr.

Flassbeck, Heiner (2000). "Lohnzurückhaltung für mehr Beschäftigung? Über eine zentrale Inkonsistenz im jüngsten SVR-Gutachten", in *Wirtschaftsdienst 80/2*, pp. 84–93. Available online at http://www.flassbeck.de/pdf/2000/Lohnzurc. pdf. (Website visited February 2018).

Flassbeck, Heiner (2013a). "Kleine Steuern und große Lügen". Available online at https://makroskop.eu/2013/07/kleine-steuern-und-grose-lugen/. (Website visited February 2018).

Flassbeck, Heiner (2013b). "Vom Merkantilismus zum Merkelantismus". Available online at https://makroskop.eu/2013/07/abo-artikel-vom-merkantilismus-zum-merkelantismus/. (Website visited February 2018).

Flassbeck, Heiner (2013c). "Sollen die Steuern für Reiche erhöht werden?". Available online at https://makroskop.eu/2013/10/sollen-die-steuern-fuer-reiche-erhoeht-werden/. (Website visited February 2018).

Flassbeck, Heiner (2014). "Der ganz normale Wahnsinn an einem ganz normalen Tag in einer ganz normalen Zeitung". Available online at https://makroskop. eu/2014/11/der-ganz-normale-wahnsinn-an-einem-ganz-normalen-tag-in-einer-ganz-normalen-zeitung/. (Website visited February 2018).

Flassbeck, Heiner (2016a). *"Löhne und Preise in Deutschland"*. Available online at https://makroskop.eu/2016/04/loehne-und-preise-in-deutschland-oder-warum-europa-der-deflation-auch-in-zwanzig-jahren-nicht-entkommen-kann-teil-3/. (Website visited February 2018).

Flassbeck, Heiner (2016b). "Milch, Schweine und die Marktwirtschaft". Available online at https://makroskop.eu/2016/05/milch-schweine-und-die-marktwirtschaft/. (Website visited February 2018).

Flassbeck, Heiner & Bibow, Jörg (2018). *Das Euro-Desaster. Wie deutsche Wirtschaftspolitik die Eurozone in den Abgrund treibt*, Frankfurt am Main: Westend.

Flassbeck, Heiner, Horn, Gustav A. & Zwiener, Rudolf (1989). *"Die Bedeutung von starken, außenwirtschaftlich bedingten Angebots- und Nachfrageveränderungen für die gesamtwirtschaftliche Entwicklung"*, Berlin: Gutachten im Auftrag des Bundesministers für Wirtschaft.

Flassbeck, Heiner & Maier-Rigaud, Gerhard (1982). *Umwelt und Wirtschaft. Zur Diskriminierung des Umweltschutzes in der ökonomischen Analyse*, Tübingen: Mohr Siebeck.

Flassbeck, Heiner & Spiecker, Friederike (2013). "Investitionen in Sachanlagen — die ungenannte Achillesferse der deutschen Wirtschaft". Available online at https://makroskop.eu/2013/07/abo-artikel-investitionen-in-sachanlagen-die-ungenannte-achillesferse-der-deutschen-wirtschaft/. (Website visited February 2018).

Flassbeck, Heiner & Spiecker, Friederike (2016), *Das Ende der Massenarbeitslosigkeit.* Frankfurt am Main: Westend.

Fratzscher, Marcel (2016). "Die Illusion vom deutschen Wirtschaftsboom", in *Spiegel online* (6th January). Available online at http://www.spiegel.de/wirtschaft/ soziales/wirtschaft-in-deutschland-die-illusion-vom-wirtschaftsboom- a-1068970.html. (Website visited February 2018).

Fricke, T. (2016). "Das Märchen von Linksgrün", in *Spiegel online* (9th December). Available online at http://www.spiegel.de/wirtschaft/soziales/cdu-csu-das- maerchen-von-linksgruen-a-1125059.html. (Website visited February 2018).

Friedman, Milton (1970). "The social responsibility of business is to increase profits", in *The New York Times Magazine* (13th September).

Fuest, Clemens (2017). "Wie steht es um die Ungleichheit?", in *Frankfurter Allgemeine Zeitung* (4th June). Available online at http://www.faz.net/aktuell/wirtschaft/ arm-und-reich/arm-und-reich-wie-steht-es-um-die-ungleichheit-15042843. html. (Website visited February 2018).

Fullwiler, Scott. T. (2011). "Treasury debt operations. An analysis integrating social fabric matrix and social accounting matrix methodologies". Available online at http://papers.ssrn.com/sol3/papers.cf.?abstract_id=1874795. (Website visited February 2018).

Grimm, Dieter (2016). *Europa ja – aber welches?*, München: Beck.

Haffner, Sebastian (1987). *Von Bismarck zu Hitler. Ein Rückblick*, München: Kindler.

Hartmann, Michael (2002). *Der Mythos von den Leistungseliten.* Frankfurt am Main: Campus.

Hayek, Friedrich A. (1988). *The Fatal Conceit. The Errors of Socialism*, Chicago: University of Chicago Press.

Heide, Dana (2016). "Gabriels Berater mahnen zur Umsetzung von Basel III", in *Handelsblatt* (21st December). Available online at http://www.handelsblatt. com/politik/deutschland/finanzstabilitaetsregeln-gabriels-berater-mahnen-zur- umsetzung-von-basel-iii/19162706.html. (Website visited February 2018).

Heidenreich, Bernd (Hg.) (2002). *Politische Theorien des 19. Jahrhunderts*, Berlin/ Boston: De Gruyter.

Heine, Frederic & Sablowski, Thomas (2015). "Zerfällt die Europäische Währungsunion? Handels- und Kapitalverflechtungen, Krisenursachen und Entwicklungsperspektiven der Eurozone", in *Prokla* 181, pp. 563–591.

Heinemann, Frank J. (2002). "Michael Hartmann: Der Mythos von den Leistungseliten", in *Deutschlandfunk* (21st October). Available online at http:// www.deutschlandfunk.de/michael-hartmann-der-mythos-von-den-leistung- seliten.730.de.html?dram:article_id=101903. (Website visited February 2018).

Heller, Hermann (1934). *Staatslehre*, in der Bearbeitung von Gerhart Niemeyer, Leiden: Sijthoff.

Herzog, Lisa (2014). *Freiheit gehört nicht nur den Reichen: Plädoyer für einen zeitgemäßen Liberalismus*, Munich: Beck.

Höpner, Martin (2017). "Plädoyer für eine aufgeklärte Souveränität". Available online at https://makroskop.eu/2017/01/plaedoyer-fuer-eine-aufgeklaerte-souveraenitaet/. (Website visited February 2018).

Huber, Joseph (no Date). "Gegenkritik an Flassbeck-Economics". Available online at https://www.vollgeld.de/gegenkritik-an-flassbeck-economics/. (Website visited February 2018).

International Monetary Fund (IMF) (2017). "Current account balance, percent of GDP". Available online at http://www.imf.org/external/datamapper/BCA_NGDPD@WEO/OEMDC/ADVEC/WEOWORLD/CHN. (Website visited February 2018).

Irwin, Neil & Paley, Amit R. (2008). "Greenspan says he was wrong on regulation", in *Washington Post* (24th October). Available online at http://www.washington-post.com/wp-dyn/content/article/2008/10/23/AR2008102300193.html. (Website visited February 2018).

Janssen, Albert (2014). *Die gefährdete Staatlichkeit der Bundesrepublik Deutschland. Beiträge zur Bewahrung ihrer verfassungsrechtlichen Organisationsstruktur*, Göttingen: Vandenhoeck & Ruprecht.

Kaufmann, Stephan (2016). "Autoritätsverlust der Ökonomen", in *Frankfurter Rundschau* (7th December). Available online at http://www.fr.de/wirtschaft/wirtschaftsexperten-autoritaetsverlust-der-oekonomen-a-729769. (Website visited February 2018).

Keynes, John Maynard (1930). *A Treatise of Money (Vol I: The pure theory of money)*, London: Macmillan.

Knapp, Georg Friedrich (1905). *Staatliche Theorie des Geldes*. Munich/Leipzig: Duncker & Humblot.

Krugman, Paul (2013a). "The Japan story", in *New York Times* (5th February). Available online at https://krugman.blogs.nytimes.com/2013/02/05/the-japan-story/#more-33700. (Website visited February 2018).

Krugman, Paul (2013b). "This age of bubbles", in *New York Times* (22nd August). Available online at http://www.nytimes.com/2013/08/23/opinion/krugman-this-age-of-bubbles.html. (Website visited February 2018).

Krull, Daniel (2016). "Freihandel: So schüren Gegner Ängste", in *Plusminus* (aired on 14th December).

Lerner, Abba P. (1943). "Functional finance and the federal debt", in *Social Research* 10/1, pp. 38–51.

Lerner, Abba P. (1951). *Economics of Employment*, New York: McGraw-Hill.

Liikanen, Erkki (2012). "Final report: High-level expert group on reforming the structure of the EU banking sector". Available online at http://ec.europa.eu/

internal_market/bank/docs/high-level_expert_group/report_en.pdf. (Website visited February 2018)

Lucas, Robert E. Jr. (1988). "On the mechanics of economic development", in *Journal of Monetary Economics*, 22(1), p. 3.

Mandeville, Bernard (1714). *The Fable of the Bees or Private Vices, Publick Benefits*, Oxford: Clarendon Press. Available online at http://oll.libertyfund.org/titles/mandeville-the-fable-of-the-bees-or-private-vices-publick-benefits-vol-1#chapter_66840. (Website visited February 2018).

Mattert, Jana, Valentukeviciute, Laura & Waßmuth, Carl (2017), *Gemeinwohl als Zukunftsaufgabe. Öffentliche Infrastrukturen zwischen Daseinsvorsorge und Finanzmärkten* (= Heinrich Böll Stiftung, *Schriften zu Wirtschaft und Soziales* 20). Available online at https://www.boell.de/sites/default/files/gemeinwohl_als_zukunftsaufgabe_-_oeffentliche_infrastrukturen_zwischen_daseinsvorsorge_und_finanzmaerkten.pdf?dimension1=ds_g20_de. (Website visited February 2018).

Mayer, Thomas (2013). "Das Spar-Paradox", in *Frankfurter Allgemeine Zeitung* (4th May). Available online at: http://www.faz.net/aktuell/wirtschaft/mayers-weltwirtschaft/mayers-weltwirtschaft-das-spar-paradox-12172266.html. (Website visited February 2018).

Menger, Carl (1892/1970 [1892]). "Geld", in *Gesammelte Werke* IV, pp. 1–116, Tübingen: Mohr (Paul Siebeck).

Michéa, Jean-Claude (2014). *Das Reich des kleineren Übels. Über die liberale Gesellschaft*, Berlin: Matthes & Seitz.

Mill, J. S. (1871). *Principles of Political Economy* (7th ed., Vol. 1). London: Longmans, Green, Reader and Dyer. Available online at https://en.wikisource.org/wiki/Principles_of_Political_Economy_(J.S._Mill,_1871),_vol._1/Book_II,_Chapter_I. (Website visited February 2020).

Mises, Ludwig von (1940). *Nationalökonomie. Theorie des Handelns und Wirtschaftens*, Genf: Editions Union Genf.

Moser, Simon (2016). "Warum Arbeitnehmer früher ein größeres Stück vom Kuchen bekamen", in *Der Standard* (13th October). Available online at http://derstandard.at/2000045793241/Warum-Arbeitnehmer-frueher-ein-groesseres-Stueck-vom-Kuchen-bekamen. (Website visited February 2018).

Müller, Jan-Werner (2016). *Was ist Populismus? Ein Essay*, Berlin: Suhrkamp.

Müller, Sebastian (2017). "Kaufprämie für E-Autos floppt". Available online at https://makroskop.eu/2017/01/kaufpraemie-fuer-e-autos-floppt/. (Website visited February 2018).

Müller, Sebastian & Flassbeck, Heiner (2017). "Deutschland droht ein Währungskrieg". Available online at Makroskop: https://makroskop.eu/2017/01/deutschland-droht-ein-waehrungskrieg/. (Website visited February 2018).

Nida-Rümelin, Julian (2016). "Ungleich ist nicht immer ungerecht", in *Frankfurter Allgemeine Zeitung* (28th December). Available online at http://www.faz.net/ aktuell/politik/die-gegenwart/soziale-gerechtigkeit-ungleich-ist-nicht-immer-ungerecht-14581266.html?printPagedArticle=true. (Website visited February 2018).

Nienhaus, Lisa & Tönnesmann, Jens (2016). *"Aufstand gegen den Freihandel"*, in *Die Zeit* (9th December). Available online at http://www.zeit.de/2016/50/global-isierung-freihandel-verlierer-gewinner-gegner/komplettansicht. (Website visited February 2018).

Nozick, Robert (1974). *Anarchy, State and Utopia,* Oxford: Basil Blackwell.

Offe, Claus (1987). "Die Staatstheorie auf der Suche nach ihrem Gegenstand", in *Jahrbuch zur Staats- und Verwaltungswissenschaft*, herausgegeben von Thomas Ellwein et al., Baden-Baden: Nomos, pp. 309–320.

Pfannkuche, Walter (2016). "Prinzipien einer gerechten Einkommensverteilung". Available online at https://makroskop.eu/2016/07/prinzipien-einer-gerechten-einkommensverteilung-1/. (Website visited February 2019).

Phoenix (2017). "Im Dialog: Michael Hirz im Gespräch mit Richard David Precht". Available online at https://www.youtube.com/watch?v=wjPJIwI-M2g&sns=em. (Website visited February 2018).

Plickert, Philip (2015). "Nehmen Roboter den Menschen die Arbeit weg?", in *Frankfurter Allgemeine Zeitung* (28th December). Available online at http://www.faz.net/aktuell/wirtschaft/automatisierung-nehmen-roboter-den-men-schen-die-arbeit-weg-13986337.html. (Website visited February 2018).

Politi, James (2014). *"US jobs: Slim pickings"*, in *Financial Times* (20th July). Available online at https://www.ft.com/content/3676ad9e-0de1-11e4-b149-00144feabdc0. (Website visited February 2018).

Polster, Werner (2014). *Die Krise der europäischen Währungsunion. Eine ordnungspolitische Analyse*, Marburg: Metropolis.

Rawls, John (2017 [1971]). *Eine Theorie der Gerechtigkeit*, Berlin: Suhrkamp.

Reuters (2015). "Investieren unsere Konzerne nun endlich?", in *Frankfurter Allgemeine Zeitung* (28th December). Available online at http://www.faz.net/aktuell/wirtschaft/konjunktur/ifo-umfrage-investieren-unsere-konzerne-nun-endlich-13987299.html. (Website visited February 2018).

Reuters (2016). *"Top-Manager in Alarmstimmung"*, in Handelsblatt (9th December). Available online at http://www.handelsblatt.com/politik/international/cryan-ma-weber-gegen-globalisierungskritik-top-manager-in-alarmstimmung/14956506.html. (Website visited February 2018).

Sachs, Jeffrey D. (2017). "Will economic illiteracy trigger a trade war?". Available online at http://csd.columbia.edu/2017/04/20/will-economic-illiteracy-trigger-a-trade-war. (Website visited February 2018).

Schieritz, Mark (2016). "Plötzlich gerecht", in *Die Zeit* (15th December). Available online at http://www.zeit.de/2016/50/globalisierung-g-20-usa-grossbritannien-unternehmenssteuern. (Website visited February 2018).

Schumpeter, Joseph (2006 [1912]). *Theorie der wirtschaftlichen Entwicklung*, herausgegeben von Jochen Röpke und Olaf Stiller, Berlin: Duncker & Humblot.

Seidl, Conrad (2016). "Industrie lehnt SP-Pläne für Maschinensteuer ab", in *Der Standard* (3rd January). Available online at http://derstandard.at/2000028414544/Industrie-lehnt-SP-Plaene-fuer-Maschinensteuer-ab. (Website visited February 2018).

Shiller, Robert J. (2017). "Die heutige Stagnation verstehen lernen". Available online at https://www.project-syndicate.org/commentary/secular-stagnation-future-of-work-fears-by-robert-j--shiller-2017-05/german?barrier=accessreg. (Website visited February 2018).

Sinn, Hans-Werner (2003). *Ist Deutschland noch zu retten?*, München: Econ.

Sinn, Hans-Werner (2014). "Sie sind wie Spürhunde", in *Süddeutsche Zeitung* (1st November). Available online at http://www.sueddeutsche.de/wirtschaft/kritik-an-oekonomen-der-grosse-irrtum-1.2198333. (Website visited February 2018).

Sinn, Hans-Werner (2015). *Der Euro: Von der Friedensidee zum Zankapfel*, München: Hanser.

Smith, Adam (1979 [1776]). *An Inquiry into the Nature and Causes of the Wealth of Nations*. Oxford: A.S. Skinner.

Spiecker, Friederike (2014). "Bontrup-Erwiderung, die dritte: Kann Arbeitszeitverkürzung die Knappheit des Produktionsfaktors Arbeit erhöhen?". Available online at https://makroskop.eu/2014/10/bontrup-erwiderung-die-dritte-kann-arbeitszeitverkuerzung-die-knappheit-des-produktionsfaktors-arbeit-erhoehen. (Website visited February 2018).

Steinhardt, Paul (2015). *Was ist eigentlich eine Marktwirtschaft?*, Marburg: Metropolis.

Steinhardt, Paul (2016). "Was ist eigentlich Geld?". Available online at https://makroskop.eu/2016/09/ist-eigentlich-geld-1/. (Website visited February 2018).

Stiglitz, Joseph E. (2014). "The myth of America's Golden Age", in *Politico* (July/August). Available online at http://www.politico.com/magazine/story/2014/06/the-myth-of-americas-golden-age-108013. (Website visited February 2018).

Stützel, Wolfgang (2011). *Volkswirtschaftliche Saldenmechanik. Ein Beitrag zur Geldtheorie*, Tübingen: Mohr Siebeck.

Suchanek, Andreas (2012). "Die Goldene Regel als Grundlage von Wirtschafts- und Unternehmensethik", in *Politik unterrichten* 1, pp. 48–51. Available online at http://3071.nibis.de/inhalte/PU/1_2012/Suchanek.pdf. (Website visited February 2018).

Thielemann, Ulrich (2010). *Wettbewerb als Gerechtigkeitskonzept. Kritik des Neoliberalismus*, Marburg: Metropolis.

Thielemann, Ulrich (2016). "Geld aus dem Nichts — oder das Geld der Vermögenden?". Available online at http://www.mem-wirtschaftsethik.de/blog/blog-einzelseite/article/geld-aus-dem/. (Website visited February 2018).

UNCTAD (2009). *Trade and Development Report 2009*. Available online at http://unctad.org/en/Docs/tdr2009_en.pdf. (Website visited February 2018).

Petersdorff, Winand von & Plickert, Philip (2017). "Die Taktiererei mit den Handelsbilanzen", in *Frankfurter Allgemeine Zeitung* (31st January). Available online at http://www.faz.net/aktuell/wirtschaft/wirtschaftspolitik/export-und-import-die-taktiererei-mit-den-handelsbilanzen-14790481.html. (Website visited February 2018).

Wagenknecht, Sahra (2011). *Freiheit statt Kapitalismus*, Frankfurt am Main: Eichborn.

Wagenknecht, Sahra (2016). *Reichtum ohne Gier. Wie wir uns vor dem Kapitalismus retten*, Frankfurt am Main: Campus.

Wahl, Peter (2016). "Zwischen Eurofetischismus und Nationalismus" (28th October). Available online at https://makroskop.eu/2016/10/zwischen-eurofetischismus-und-nationalismus/. (Website visited February 2018).

Weidmann, Jens (2012). "Begrüßungsrede anlässlich des 18. Kolloquiums des Instituts für bankhistorische Forschung (IBF) Papiergeld — Staatsfinanzierung — Inflation. Traf Goethe ein Kernproblem der Geldpolitik?". Available online at https://www.bundesbank.de/Redaktion/DE/Reden/2012/2012_09_18_weidmann_begruessungsrede.html (Website visited February 2018).

Wetzel, Daniel (2017). "Bundesregierung gibt Alleingänge im Klimaschutz auf", in *Die Welt* (11th March). Available online at https://www.welt.de/wirtschaft/article162762773/Bundesregierung-gibt-Alleingaenge-im-Klimaschutz-auf.html. (Website visited February 2018).

Wicksell, Knut (1958). *Selected Papers on Economic Theory*, Boston: Harvard University Press.

Wolf, M. (2017). "Dealing with America's trade follies", in *Financial Times* (18th April). Available online at https://www.ft.com/content/fca7e9a4-2366-11e7-a34a-538b4cb30025. (Website visited February 2018).

Wray, L. Randall (2012). *Modern Money Theory. A Primer on Macroeconomics for Sovereign Monetary Systems*, London: Palgrave Macmillan.

ZEIT ONLINE, bb. (2016). *Mindestlohn zeigt kaum Wirkung*. Abgerufen am 23th October 2017 von Die Zeit Online. Available online at http://www.zeit.de/wirtschaft/2016-10/mindestlohn-wirkung-statistisches-bundesamt.

Index

migration, 23
mobility, 224
productivity, 27–28
saving technologies, 41
labour market, 5, 11, 23, 25, 47, 53,
  92, 95–98, 101, 106–107, 117–118,
  131, 136–137, 151, 200201, 206–
  208, 215, 218, 220, 224–227
  2008/09 episode, 137
  flexibility, 225
Lamy, Pascal, 3
language, 24
Law on the Promotion of Stability
  and Growth of the Economy, 1967,
  233
legal
  documents, 56
  framework, 23
  regulations, 184
  separation, 156
legislation, 51, 70–71
legitimate expenditures, 183
Lehman Brothers, 233, 245
  insolvency of, 233
lender, 158, 183
Lerner, Abba P., 239
Lewis, Michael, 148
liabilities, 155, 158, 175, 179, 181,
  190, 233
liberal, 63, 67
  critics of state, 65
  economic orthodoxy, 38
  globalisation, 2
  parties, 112
liberalism, 36, 54
Libyan crisis, 138
Liikanen Commission, 157
Liikanen, Erkki, 156
liquidity, 79, 152, 170–171, 184
Lisbon Treaty, 70

loan, 154, 156, 160, 169, 176,
  178–180, 186, 233–237
  contracts, 57
  liability, 175
  questionable, 63
  revenue from, 246
  volume, 164
lobby organisations, 244
low-wage country, 14, 16, 19–20, 22,
  25, 209
low-wage jurisdiction, 24
Lucas, Robert E. Jr., 52
luxury, 125

M
machine tax, 35
macroeconomic, 5, 37, 53–54, 77,
  120
  analysis, 230
  conditions, regression in, 138
  control task, 271
  dynamism, 211, 230
  income, 72, 75
  interrelationships, 74
  perspective, 35
  policy, 228
  relationships, 69, 137
  requirements, 205
  stagnation, 134
  trend of poor development, 136
macro-foundation, 86
Mandeville, Bernard, 36
marginal productivity, 105, 107–108
  theory, 220
marketability, 161
market-centred organisation, 151
market discipline, 185
market-economy, 36, 109, 123, 125, 231
  organisation, 156
  system, xi, 226